AF477046

TED KID LEWIS

His Life and Times

TED KID LEWIS

His Life and Times

Morton Lewis

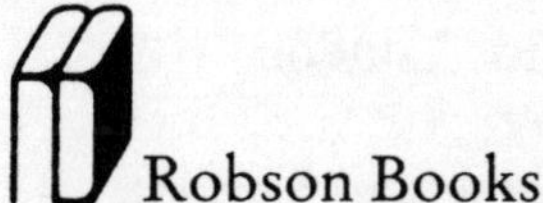

Robson Books

First published in Great Britain in 1990 by Robson Books Ltd,
Bolsover House, 5–6 Clipstone Street, London W1P 7EB

Copyright © 1990 Morton Lewis

British Library Cataloguing in Publication Data
Lewis, Morton
  Ted Kid Lewis: his life and times.
  1. Boxing. Lewis, Ted, Kid
  I. Title
  796.830922

Typeset by Selectmove Ltd, London
Printed in Great Britain by
Butler & Tanner Ltd, Frome and London

I dedicate this book to my wife Sally for extending her love for me to my mother and father, for sacrificing the first twenty-seven years of our married life by undertaking and sharing my responsibilities, without her support, I know not what would have happened. And to Elsie, whom Sally and I considered to be the eighth wonder of the world – our world anyway. She was without a doubt my father's engine. I cannot describe the love and loyalty she had for her husband, which made it all worthwhile to Sally and me.

Contents

Acknowledgements   ix
Foreword by Reg Gutteridge   xi
Introduction   xiii

Part One: A Star Rises in the East
 1 The Cabinet-maker's Son   3
 2 The Judean Club   10
 3 Premierland Début   15
 4 Apprentice Days   22
 5 Title Contender   28
 6 The Lonsdale Belt   35
 7 Champion of Europe   41
 8 The Australian Adventure   47

Part Two: The Smashing, Dashing, Crashing Kid
 9 Early Days in the USA   57
10 The Havana Interlude   64
11 Chasing Titles   68
12 World Champion at Last   75
13 The Kid Meets His Match   82
14 The Title Slips Away   93
15 The Kid Gets Hooked   101
16 The Title Regained   108
17 The Birth of a Son   113
18 The End of an Era   120

Part Three: The Prodigal Returns
19 The Lonsdale Belt Again   133
20 Transatlantic Commuter   145
21 Carpentier   157

22 Britain's Premier Fighter   163
23 The Continental Tour   171
24 Hollywood Calling   180

Part Four: I Knew Him Before You Were Born
25 Further Continental Adventures   195
26 The Comeback Treadmill   201
27 Desperate Days   207
28 The USA Bids Farewell   214
29 Mosley Kids the Kid   220
30 Clubland   229
31 The Living Legend   237
32 Final Days   247

Epilogue   255

Ring Record 1909–1929   258

Index   267

Acknowledgements

I should like to thank the people who have helped me over the years with the editing, research and production of the manuscript. My thanks to, Harry Mullan, Ron Olver and Gilbert Odd of Boxing News. Tony Vandenburgh, Jack Kid Berg, Peter McInnes and Steve Powell. To Zena Swaab for deciphering my longhand and typing the original manuscript. To Jeremy Robson for his encouragement and courage in publishing this book. To my many relatives for the use of their private collection of photographs. And in particular to my chief cook and bottlewasher, sparring partner, researcher extraordinary and editor, John Harding, for keeping me on the right track.

Foreword

Being invited to provide a foreword for the first, and long overdue, complete story of Ted Kid Lewis is an honour. He was exceptional – as both champion and man. A poll amongst the boxing fraternity would undoubtedly vote him the best all-round British box-fighter of them all. His record is outstanding. Greatness in the ring should not be entirely judged by titles won – during the eighties they were ten a penny – but by the strength of the opposition.

Ted Kid Lewis fought the best in Britain and in the USA at several weights. He conceeded poundage without a murmur of protest. Imagine a natural welterweight (10 st. 7 lb.) of today being able to flatten a full-blown light-heavyweight (12 st. 7 lb.). He did it without working up a sweat.

But this book is much more than a complete and proudly accurate record of a champion. His only son, always close to the ring scene and frequently producing films, spent months of diligent research to provide a fascinating insight. The 'Ole Man', as they would say where Lewis was born, would have been proud of him.

Regrettably, I weighed-in too late to have seen Ted Kid Lewis in action. But I knew him well in later years and have seen the flickering family films of the man in his prime. He popularized the now modern 'combination punches' during World War I. He rarely bothered to hit an opponent with one punch when six would do. His sinewy physique with a milk-white skin and boxing with an open mouth disguised a sheer ruggedness and essential desire to land a pay-off punch. Or punches. They also came no braver than the Kid. My grandfather, Arthur, seconded Johnny Basham against Lewis and rarely stopped relating, round by round, how Lewis overcame the smart Welshman by sheer pressure and superior power. In today's inflated market with telephone number TV fees, the irrepressible Lewis, with such a gritty and flamboyant style, would have been perfect for the home screen. He would have become a multi-millionaire.

But, as this story relates, he was generous to a fault and gave most of it away to the under-privileged. I frequently meet old fans, most of them retired and wealthy businessmen, who still talk of the times as kids when their hero tossed coins to them during the hard times of London's East End.

Jack Kid Berg, another of the East End greats in a later era, is often introduced as the best of Britain's fighters. 'Only now that Ted Kid Lewis is no longer with us' he says. That says it all.

Reg. Sutteridge 1990.

Introduction

Since as long as I can remember, I would thrill whenever Father was halted in the street by a perfect stranger anxious to talk to him. Or to be seen talking to him. It was a frequent occurrence and, indeed, the mere shadow of Father was enough to invest me with the sense of importance – the sire of self-confidence which is so vital in vulnerable youth. Today, having passed through three score and ten years, the thrill of having stood beside him has not diminished in the slightest.

I have no apology to make for the pride I have in being the son of my father. 'That's my father,' and in the same breath, 'Would you like to see some of his fight films?' I don't know whether or not the showing of those films was an asset to my business, but what a conversation-piece to be the proud possessor of! After all, isn't he one of the all-time greats in a profession that can be traced back to the days of the Romans?

In Nat Fleischer's *Record Book and Boxing Encyclopedia* no boxer figures more frequently than Ted 'Kid' Lewis. However, my pride in him does not stem so much from his unsurpassed fighting record as from the character of the man. Vicious he undoubtedly was in the ring, but outside the ropes no greater gentleman was ever born and no son had a more lovable father.

That he had his faults – serious faults – I cannot deny. He had the inability to say 'no', for Father was the easiest touch in the world in a profession in which 'touching' has been cultivated into a fine art.

On one occasion in 1936, TK and I were walking across Leicester Square to Jones's tea shop. He was stopped by the usual tapper, a few words were spoken, TK gave him five shillings, he thanked him and walked off. A few moments later, another man came over, 'Can I have a word with you, Ted?' TK's hand went to his pocket, when the man said, 'No, it's OK, thanks, but that tapper you just gave some money to said, as you were coming over, "Beat it, here comes my mug". I just thought that was a lousy way to repay your generosity.' TK thanked him and said, 'I'd like to be his mug all my life.' It said a lot about TK's character and I still use that thought as my philosophy in life.

He had an ultra-sentimental streak which increased with age, and an engaging naïveté which allowed him to let himself be drawn – with the best of intentions – into things which he did not, and could not, understand, such as joining Oswald Mosley's new party as boxing instructor, a movement from which he freed himself, after discovering his mistake, with four of the best punches I have ever seen. His faults were all human, warm frailties, without a shred of meanness or spite in them, and I loved him for his faults every bit as much as for his virtues.

The last six years of his life he spent in a hotel in Brighton and at the Nightingale Home for Aged Jews. He was half-blind in one eye. His features – those sculpted granite features – bore unmistakable evidence of his 299 recorded ring battles. He would, with the smallest encouragement (and he received plenty), recall his younger days in the East End of London, when the ragamuffin, shoeless little Gershon Mendeloff, rose to lead the Jewish children through the jungle of streets, where they were fair game for all and sundry. Thank God those days of racial intolerance are since long dead in this country. Casual remarks from strangers would jolt his memory back to his many battles in South America, Australia, France, Germany, Italy, South Africa, Canada and the USA. He would talk about the twenty bouts he had with Jack Britton from whom he twice took the world title, and Alec Lambert, whom he defeated for the British featherweight title, in 1913, his first championship – when still only nineteen.

Father sparred with Jack Johnson, whom he described as the 'cleverest of them all'. He topped the bill and appeared with half the music-hall top-liners of his day. The then Prince of Wales was his host on more than one occasion and the stars of stage and screen of Hollywood, Broadway and the West End of London were proud to call Father a friend. And he gave me as my godfather no less a personage than Charlie Chaplin.

Most days when I visited Father in Brighton we would stroll along the promenade, and rarely had we walked more than a few yards before someone recognized him and introduced himself, or I would be asked, 'Is that Ted "Kid" Lewis?' and would I introduce him to the great man? He would shake his hand, and Father's face would beam with friendliness. I would watch the admiration in the stranger's eyes when asking for Father's autograph. If the stranger was lucky enough to have a camera with him, I would offer to take a picture, which immediately prompted my father to put his arm around the stranger in an embrace, cheek to cheek, in his attempt to bring some pleasure, however small, to friends and strangers alike. A few yards further on and once again we would be stopped. This time it would be perhaps someone I had known for years. Nevertheless, Father would be almost certain to introduce me with, 'This is my son,' and I would warm to the pride in his voice, however unearned it might have been. And always I would hear those words which have become a part of my life, words which never fail to recapture for me that first boyish thrill: 'I knew him before you were born.'

It is through such people that I have been tempted to write this book. I have gathered clippings, stories and photographs that conjured up memories. I remember the stories that Alec 'Zalig' Goodman, my father's first trainer, told me. I was, so I am told, the one person he warmed to. Perhaps grown-ups could read him better. Nevertheless, he was a great source of information until the time I last saw him. In later years, I was able to meet and talk to some of the great fighters who faced my father across the ring: Jack Britton, Willie Richie, Johnny Basham, Jack Perry, Matt Wells, Phil Bloom, Maxie Rosenbloom and Georges Carpentier. And to the men who managed my father: Sam Shear, Charlie Harvey, Jimmy 'Jay Jay' Johnson and Joe Morris. I have met and spoken to, over the years, his friends with whom he grew up in the East End, to those who never left there, and to those, like Father, who managed to break out and make their way in the world. I have met and spoken to other names in the boxing world, including Major Arnold Wilson, Jeff Dickson, Sir Arthur Elvin, Ted Broadribb, Jack Cappel, Harry Levine, Jarvis Astaire, Mike Barrett and Micky Duff. The list is endless and continues to this day. I have checked and double-checked with my aunts and uncles. But most of all, I have obtained the inside stories from my mother and father.

My first attempt to write this book was after my mother passed away in 1962, but my heart was not in it. We did not think that my father would last six months without her, because Elsie Lewis was his engine. She was a remarkable woman, whose personality finally filtered through to my father and gave him the education he needed outside the ring, which he had not received in childhood.

I tried again to write the book in 1966, only to find that I was spending more and more time with my father, accompanying him to boxing shows, dinners, to many, many shows where he was the guest of honour and, consequently, I was meeting more and more people. Their stories were never-ending. Finally, it reached a stage where I did not know where or how to start. I kept learning more about him as time went by, especially when he was spending his last four years in the comfort of the Nightingale Home. I would call to take him out for the day. The feeling of pride and pleasure which went through my body cannot be described. I treated him like my son. After all, he was my responsibility. I would guide him in how to dress, in where we should go, which invitations to accept, which to refuse. Not that many refusals were necessary because they were all his admirers. I was worried that people would forget his name. Fortunately, the press never did. I think they enjoyed writing about him. After all, they didn't have to invent a story! There were a million stories and incidents from which they could draw – he was good copy. Then came the time when I decided I was not capable of writing his book and stopped other people trying because I did not want another boxers' book, which would most likely be a record of his fights, as they can be seen in any one of the many boxing record books.

I wanted to enjoy being with him for the rest of his days, not write about his past. We enjoyed the last eight years of his life. I grew to understand him in a way in which no one other than my mother could. It was a sad day when, after one week in bed with a cold, he passed away peacefully in his sleep on 20 October 1970. The press gave him a memorable send-off. Here are just a few paragraphs extracted from the papers the next day: George Whiting – without doubt one of England's leading sports writers of his day – wrote in the *Evening Standard*: 'The Dashing, Crashing, Ted Kid Lewis dies at 75. Ted Kid Lewis, whose ice-cold fist used to crush bones, cried like a baby when the Boxing Writers' Club, early in 1964, gave him a silver trophy inscribed "To the Best Old Boxer of This or any other Year, Ted Kid Lewis, from the Boxing Writers' Club 1964". Now that the Dashing, Crashing Kid is dead – he would have been 76 next Saturday – and it is we who should be weeping. We shall not again see his like. He fought like a killer. He ended his days a kindly old gentleman, a pugilistic patriarch – and the softest touch in the business. He was the last British boxer to win a world title abroad. If there are punch-ups in paradise, rest assured that Ted "Kid" Lewis will be there – ringside.'

Neil Allen wrote in *The Times*: 'In the ring Lewis was a hard man, but outside the ropes, he was generous to a fault. He will be remembered not only for his fiery attack and incredible determination, but also for his dignity and modesty in old age whenever lesser men, all of us, toasted him for his deeds of long ago.'

Reg Gutteridge summed it all up in the last paragraph of his obituary in the *Evening News*: 'The man whose fighting heart was second to none literally "gave up the fight" when his 65-year-old American wife Elsie died in 1962. They had been married 45 years.'

Among the numerous letters sent to the newspapers, paying their respects, several wrote to say, 'My first sight of the seaside was thanks to the generosity of Ted Kid Lewis.'

The television news and sports commentators on both the BBC and ITV were generous in the time they gave to inform the public of the passing of the great sportsman. The sad news was given out by the press and television in the USA and in countries wherever he had boxed.

The turnout at the cemetery was something I shall never forget. I arrived to see hundreds of people, faces that I had seen around for years, tough faces with tears, faces that could frighten a lot of people who might oppose them in other circumstances. All were there to pay their respects to their friend and idol. It looked like a *Who's Who* of sport and from all other walks in life. There he was counted out for the last time. As they lowered the box, my 15-year-old son put his arm around my shoulders to comfort me. How good it felt. It took me back eight years to my mother's funeral. I hope my father felt the same when I put my arm around him. I remember sitting on a wooden bench in the small synagogue as an unending line of people came past to shake my hand, to wish me Long Life – a traditional blessing in the Jewish religion. I could not control the tears streaming down my cheeks. I was not embarrassed because I drew consolation from seeing tougher men than I will ever be openly crying. The last person on the line was a tough-looking fellow, 'one of the London boys'. He placed a small folded piece of paper in my hand, wished me Long Life and said, 'Here, put this in your pocket, read it later.' During the next few weeks I received hundreds of letters from friends and from people I had never heard of, each one remembering my father, describing their feelings. Among these was a letter from Lord Avon, then Sir Anthony Eden. I then came across the piece of paper I had been given in the cemetery. I unfolded it. It was an envelope and scribbled on it was, 'Ronnie, Reggie send their deepest sympathy to their best friend Ted Kid Lewis and also myself. Mrs Kray.' One could not conceive a more extreme contrast than that between Sir Anthony Eden and the Kray brothers, but it does demonstrate that my father loved everybody alike, as I am sure they loved him.

He was a living legend who spent 62 of his 76 years achieving something that very few people in England have done. He 'made it' and was loved for doing it. He will be remembered for the man he was as much, if not more, than as the boxer. Yet I still hesitated to write his story, inwardly afraid that these last few generations would not have heard of Ted 'Kid' Lewis, that is until I went to a recent Boxing Writers' Club Annual Club Dinner. No, they had not forgotten him. Several people at the dinner said the book should be written, so I decided then and there to finish it and if a publisher wasn't interested, then I would print and publish it myself. Fortunately, this wasn't necessary. Robson Books offered to publish it. I accepted the challenge and went to work. I would treat the early years as a biography, until such time as I could take over. Although I called him 'Daddy' all our life together, I shall refer to my father as TK in all cases and try to avoid writing it as a film script. The theme would be about a son finding out about his father from people who knew more about him than I did.

My main problem in writing was not what to put in, but what to leave out. I kept meeting people; they all had something to say. I would find notes TK made for his story that never got started. Photographs were sent to me; they all acted as a catalyst to my memory and I think are interesting enough to be included. So I wrote it my way – doing the best I could in a field in which I felt absolutely inadequate – where I was a complete novice. Nevertheless I have enjoyed doing it. I hope that those of you who read it will understand what I have tried to do and perhaps find it interesting. And finally, people often used to ask me, what was it like to be in the shadow of such a great man? I wish I could have thought of the answer Edwina Dixon, Winston Churchill's granddaughter, gave to a similar question, 'It was not being in his shadow, I was basking in his sunlight.' That said it all for me.

Morton Lewis
1990

PART ONE
A Star Rises in the East

1 The Cabinet-maker's Son

'His fighting career was a real ring romance. Nothing I
have ever seen in boxing films has matched his story'
Charlie Rose

My father was born Gershon Mendeloff, son of Solomon Mendeloff, cabinet-maker, on 28 October 1893. Place of birth, 56
Umberston Street, St George's-in-the-East, in the heart of what
was then, in fact if not in name, the Jewish East End.

Life was hard. TK was the Mendeloffs' third child and in the next
twelve years mother Leah had five more. Thus, even when Solomon
was in full employment, it was difficult to make ends meet. TK
recalled: 'Often as a child I lived a hard day on a cup of water and
a slice of bread covered thinly in sugar.'

While his brothers and sisters seemed to thrive on such fare, he
struggled, and for a time it was thought he was consumptive. As a
small child he was all bones and pipe-stem arms with a body that
was no more than a cage of ribs covered with the leanest possible
sheath of dead-looking white skin.

Though apparently sickly, he was in fact a restless, energetic child,
never able to keep still for long, and in the days when boots and shoes
were scarce and of poor quality it meant he was always wearing them
out. Which only made matters more difficult for his mother. As TK
recalled: 'My dear mother worried a lot about me because I was so
different to my five sisters and two brothers . . . often she protected
me from the wrath of Dad who could always see holes in my boots
while missing those in my brothers' and sisters'.'

TK's relationship with his father would always be a difficult one.
Solomon Mendeloff was a quick-tempered man, obsessed, even
soured, by the day-to-day struggle to earn enough money to feed
the family, a struggle he all too often lost. He was a proud man,
too proud perhaps, for TK claimed that there were times when
the family went hungry when a word to the neighbours might have
helped.

Solomon had even taken the drastic step of setting off alone for South Africa in search of work. The rest of the family – TK was then five and Leah was pregnant with the third daughter – were left to fend for themselves until Solomon could send money. Money did eventually arrive, but never enough and after two hard years he was forced to return, having achieved nothing. The losing struggle resumed – no wonder TK later excused his father's avariciousness with the words: 'His was a hard life, enough to embitter the temper of an angel.'

It did not help the father–son relationship that TK was, until the age of ten, the only boy in the family. Solomon was anxious that TK should, as soon as he was able, lend a hand in the family cabinet-making business. Solomon seemed less inclined to restrain himself when venting his frequent rages where TK was concerned – Solomon would never strike a daughter. No wonder, then, that Leah treated TK like her 'ewe' lamb. Not that he ever looked particularly ewe-like. His face – which lent a clue to his Russian ancestry, being sculpted with high, prominent cheekbones – was striking, with eyes that, being deep-set and of a steely blue, could look disconcertingly at you as if he were weighing up a possible enemy and estimating just where your weakness might be. The body might have been that of an undernourished street urchin, but the face, even then, was that of a fighting man, fighting for survival.

With the advent of schooldays, however, life began to change. 'It was the proudest day of my life when I passed the exam which admitted me to the famous Jewish Free School, for I knew that no more would I go ragged nor wear boots through which my toes peeped out on a cold hard world.'

TK's health began to improve at the school; he saw the world beyond the confines of the ghetto streets on regular trips to the countryside; he even learnt, much to his surprise, that London was just a tiny dot in a great big world. . .

In fact, Rothschilds' Jewish Free School made a deep impression on TK as a boy, deeper perhaps than he knew. That such dramatic changes as had occurred in his own life could be brought about by the application of simple charity was a lesson he never forgot. And though he left the school with hardly any academic qualifications, he graduated with honours – in philanthropy.

In the decades to come, his open-handed generosity became a byword in the East End, particularly among the children who would flock like starlings around scattered breadcrumbs – only TK would be scattering gold and silver coins.

But then, kids had always flocked around him – even when he had been a child himself: 'I was a bad boy at school in as much as I was nearly always fighting. I had only to hear that Jack so-and-so fancied himself as a fighter than I went looking for him to test him out! Victory wasn't always mine, but I generally won in the end owing to my stubbornness in refusing to admit defeat. Would you believe I fought a fellow every day for a week? He was a tough guy, that chap, but on the seventh day he quit saying, "You ain't human, so I'm quitting".'

What the origins were of his pugnacity, or of his innate courage, no one could say. Perhaps he inherited them from his father, Solomon, even though the cabinet-maker professed himself to be a man who hated all forms of aggression. . .

Among the older generation such apparent antipathy towards overt violence was understandable. Solomon and his family had fled Russia to avoid terrible pogroms; it was said Solomon had himself witnessed the slaughter of relatives and friends, and even in London the reality of ghetto life suggested that turning the other cheek was the best policy.

But such instincts of self-preservation were not being passed on to a generation born in England and educated to expect equality, in principle if not always in fact.

And when on the route to school groups of Gentile boys hurled mud and stones at Jewish children, and called out 'Dirty Jews', 'sheenys', 'Christ murderers', it seemed the natural thing for Jewish boys to form their own gangs for self-protection. TK later recalled: 'When it was time to go to school in the morning, my best friend Curley would be waiting for me on the corner with the rest of the Jewish neighbourhood boys, to lead them and run the gauntlet through the "Goys" that waited for the Jew boys. I would wrap my belt around my hand and we marched through as one, defying any attack. If they did chance their arms, we would usually drive them back running to their parents.'

In this respect the children of Umberstone Street could now hold their heads up high, for in Gershon Mendeloff they had a champion, who would fearlessly face the impending trouble generally with boys much bigger than himself. Indeed, stacking the odds against himself seemed to fire him up – a clue to his subsequent successful career in the ring.

TK would always tell me of how much he revelled in fighting from as far back as he could recall. I have a vision of him leading his followers to school and back through the streets made infamous by Jack the Ripper, leaving a trail of bloody noses and black eyes behind him. In the evening, when returning home, bright-eyed and panting from the exertion of mounting a running street fight, in the alleyway he would pause to brush back the blond hair, arrange his ragged little jersey and wipe the tell-tale blood from his lips.

It would usually be in vain, however. Solomon Mendeloff was rarely deceived. His eyes would note the signs of conflict. In the evenings, as soon as he was old enough to hold a chisel, TK helped out in the small workshop his father rented, and here he had to be doubly careful. Any tell-tale abrasion on his face and: ' "Fighting again?" Dad would say. "Come on, fight me, my boy," and then he would either clip me around the ear, or he would throw lumps of wood at me! I think I preferred the blocks of wood, I'm sure it helped me learn to duck and side-step, in fact I began to parry them with my hands. It really used to annoy Dad, he'd stop and scowl at me.

' "Pick up the wood," he would say. I kept my eye on him as I picked the blocks up – I wasn't sure whether he just wanted them for more ammunition. Fortunately he got tired before me and we would go back to work. But the injustice of it made me mad. I was never a "squealer" myself. That is to say, any hidings I took while I was fighting I took with a good heart, but the kids I beat, most of them went home crying to their fathers and mothers who came and complained to my parents! And then there was another beating!'

Street-fighting soon became a poor substitute for the real thing, however. By the time he was ten, TK was dreaming of prize-fights and the fame they would bring him. Prize-fighting was, of course, an important part of the East End sub-culture. From the 1850s right through to the late 1930s, the area east of Aldgate Pump was the largest nursery of boxers in the country, and in the years leading up to the First World War boxing as a spectator sport had rapidly become something of a craze. The music-halls and theatres of the East End staged more and more tournaments, much to the disgust of the social reformers and 'respectable' inhabitants. An editorial in the *East End Observer* of 1911 commented: 'The so-called boxing matinée – which is neither professional nor amateur, scientific nor artistic – is the lowest form of sport which ought not to be tolerated by even a veneer of authority. The consequent gathering of human scum and villainy constitutes at once a public danger and a local nuisance of the first magnitude.'

And at an LCC weekly meeting some weeks later there were complaints concerning boxing exhibitions at the nearby Paragon Hall: 'The most disgusting operations they had ever seen and the respectable inhabitants were loud in their complaint, being unable to leave their doors owing to the crowds in the vicinity of the halls where the performances were going on.'

It was among these crowds, however, that TK increasingly found himself, caught up in the excitement, the frenzy of the betting, the scuffles and the shouting – the sense of something happening! It was rare in those early days before he left school that he had the money for even the cheapest ticket to a tournament. Nevertheless, he would stand outside the hall, sharing in the passion as the roar of the crowd inside reached its climax.

He claimed he could describe the style of every local boxer even before he had seen his first professional bout! And when he did at last become a regular patron of the theatres and halls he was instantly captivated, adopting heroes whose names and images would remain with him all his long life.

The first fighter to catch his imagination in a big way was the great American Jimmy Britt: 'He was the idol of my boyhood . . . I first saw him at the Memorial Football Ground, West Ham, on the afternoon he was KO'd by Johnny Summers.'

Though Summers was the Englishman and all of TK's friends (and indeed the whole crowd) were on his side, TK was gripped by the sight of the fair-haired American. 'And when I saw him sink to the canvas under a hail of blows I felt quite sick. As young as I was, I could see he was past his best, but somehow I loved him for the smile that he wore when he must have known his chance of winning was hopeless. It was his smile that got to me.'

There were other heroes, of course, much closer to home: Sid Burns, Jack Scales – Young Joseph. In fact, when Young Joseph fought Harry Lewis (the man whose name TK had previously stolen!) for the world welterweight title in June 1910, TK stood outside Wonderland on the Whitechapel Road until the fight was over and then followed his defeated hero all the way to Aldgate in silent admiration: 'He had previously gained my respect by diving into the water at Goulston Street baths and giving first aid to a boy who had fallen from the gallery during one of the swimming sessions and injured his head on the bottom of the bath . . . in fact, his family lived near my school and kept a clothing store; they hired out roller-skates after school hours

and I was a frequent customer in order to get a glimpse of my
hero. . .'

Thus for TK the romance of the prize ring was a real and tangible
thing. His heroes could be seen in the flesh, even touched, and he
could participate closely in their struggles and triumphs – they were
a part of his everyday life.

In 1906 he left the Jewish Free School and started an apprenticeship
in his father's workshop. His father lied to the school authorities
about TK's age, saying he was fourteen when in fact he was
twelve, but TK had no complaints. Like many boys of his age
he felt school had become an irksome thing; to work and earn
some real money appealed to him: 'So as a dutiful son I followed
in my Dad's footsteps and became a cabinet-maker. I was already
pretty good for I had been taught carpentry at school and because
I wanted to be better than my classmates I used to practise at home
in the evenings – when there was no fighting to be done. In fact
later on I made a cabinet that even pleased my Dad. At least I
had accomplished something. In this way I won first prize at the
end of the year for being the best woodworker in the school.'

First prize was a set of tools; together father and son progressed
to having a workshop of their own. Instead of having to pay for an
apprenticeship TK learned his trade from his father who paid him
2s.6d. for a fifty-two-hour week. Two shillings went to his
mother for housekeeping: 'And I spent the rest, the odd tanner, in
riotous living. . .'

And where was the riotous living to be had? In the local music-
halls, then in their heyday.

Within easy walking distance of TK's house was the Cambridge
Music Hall in Commercial Street where Charlie Chaplin – who
became a close friend of TK's – first found fame in the *Humming
Birds*; and round the corner was the Olympic Music Hall where
for 2d. you could buy a seat in the gallery. It was here that the
incident occurred that was to lead TK into the world of his dreams:
'Several of us were in the habit of having twopennyworth up in
the gallery of the Olympic Music Hall, and one night I noticed a
chap about to strike a girl. I felt moved to interfere, but instead
of being grateful she turned on me, asking, "Why can't you mind
your own business?"

'Her heavy-handed boyfriend was a rival gang-leader and a "tough
guy", and was not prepared to let the matter drop, so before you
could say Harry Lewis, we were in the street, coats off, and shaping

up, when a policeman interrupted the proceedings – but instead of pinching us, he proved a rare sport.

' "Why don't you boys go down to the Judean Club?" he said. "You'll get paid for fighting there." '

And off they went. Destiny, it seemed, had decided to beckon TK at last.

2 The Judean Club

'You wanna be a box-fighter? You? Never!'
Solomon Mendeloff

The Judean Club was situated just off Cable Street in Princes Square. Part boxing-hall, part gymnasium, part social club, it took as its unusual model the National Sporting Club in Covent Garden, dubbing itself, tongue-in-cheek no doubt, the National Sporting Club of the East, although there were members of the Club committee who did indeed become NSC members.

There could hardly have been two more dissimilar institutions: the Covent Garden club (virtually the headquarters of British boxing) being on a par with gentlemen's clubs such as White's and the Garrick, patronized by the nobility and the wealthy, while the Judean Club was once described by TK himself as being 'little more than a big room over a cowshed'.

It was small and often packed to suffocation and was extremely noisy on fight nights. As a *Boxing News* correspondent observed on the very afternoon TK was due to make his first appearance in September 1909: 'Oh ye Gods! You could not hear yourself shout! We would impress upon the good boys of the Judean Club to maintain silence, if not all the time, at least during the boxing. Howling and bawling to your pal in the ring does not help him; as a matter of fact, it tends to hinder him.'

Not that the Judean patrons would have taken much notice of any calls for 'hush'. Money was usually at stake and shouting was more often than not being directed at the referee in an attempt to sway the verdict.

It was a rough and ready place and could be dangerous. No doctor supervised the endless contests; no Board of Control checked the safety regulations. In fact, on that same September night, as *Boxing*'s correspondent stood enduring the noise, he watched as one unfortunate young fighter was punched against the ropes, which failed to support him. He toppled out of the ring on to the referee's table where he gashed his arm on a bottle of Tizer and had to be rushed to the nearby London Hospital. Secretary of the club, Sam Kite, hurried up to the journalist with assurances that the ropes would be tightened and strengthened. . .

And it was into this unprepossessing atmosphere that TK strode on that fateful September afternoon: 'I clambered up a steep flight of stairs which I found opened into a large room with a boxing ring in the centre. It was my first visit to a recognized boxing hall. Right in front of this was a small enclosure, to sit in which cost sixpence. Scattered around the room were people of all nations – mostly Jewish, it being the Gentile Sabbath.'

What happened next is part of boxing legend. The boy from the theatre never turned up. Secretary Kite, when prevailed upon by TK to produce a substitute opponent, obliged by pairing him with Johnny Sharp, one of three brothers of a famous East End fighting family which included Young Cohen, who was to figure in TK's career in later years. In the official record book this fight features as TK's first.

He fought, understandably, like a novice, but he gave the crowd a great deal of entertainment with his stubbornness. 'I ducked under the ropes to a roar of laughter. I remember little of the fight. I know I started with a southpaw stance which was quickly corrected by my second, Alf Goodwin. I also know that something was hitting me far too often to be pleasant and that something was my opponent's glove. I hit back, mostly with wild swings, and I know that some of them connected. I still lost the decision.'

The very sight of him must have caused the majority of the crowd to back his opponent. With no proper kit, borrowed gym shoes and faded black shorts tied at the waist with a frayed sash, with ribs jutting out of a painfully thin chest and sharp elbows, he must have cut a sorry sight. In fact, it is just possible that *Boxing*'s correspondent had TK in mind when he lamented: 'We will not, we hope, be thought unkind when we say we have no love for kiddies fighting each other. It is all very well when a boy has finished his schooling and when afterwards he expresses a desire for the game to let him learn the tricks of the mystic square, but not before. . .'

For TK, however, now was the hour. There would be no turning back. From that first prize fight (for which he was paid 6d. and a cup of tea!) there is no doubt that he was back the following week earning another 6d., this time winning for the first time, again over six long rounds. By the end of the year he had fought five more times, winning four and drawing one. He was, by then, a Judean regular, training every evening he could, and acting as 'stop-gap' for any pros unable to turn up for scheduled bouts.

He knew that nothing could now stop his becoming a fully fledged professional himself: 'I thought of it every day and dreamt of it every night. It became such an obsession that it detracted from my work as a cabinet-maker.'

His father and now employer did not learn of his son's obsession for some time. Though his mother suspected, she said nothing, and though he fought frequently, his name – his real name at least – did not appear on any bills or posters. For he had assumed his pseudonym – Kid Lewis.

How he had come to choose such a name is also something of mystery. It had, he claimed at various times, been just a flash of inspiration, prompted by fear. When asked his name by the Judean Club MC prior to his first fight, so that patrons might know upon whom they were placing their pennies and shillings, he had at first been struck dumb. He could not say Gershon Mendeloff – his father would have known about it before the evening was out. 'The only name I could think of was Harry Lewis – a great fighter and the welterweight champion of the world. "Kid Lewis," I blurted out.'

And Kid Lewis it was to remain. (The 'Ted' was added some years later in America.)

But if the name he carried with him into the Judean ring was unoriginal ('Kids', with their Wild West connotation, were almost as plentiful as 'Youngs' in the professional ring) his gradually evolving boxing style was certainly something new to the Judean patrons.

TK had received no formal boxing training as a boy. His father would have prevented it even if there had been a boys' club near by that he could have joined. Thus, being keen and observant, with each fight that passed he learnt something new, either from his opponent or from the experienced seconds and fighters with whom he mingled at the Judean Club.

For the Judean Club was undoubtedly a repository of experience and no little excellence. It had produced and would continue to produce champion-class fighters right up until its destruction by Zeppelin bombs in the First World War. Young Joseph, Joe Fox, Harry Reeve, Mike Honeyman, Fred Halsband, Sid Burns, Jack Greenstock – all had cut their professional boxing teeth at the old Club.

However, whatever TK learned he was to graft on to a style that was, at first, peculiarly his own, a style formed partly through realistic analysis and partly through a physical deformity that would later exclude him from the British armed forces.

He noticed that many of the swiftest moving fighters boxed high on their toes (at this stage he was little more than 7 st.). But for him to box on his toes was extremely difficult. His poorly shod feet from childhood days had developed hammer toes and insteps flattened from running over cobbles – thus he was more at home moving flat-footed, which had the advantage of producing punches of greater power. To compensate for the lack of speed such a style entailed, he developed swift fist work: fast hands. With his deadpan expression, his jaw half-open, eyes unblinking, he presented a strange, sometimes unnerving sight, continually edging forward towards his opponent, his left hand carried low touching his left thigh and his right hand clenched across the top of his trunks, feinting, shuffling forward all the time ready to spring through the briefest opening.

As such, he would have been unrecognizable to his father, who regarded his growing son with a mixture of impatience and disdain, particularly as TK was now increasingly often late, lacking in diligence and occasionally suspiciously marked about the face.

As the months went by and his secret life became more onerous, TK felt the pressures mounting: 'My willingness to fight anybody, at any time, meant that I had no trouble getting a fight at one of the Saturday matinées put on by local music-halls. Boy, how I had to scratch gravel in those days. At one o'clock sharp I knocked off work, took my weekly wage of 2s.6d., gave Mother two shillings, and then made a beeline for the arena where I was to fight. Later the same evening I would probably go to the same theatre to see a show. It gave time for my face to heal and get back to normal.'

Eventually his parents, and especially his father, had to find out. A competition was held at the Judeans' to find the best boy at bantamweight. A cup was offered and a 5s. prize. TK won, and suddenly, to his horror, he was a local hero, with small boys calling at his home asking to see the cup.

Though he gave the five shillings to his mother and she hid the cup, his father, on hearing of his son's sudden fame, demanded to be shown it. To TK's surprise, Solomon was momentarily impressed: 'My boy Gershon has won this against all comers! At his age!' he would announce to friends and customers – a clue to things to come. But it was an uneasy truce.

When the furore had died down and the celebrity value had waned, Solomon took to ridiculing TK, mocking his pretensions at being a professional, denigrating the opposition TK had beaten to win the cup. Solomon was angry, of course, at having been deceived but also, and more painfully perhaps, not a little resentful of his son's growing strength and independence.

As life at home became more and more intolerable, TK was forced to consider his future: 'I got so fed up that I began seriously to think of leaving home. It wasn't fear that I should be unable to earn a living that kept me beneath the family roof but the knowledge that my mother would be awfully upset by the departure of her "David".'

And this tug of loyalty was to cause TK more anguish than he would ever experience in the ring. Though his mother quite naturally disliked the idea of his fighting, she accepted that it was what he wanted to do and did her best to keep the awful truth from her volatile husband. Mother and son devised a strategy – they would keep the truth from Solomon until TK was established, and present the old man with a *fait accompli*. In the meantime she found the extra money TK gave her extremely useful, though she paid a price in terms of the almost weekly dread she experienced at the possibility that TK should come to permanent grief in the ring. At least the incident of the Judean cup had brought matters out into the open; now she was faced with the acrimonious struggle of wills between a proud father and a determined son.

When the prize cup was eventually revealed as being made of base metal and not silver, Solomon seemed to have won a psychological victory; when TK suddenly announced that he would be taking a Monday afternoon off to fight at the famous Judean Club, Solomon decided that enough was enough.

There followed a heated argument culminating in TK's being ordered out of the house. He left, went to the Judean Club and won, but when he returned home found himself confronted with an ultimatum. Either he settled down and became a cabinet-maker or, if he insisted on boxing, he was to leave home. He had a fortnight to mull it over.

In a sense, however, it was Solomon Mendeloff's last stand. Though TK was only a sixteen-year-old boy, he was rapidly becoming a seasoned fighter. By now, September 1911, two years after his first fight, he had notched up over sixty bouts – and he had lost only five.

And it was during the fateful fortnight that he was to make the big breakthrough – stepping up from the ranks of journeyman into the promising contender class.

3 Premierland Début

'I really loved to fight – I would take anyone on – the bigger
the name, the better.'

TK

To appear at Wonderland, the famous old boxing hall just off the
Whitechapel Road where world title fights had been staged for
almost a decade, had long been TK's ambition. 'During the period
that I kept up my training at the Judean Club I often stood outside
Wonderland allowing my imagination to run riot, seeing visionary
pictures of my name in large type in company with the stars then
showing – Sid Burns, Jewey Smith, Cockney Cohen, Jack Scales,
Young Joseph, etc. . .'

During the short period in which Solomon Mendeloff allowed TK
to make up his mind – boxing or cabinct-making – Wonderland
staged a novices' bantamweight competition which TK entered, not
so much for the cash prize but for the chance of a real six-round bout
and a place on a proper Wonderland bill.

TK duly knocked out one Young Kline in three rounds in the
final and collected, along with 30s., the long dreamed-of contract to
appear at the famous hall the following Saturday. Unfortunately, he
had also collected a cauliflower ear at the sight of which, he recalled,
his mother almost passed out: 'To this day I can see her face change
from its normally healthy colour to a ghastly white when she saw what
had once been a decently shaped ear. I thought she was going to faint,
and I think she would have done only she realized that Dad was in
the next room. Pulling herself together she quickly put on her hat
and coat and, grabbing me by the hand, dragged me to the nearest
doctor.

'Well, the doctor hurt me. He must have thought that because
I was a boxer any kind of handling would do. It may be that
he was cross at being pulled out of bed. At any rate, whatever
the reason, he pulled and probed my ear this way and that and
made my mother wince. She was in a terrible state of mind

wondering what my father would say when he found out I was still boxing.'

With his ear in such a state he could no longer stay at home. The decision had been made and he left with his clothes before his father could create a scene. He took a room at a local Whitechapel boarding house called Fusco's at 5d. a week. There were other young boxers staying there: Alf Mansfield, Young Brooks, Jackie Phillips. It was easy-going and homely, to a degree – Fusco was a fight fan and never pressed too hard for rent arrears.

But it was not home; home for TK meant his mother: 'It was a rotten life. Home was clean, though the bedclothes may have been scanty. I got fed up with cook-shop food and I missed the daily talks with my mother and her loving care.'

All might have been bearable, however, had the treasured Wonderland fight come off. However, what TK described as his 'first tragic moment' arrived on the very night he was to make his début. Though he saw his name on a Wonderland poster, an achievement in itself, the building mysteriously burnt down: 'I cannot describe my feelings as I watched the building burn . . . something I had dreamed about for so long had gone up in smoke. It seemed my big chance had gone.'

To augment the shillings he earned in the Judean ring, he started selling papers on the Commercial Road with Alf Mansfield; he seemed to be going nowhere, the possibility of a humiliating return home loomed large. And then came a slim chance – at the Judean Club.

Fred Halsband was a top Judean fighter, undefeated at the club and a big draw. On one particular evening in September he was due to fight Tom Briggs, but Briggs failed to turn up. TK recalled: 'Although I had been acting as second for most of the evening and I was feeling a little tired, I thought this was a golden opportunity. I amazed Sam Kite by suggesting that I should fight Halsband.'

The offer soon reached Halsband's ears; he was unimpressed. But TK persisted, even holding out for the full purse, or what he thought was the full purse. Halsband, angered by TK's cool, cheeky attitude, pointed to the dressing room and told him to strip but, 'I added coals to the fire by retorting, "Don't get excited. I haven't arranged terms yet." He asked how much I wanted and I offered to accept thirty shillings. Halsband was about to start the fight there and then when Sam Kite intervened: "Why, Fred himself is only receiving a quid!" '

Eventually TK agreed to accept two shillings.

This cheeky approach paid dividends in more ways than one. Boxing being, more than many sports, a physical one-to-one confrontation, it involves a great deal of pride and self-control. Niggles and arguments before the fight, though often seemingly innocuous, very often serve as a mood-setter for the coming encounter, a psychological game in which opponents try to win the upper hand before throwing a punch. Throughout his career TK, more by straight talking than by devious intent, often gained the upper hand in such pre-fight encounters. His subsequent trainer, Alec Goodman, however, was a past master at 'riling' opponents and their handlers, and he would regularly upset, demoralize and fluster men usually noted for their cold, calculated approach.

Fred Halsband had certainly been flustered: 'At the bell, he went in for the kill, but he had made two foolish fatal mistakes – he underrated me and he lost his head.

'I kept mine, my brain was like an icebox, and I used the ring as much as possible, jabbing him with my left hand whenever I had the opportunity. No one knew better than I that Fred was a very good boxer, but I also knew that he had allowed his outraged dignity to confuse his judgement and the cooler I boxed, the more ragged he became. The decision was a draw and my stock shot up like a rocket, the fact that I had run the Club champion to a draw doing me a power of good.'

Upon such chances, whole careers turn. Quite suddenly, he was able to ask for more money for each fight, sometimes up to fifty shillings a bout, and with his name now an attractive draw, promoters from various nearby music-halls in the East End who used the Judean Club as a recruiting hall began to seek him out. Not only that, he was able to fill even more last-minute vacant spots on prestigious bills although even then his luck stretched only so far: 'On one occasion when it was time to go in for my fight for which I received the princely sum of seven shillings and sixpence I discovered that my new pair of shoes had been stolen, with the result that I had to walk home barefooted.'

The thief, had he known from whom he was stealing, might well have decided to conserve his energy and simply ask for them; the result would have been the same: TK would have walked home barefooted, so soft a 'touch' was he.

However, it was this sudden leap in his earning power that turned the head of Solomon, his father, although the older man took some time before relenting. A chance encounter in the street with his mother who had been searching high and low for him – the very stuff of Yiddish theatre – led to TK's returning home: 'She found me at the newspaper stall; I must have presented a sorry sight in my tattered clothes and gaping boots. It was a touching reunion and I am not ashamed to admit that my tears mingled with those of Mother. She begged me to return home with the promise that Father would relent.'

But it was not to be quite so easy. TK related how that same night he slipped into bed without his father hearing. The following morning he made no effort to go in for breakfast, hoping that his father would simply go off to work: 'But I think he must have smelled a rat. Perhaps Mother's anxiety to get him out of the house aroused his suspicions. Anyhow, he would not budge, so, putting on as bold a face as I could, I walked into the room and sat down at the table. Well, you should have heard Dad go off! It would have been far easier to tell you what he did not say. He raved and ranted, stormed and swore by his father's beard that he would sling me out of the house neck and crop. Mother burst into tears and then something seemed to turn over inside me. Rising to my feet I told him plump and plain that I was through with cabinet-making and had determined in future to spend all my time in perfecting myself in boxing.

'He sneered, "What good will that do you?" '

'Mother's answer came pat enough. "It's done you a lot of good already!" And then, gathering courage, she continued, "You and the children would have gone hungry many a time if it hadn't been for the money Gersh has given us out of his earnings from boxing."

'He looked at Mother, then at me – then he left the room without uttering another word. For weeks he never addressed a word to me and I might just as well have been dead, so completely did he ignore me.'

But Solomon eventually relented, though he offered no word of apology or reconciliation.

Established once more at home within the beloved family, TK looked out on a world suddenly filled with promise. 'At the age of sixteen I was receiving an average of 50s. for bouts of eight and ten rounds and boxing with fair regularity. But what was much more important, I was learning the finer points of boxing and ring-craft and consequently going into the ring with greater confidence and faith in my ability.'

What is more, he was approached towards the end of 1911 by a significant figure in British boxing history: 'One day I met a promoter. He told me that he was building a boxing hall not a stone's throw from where I lived and before I could ask him for a job he said, "How would you like to sign a contract with me for sixteen fights at £4 a fight?"

'I thought he was joking with me. Just fancy, £4 a fight for sixteen of them and to be fought at the rate of two per month. Why, that would mean an income of two pounds a week!

'All this flashed through my head as he stood there waiting for my answer and for me in those simple days two pounds a week seemed to be fabulous wealth. I said, "Yes", I would sign.'

The promoter in question was Harry Jacobs and the hall he was building, or rather refurbishing, was to be called Premierland.

Jacobs had seen his previous arena, Wonderland, which he had run in partnership with Jack Woolf, burn to the ground in August of that year. By then he had parted company with Woolf after many bitter arguments and hurling of insults which had all too often spilled over into the Wonderland ring between bouts. . .

Having failed to establish the Paragon Music Hall as a venue in competition with Wonderland during the summer he had rented an empty warehouse on Back Church Lane which led down to Cable Street and the river. At considerable cost he re-created Wonderland beneath the glass roof of the one-time meat store, and in December 1911 he opened with a showman's flourish.

Top of the bill had been Harry Mansfield versus Bill Curzon, a middleweight clash with local interest; further down the bill had come Sid Burns, Nat Brooks, Jack Bunner, Harry Reeve and, almost at the bottom but not quite, Kid Lewis versus Jewey Murray. TK recalled little of the evening except that, 'Murray was a nice-looking youngster and it seemed a shame to hit him but it was a job that had to be done so I went to do it with all my might and knocked him out in the first round.'

' "No Shenanigans," said the promoter before we started. Without in the least knowing what he meant I suppose he was satisfied after it was over since as I was being handed down the steps leading from the ring after winning he patted me on the shoulder and said, "Good boy, Lewis".'

However, TK was anything but pleased at the prospect that suddenly stretched out before him. He had not realized that he could box nowhere else but Premierland for quite some time: 'It was sheer bad luck that my father had so sternly set his face against me adopting the career of a professional boxer. If only we had been friendly then I should never have signed on for so long. The contract bound me down not to box elsewhere for the next eight months, which was, to say the least of it, a very harsh clause. But it was useless to cry over spilt milk and rightly or wrongly I had put my signature to the paper.'

Whether his father would have been quite as beneficial an influence at that stage is open to doubt. Solomon certainly made determined efforts in the following months to wrest his son from Jacobs's grasp – this, after appearing to have experienced a conversion almost as surprising and complete as that of the Biblical Saul.

On that first Premierland night, TK was hurrying on with his clothes in order to be first at the paying-out box when he was told that his father was in the audience. . . 'He had apparently caused much laughter and amusement by his encouraging shouts and his offers to back me for fabulous sums of money. "It's my son, I tell you, and he can beat any boy his weight or heavier already!" he would say to those around him who told him to shut up.

'I told my mother all about him and she was tickled to death to think that Father should go to see me fight. Just then we heard a footstep on the stairs. My boyish vanity would scarcely allow him to get inside the room before I said, "Well, Dad, what do you think of me as a boxer now?"

'What do you think his reply was? This – "Don't bother me. I always thought you would be a champion."

'Would you believe it? Always thought I would be a champion! Then I thought of all the times he had hurled blocks of wood, and hit me to try and stop me – and I went to bed.

'Father's conversion was complete from then on. He used to walk boldly up to the pay-box and demand a free ticket saying, "I am 'Kid' Lewis's father." He always got one right away unless a new man happened to be in the office when, of course, there would be trouble, out of which Dad would always emerge triumphant.'

TK's father's pride in his son's achievements carried a price, of course. TK's devotion to his family, his tolerance of their ever-increasing demands, combined with his open-handed generosity, were to prove disastrous to him financially. To put it bluntly, from being a mere supplement of the family income TK rapidly became the family's meal-ticket – a teenager supporting a family of nine! Free entrance to fights demanded as of right by his father were extended to complete financial dependence, which TK bore without so much as a murmur of complaint.

Not long after the Premierland début, Solomon introduced TK to Sam Shear, a boxing manager who already had Young Jack Cohen on his books. Shear was to prove a dubious addition to the Lewis entourage – in fact the relationship ultimately ended up in court. At the time, however, TK allowed his father to talk him into signing: 'Naturally I wanted to know what I was signing, but Father told me he had arranged for me to have a manager who would be the means of making a lot of money for all concerned.'

In fact, Shear had already paid Solomon a £20 bribe to sign, a secret he kept from TK for some years.

Thus within a matter of months, from being alone, down and almost out, in Fusco's doss-house, TK had acquired a promoter, a manager and a devoted, enthusiastic father.

Kid Lewis was obviously a very valuable commodity.

4 Apprentice Days

'For years I had dreamed of this first night at the National Sporting Club, but never in my wildest dreams had I pictured myself being counted out . . . and in the first round at that.'

TK

In January 1912 TK's picture appeared for the first time in *Boxing*, the weekly bible of British boxing, posing in training briefs above a caption, 'A most promising bantam who has met with only three defeats in the course of his career to date.' He stands looking all of his sixteen years, though not quite as frail as he had appeared a year before. In fact, the *Boxing* caption was out of date. He was now a full featherweight and within six months he would regularly have to reduce himself from near lightweight to make the nine st. featherweight limit. More often than not, he would fight at a few pounds above the featherweight limit. What is more, over a period of twenty-seven months he had fought 83 contests, losing just five. For a boy of sixteen it was an incredible record and takes no account of the numerous matinée bouts he had taken on at local music-halls, not to mention the hundreds of sparring bouts he managed to fit into his busy schedule.

Harry Jacobs certainly obtained his pound of flesh, for the year saw TK fight at Premierland no fewer than 35 times! Sam Shear at least managed to negotiate slightly better terms when he took over his new protégé – although the fact that Shear already had a poor relationship with Jacobs did not help matters. But the Lewis–Shear relationship was never to be a happy one. TK resented the fact that Shear was able to negotiate much better terms for his main fighter, Young Jack Cohen. In fairness to Shear, Cohen was a hot property having just returned from the States where he had fought the legendary Abe Attell; he was a bona fide contender for the featherweight title while TK had yet to fight anyone of similar class.

Shear, however, never seemed to have any real ambitions for TK, seeing him more as a willing work-horse who would fight at the drop of a hat and thus produce a regular, if limited, income. Shear was even accused, in the subsequent court case when TK broke the contract, of suggesting to TK that he would get more money if he 'threw' his subsequent featherweight title match.

TK could console himself, however, with the fact that early in 1912, some months before Shear took over his contract, two wealthy and influential 'backers' – Tom Williams, a bookmaker, and Ernest Mogford – had offered to stake him whenever he fought. With backers to secure attractive side-stakes, challenges could be issued to established men and with challenges came much bigger purses. It was in this way that real money could be made rather than via the regular fees paid by promoters such as Jacobs.

The two backers had almost stumbled across TK, arriving at Premierland one evening to watch another fighter of promise, Darky Harris, who happened to be TK's opponent. It took them no longer than a round, however, to change their minds and they were to remain loyal backers for many years to come (although their loyalty was always tempered by hard financial sense, as we shall see).

More significantly, their interest and the subsequent challenges they issued to featherweights to take on 'their' man resulted in TK's making his début at the NSC – the 'headquarters' of boxing, home of the Lonsdale Belts. 'Having a backer I blossomed forth, throwing out a challenge to anyone in the country at 9 st. This was quickly snapped up by a man whom I had already defeated – Duke Lynch. The match was fixed to take place at the National Sporting Club for £25 a side, but it proved a fiasco for me.'

The earlier win over Lynch had convinced everyone connected with TK that it would be easy money. 'A big crowd of members turned up to see this, the latest Star of the East, namely me, shine. I never even glimmered for I was down and out before I realized the fight had begun. I shall never discover how or why this disaster happened. Perhaps it was the grand array of cigar-smoking faces and polished shirt-fronts gleaming with diamonds which surrounded the ring – or perhaps it was not.'

The *Boxing* report of the fight suggests an answer. Under the headline, 'Will You Please Keep Your Jaw Fairly Safe?', a correspondent wrote: 'Through an indifference and almost reckless disrespect of this, one of the first principles of the game, he went down to defeat in inside two minutes.'

It seemed that TK had taken Lynch too lightly, 'and very unwisely jumped gaily into a positively savage exchange of swings and hooks after the very briefest of preliminary spars'.

TK, it was noted, had a tendency to slog it out on occasions when what was required was restraint and judgement. What is more, when hurt, he simply waded back into the fray. As *Boxing* said: 'One would have imagined that he would learn wisdom during the rest (he was put down for eight seconds), but he rose to mingle matters again, only to receive far more than he could hand out.'

It was purely experience that he lacked; he had lost on points before but had rarely been in much trouble during the course of his brief, prolific, relentlessly victorious career.

Add to that his tendency to react immediately whenever he was hurt – a desire to re-establish self-belief swiftly no matter what the risk – and the defeat by Lynch can be understood.

It was a blow to TK's pride, however, and a potentially disastrous stumble on his road to the top – of all the places to have failed so lamentably!

He hurried away from the Club without a word to his backers and the very next day was on a boat-train bound for Paris where he was to meet featherweight Leon Truffler within twenty-four hours.

At least he had something to take his mind off Lynch – the contest with Truffler was to take place at the Cirque de Paris, and topping the bill was Georges Carpentier, fighting the great coloured fighter, George Gunther.

If TK had been impressed by the dinner-jacketed ringsiders at the NSC, he had certainly never seen anything like the audience at the Cirque de Paris. In England it was not then the custom for women to attend fights, certainly not at Premierland and the Judeans! But at the Cirque de Paris there were many women, most of them in evening dresses, all having flocked to the arena to see the new French idol of the ring, the man who was to become known as the Orchid Man or Gorgeous George: Georges Carpentier.

It was the first sign for TK of the increasing popularity of boxing, the way in which the 'noble' art was rapidly becoming fashionable, with good-looking men like Carpentier becoming sex-symbols in a way that would have been impossible a few years previously.

But if the audience was proving an eye-opener to TK, the appearance of his opponent had him staring in disbelief. Apart from his magnificent green satin robe with the cockerel of France emblazoned on the back, Leon Truffler's hair had almost certainly been waved, his features powdered and his eyebrows plucked. His general appearance, added to the cloud of perfume which accompanied his introduction, left TK not a little dumbfounded.

He recalled turning to his second, Alec Goodman, and whispering, 'Am I meant to fight him or ask him for a dance?'

TK quickly discovered that though the Frenchman might be rouged and powdered, he was no powder-puff fighter. . .

The unfortunate result against Lynch had preceded TK to Paris; indeed the French promoter had tried to call the contest off, but had been held to the contract. TK won with some ease, however, and as soon as he had showered he returned to the arena to stand at the back of the hall in order not to miss an opportunity to watch Carpentier in action.

More than anything else that evening he was to recall the set face and the gimlet eyes of the handsome Frenchman; the day would come when he too would face the Orchid Man in a contest that gave rise to arguments that continue to this day.

The good notices he received after the Truffler fight helped him recover some of his confidence; his backers, however, had never wavered. On his return from Paris TK went to see Tom Williams to apologize for the Lynch fiasco: ' "Hullo, Kid," was his smiling greeting, and I knew at once that here was a great sportsman. He cut my apologies short and offered to back me again. "Don't be silly," were the words he used. "The best of them lose sometimes," and then he asked me if I wanted any money. I left his house feeling on top of the world because of his consideration and encouragement.'

By June TK was back on course and being talked of as a possible successor to Jim Driscoll, the featherweight champion now close to retirement. With each succeeding Premierland fight there was great excitement and large enthusiastic crowds. Yet still the doubts remained concerning his technique and his inexperience. When he met Seaman Hayes in mid July 1912, the odds were all on the experienced hard-hitting opponent: 'A really tremendous concourse of wise men of the East wended their way Premierland-wards on Saturday night to see how Kid Lewis would fare opposed to that redoubtable wrecker of prospective champions, viz Seaman Hayes . . . but all the wiseacres were confounded. I confess it myself. I also thought the Kid's supporters were trying the youngster too highly and that his lack of generalship would succumb to Hayes's far greater experience. Strange to say the boy was never in trouble, although he sometimes traded right-hand punches with his formidable antagonist – a proceeding which had heretofore brought disaster to so many of the Seaman's opponents.'

Surveying the *Boxing* report it is clear that since his early days of flat-footed shuffling, TK had rapidly developed into a fleet-footed tactician, able to dodge and weave, to anticipate punches almost before they were thrown, to side-step danger and to reduce his opponents to aimless swinging. When the end of the Hayes fight came: 'A roar went up the volume of which I have seldom heard equalled. Hats, sticks, in fact every moveable object within reach was thrown high in the air and when the referee's decision was rendered during the temporary lull the excitement was redoubled, if that could have been possible, and Lewis was carried from the ring shoulder-high.'

TK was, however, still far from being invincible. Four weeks and two more wins following his victory over Seaman Hayes he met his good friend Young Joe Brooks at Premierland. Brooks was a top-rated featherweight, too, just returned from the USA where he had done well. TK ventured to criticize Shear for having made the fight: 'My manager made the match for me and the making does not suggest any great managerial ability on his part since Joe had had vast experience. Still, I had to go through with it. . .'

It would seem an odd criticism to make of Shear, however – Hayes had had even more experience than Brooks, and had been a considerable feather in TK's cap.* And yet the speed with which he was being rushed into such important contests cannot have been good for his overall preparation. TK admitted that his subsequent defeat by Brooks over ten gruelling rounds was due in part to his own lack of confidence. It was also a controversial battle: 'We both bled freely and during the fight his three brothers jumped into the ring, an action which should have immediately brought about disqualification. They were ejected and the fight proceeded.'

Though TK felt he had won, Brooks was given a close decision. There ensued a typical Premierland 'free-for-all' with fist-fights around the ring and bottles flying, further damaging Harry Jacobs's efforts to present a 'respectable' image to the world. . .

However, the Brooks defeat had a great significance for TK's immediate future. He was still one of a select band of featherweights who would soon be contesting the new Lonsdale Belt. Young Brooks was also a contender and their close exciting battle suggested an ideal eliminator, guaranteed to draw the crowds.

TK soon rehabilitated his image at the NSC, defeating Fred Halsband there in early November 1912 over ten rounds.

Indeed, 'Peggy' Bettinson, Secretary of the NSC and one of Britain's most powerful boxing figures, had got to know TK quite well. TK even claimed that Bettinson had taken him into the NSC

---

* Hayes had contested the first ever featherweight belt with Jim Driscoll in 1910.

office after the contest to show him how to use his left hook. As his career rapidly approached a climax, he would need all the expert advice he could get, though he probably learned more about ring-craft from those who actually performed day in, day out, than from the gentlemen gamblers at the NSC: 'During this time I would go to the Black Bull, Whetstone. Sid Burns was training for his match with Johnny Summers for the welterweight championship of England, which Summers won on points. Sid was a wonderful tutor. He "pasted" me unmercifully but the knowledge gained from him stood me in good stead. I even paid my own fare to Whetstone, bought my own tea and took the "mother and father" of a hiding, but it taught me quite a lot. . . Years later I got my own back on Sid – he became my sparring partner!'

5 Title Contender

'I never suffered from nerves. I knew what I had to do
and that was that.'

TK

As 1912 ended, TK could look back upon a year that had brought
him 35 wins and just five defeats. He was now talked about as being
in a different class to most of the men he faced, though he was still
regarded by many experts as well short of championship class.

In December 1912 he beat Harry Berry, billed as the featherweight
champion of Ireland, and once again a fine performance appeared
marred by certain youthful indiscretions, touches of inexperience.
Under the headline, 'Lewis Must Curb His Impetuosity', the
Boxing correspondent wrote: 'The Aldgate boxer is possessed of
an extremely combative temperament – I may say here a most
unfortunate heritage. Should he receive a punch it immediately
becomes an obsession with him to return a Roland for an Oliver.
He slings caution to the winds and hops into the fray, determined
to get back his own. This habit didn't matter much in the fight
under discussion, although he very frequently gave it rein because
he was always – with a few intermissions – the top dog. But this
temperamental trait will surely work his undoing yet, unless it be
firmly restrained.'

Partly because of this and other apparent deficiencies in his
technique, as the 1913 boxing season got under way TK was not
considered the hottest favourite for the featherweight Lonsdale Belt.
In fact, although he was to go through the year undefeated and crown
it all by taking the coveted title, he was regularly the 'underdog' in
the ante-post betting.

One refreshing change in 1913, however, was a new contract and a
different venue. The Premierland treadmill was now to be a thing of
the past. From having 39 fights in 1912 he was to reduce his work-
load to just 12 undefeated contests in 1913; from now on it would be

quality rather than quantity. He even began to travel. In January he made two trips to Liverpool to defeat Jim Lloyd and draw with Nat Williams. However, the majority of his 1913 fights took place at Dick Burge's fistic emporium across the river, the Ring, Blackfriars.

Although no more than a mile or so from 'home' territory, the Ring was, for TK, foreign ground, and the audience was almost always unanimously against him. But he was now a 'draw', and whether fans flocked to see him win or lose made little difference just so long as they came along.

His opening contest was against George Buswell of Fulham, which TK won in round 14. Buswell was outclassed from start to finish, but once again it was noted in *Boxing* how on occasions TK was careless in defence: 'Lewis came in with his usual left-jabbing and finding he was getting home pretty frequently took little if any care about guarding his chin.'

Buswell, on three occasions, caught him with a hard right that had TK holding on. For the most part, however, 'Lewis was always there (or rather his gloves were) when he wasn't wanted and never there when he was.'

TK was also praised for his skill at blocking and ducking, and towards the end of the fight he was obviously much the stronger man. In the fourteenth poor Buswell was put down for five successive counts before the referee exercised some belated mercy.

With the first eliminator now arranged for 7 April with none other than Young Brooks, TK, in the meantime, drew with Nat Williams and then took on and beat the experienced Johnny Condon twice in the space of a week. Condon was a skilful fighter who had taken on Digger Stanley for the British bantamweight title in December 1910, only to be defeated after twenty close rounds.

Then came the almost unheard-of (where TK's career was concerned) luxury of a full month's training before the eliminator, a match that seemed, even to his normally fiercely loyal backers, not quite the cast-iron certainty they were used to. In fact, because of the result of their previous encounter, most money was on 'Bayardo', as Brooks was known, and Sam Shear could not even raise the £50 side-stake agreed on when contracts were signed.

In a rare break with tradition, the NSC (or rather Peggy Bettinson) allowed the bout to proceed with the unusual purse set at £37 10s. – all the money Shear had been able to raise.

Prior to the contest, in the dressing room, the usual psychological jockeying proceeded; TK recalled: 'Ten minutes before the fight I gave my few remaining supporters a rare fright by vomiting my guts up and looking really sick. This had occurred in several previous contests but after my stomach had settled I always felt better than ever.

'There was an attempt by my rival followers to gain a psychological advantage over me. Brooks's dressing room was next to mine and they knew everything spoken in a loud voice could be heard in my dressing room. We listened to a running commentary on what was going to happen to "that kid next door". What Brooks was going to do to me was nobody's business. But they were barking up the wrong tree.'

Though the betting was 3–1 on Brooks, 5–2 against TK, he had the great comfort of having two of his childhood heroes (a childhood hardly that distant!) in the corner working for him: Young Joseph and Harry Lewis. And his trainer, Alec Goodman, was one of the few good things to have been introduced by Sam Shear. Goodman was to play a crucial role in TK's subsequent campaigns in Australia and the United States.

The fight opened with a surprise for Brooks. He rushed in, as was his style being stocky and short, and was met with straight left drives flush to the face, which brought him up with a jolt. He rushed again, only to be neatly and smartly side-stepped, 'while, just to add insult to injury, the Kid would whang him good and hard with the right on the ear or cheek as he plunged into space.'

'When Brooks stood still and tried to mix things, he was hit with long-range combinations of four and five punches. He would start to move and dart and dash again, only to find himself out-danced and out-feinted. As the fight progressed, poor Brooks was reduced to having to bore in with his head, but even this resulted in TK's employing a back-handed uppercut 'which repeatedly jarred Brooks's chin and bruised his lips'.

At the end there could be no other verdict possible but a points win for TK. Such a surprise was this, that the *Boxing* headline was: 'The Kid Upsets The Hotpot'.

A lot of people who should have known better lost a lot of money as TK sailed into the next eliminating round.

The boxing connoisseurs were still not happy, however. *Boxing* ran a full-page feature on the fight entitled, 'An Object Lesson In Boxing', and while conceding that TK was the clear winner and obviously a talented fighter, it was declared that he was nowhere near as good as Jim Driscoll, the retiring champion: 'Our complaint is that he swung dozens of times without getting within a foot of Brooks and our further complaint is that he missed most frequently when he had Brooks almost stationary.'

As had been noted in previous fights, his tendency to swing wildly with both left and right appeared to leave him defenceless: 'For Lewis stood as wide open as a cart-shed most of the time and should have proved an easy victim to a man who could force his way in and deal out telling short jabs.'

It was simply, the correspondent ruefully concluded, that TK lacked knowledge of several rudiments of the game. The answer to such complaints most certainly lay in the fact that, for most of his short, crowded career, TK had spent too much time in the ring with run-of-the-mill fighters, over-used by greedy promoters and managers – a willing, amiable teenager with the increasingly onerous task of supporting a large family.

It is interesting and instructive to note that the much-praised Jim Driscoll, undoubtedly one of Britain's finest fighters, fought just 71 times in eighteen years (though he had had an earlier career in fairground booths). TK had already passed that total in his first two years – and he was still sixteen!

As evidence of the tendency to milk him for all he was worth (though it must be said that TK himself was always anxious to climb into the ring and hardly ever turned down a bout), after defeating Joe Starmer in the semi-final of the eliminators three weeks later at the NSC, and with the title fight itself against Alec Lambert set for four months hence, instead of going into intensive training, he took on four more tough, demanding contests, all at the Ring.

The Starmer eliminator was significant for two things: first, there was now no trouble in raising the £50 side-stake money, and second, his Kettering opponent had none other than Jim Driscoll working for him in the corner. Despite this, the fight went according to the pattern of the Brooks fight: 'Knowing that Joe would force the fight I let him do all the attacking from the first bell. I was content to feint and spar and catch him with heavy uppercuts whenever an opening presented itself.

'When Joe began to tire I changed my tactics and started to attack and I increased the pace the further the contest went. By the last round I had Starmer wobbling around and dropped him with a right to the chin. He left the ring badly bruised and beaten, knowing he had been in a fight.'

Thus emboldened, TK and his backers promptly issued a challenge to none other than Owen Moran (for a fight at either 9 st. 4 1b. or 9 st. 6 1b.). Moran was a Welshman who had spent much of his highly successful career in the USA. He had fought men like

Abe Attell (five times), Ad Wolgast (twice) and had recently knocked out Battling Nelson – all world champions. In January 1913 he had drawn with Driscoll in a British title fight.

TK claimed he was willing to wager £200 for a fight with Moran at the NSC – he even suggested they fight on a winner-take-all basis. But Moran was used to much bigger pickings. He wanted £500 a side plus various other perks. Such were the terms for men of his stature. Indeed, he did not even respond to TK's offer, but took himself off to Australia where the money was reputed to be much more plentiful; it was a pointer to TK's immediate future.

For TK, therefore, it was back to the Ring, Blackfriars to defeat Harry Sterling over 20 rounds, then the following week, a 20 round return with Duke Lynch, his conqueror in 1912. Once again, *Boxing* was hard to please: 'Certainly he won, and won very easily, but the manner of his winning was not convincing enough to put him any higher on the championship ladder. On the contrary, in the opinion of the experts those last two contests dragged him down a step or two.'

Once again, it was TK's 'impulsiveness' that irritated the experts, his swinging right hand: 'Real champions seldom devote so much attention to the atmosphere with right punches as Lewis did in his attempts to hand Lynch a sleeping draught.'

However, his last fight at the Ring prior to his championship bout with Lambert in October swept away all doubts – he met and beat a Frenchman, Ferdinand Quendraux, in what he would always regard as one of his most memorable bouts.

The match had come about following a chance remark TK had made to Shear. The two had watched Quendraux defeat Alf Read, a promising welterweight from Canning Town, and afterwards TK had said, 'I can beat that Frenchman'.

Later, at the Ring offices, Shear repeated TK's remark jokingly to Ring proprietor Dick Burge. After all, a featherweight taking on a hard-hitting welter? '. . .but Dick Burge took it up seriously. "And why not?" said he. "To blazes with this old saying that a good big 'un will always beat a good little 'un. It doesn't always follow – in boxing at any rate. It may be okay as far as horse-racing goes, but not scrapping." '

And Burge set about arranging the match. It was eventually made at 9 st. 4 lb, four pounds over the featherweight limit, which put all the strain on Quendraux, who had to come down considerably, yet all the betting was on the Frenchman who packed a considerable punch.

Once again wiser heads among boxing's fraternity saw the match as another exploitative move on behalf of a grasping manager. What was more, TK's newfound trainer, Alec Goodman, had decided to follow Moran's example and depart for Australia, despite the £200 side-stake set for the Quendraux fight. By the time TK got down to training, Goodman had set sail with Sid Burns and Harry Mansfield. TK was unmoved: 'Sam Shear immediately hired Harry Stokes, a hardworking and conscientious trainer, as honest as the day is long. We made Whetstone our headquarters, staying at the Black Bull. This was an ideal training centre where practically everyone of note in those days had done all or part of their training, from Eddie Morgan to Jack Johnson, and where Sid Burns used to work me out. The food and accommodation were excellent and there was a swell gymnasium. . . I worked hard and in good company – Young Brooks, Eddie Morgan and Bandsman Rice. I trained hard for two weeks and on the morning of the fight turned the beam at 9 st. 2¼ lb.

'Now Dai Dollings, an ace trainer, was looking after Eddie Morgan and also helping me quite a lot. He had a fetish of never bringing his man to the scales more underweight than was necessary. He considered me too light and made me a pick-me-up consisting of an egg, milk and butter.

'When I next weighed myself fifteen minutes before the official weigh-in time which was to take place at the offices of the *Sporting Life*, I was three ounces overweight. There was £100 forfeit and for the contest I was receiving £80! Dolling and Stokes got busy and easily rubbed off the three ounces, with the result that just on 2 pm I had made the weight.

'I could hear the betting boys offering 5–2 on Quendraux, but Tom Williams and Ernie Mogford were taking all that was on offer, and as Dan Sullivan, the match-maker of the Ring had a lot of French money with which to back Quendraux, it made it a big betting fight.

'The premier referee of the day, Eugene Corri, was the third man in the ring and it proved a gala occasion, one that I shall never forget. There were quite a number of ladies present wearing evening dress, a unique sight in 1913.'

After spending the first round testing the strength and punching power of Quendraux, and deciding he had little to fear as long as he kept out of danger, TK set out on a strategy to baffle and disconcert the more powerful man, using his right hand more often than his left at times – and for a long period it seemed as though the Frenchman was content to bide his time, to take TK's stiff counterpunches until the moment came when he could land his reputed KO left.

However, after ten rounds of TK's dodging, ducking and scoring points almost at will, the Frenchman decided to force matters. The *Boxing* correspondent wrote: 'As always, he was the first to open with a rush that was met with a really beautiful left-hand counter. It took Quendraux flush on the mouth, jerking his head back and leaving the angle of the jaw exposed. Quick as a flash, the Kid shot a right directly to it. Ferdinand quivered to his heels, got another and yet another before going down. He arose, obviously dazed, but still he took three more before he sought the floor. Five times he was down and up almost as quickly and yet it was not until he rose for the sixth time that he went in and hung on for recuperative purposes. Thrice more he was spreadeagled and was rising again with unconquerable pluck when Mr Corri interposed. . .'

It was a famous victory, again against the odds. TK was elated: '. . . and even today I retain vivid memories of the fight. The one which stands out foremost being when Dick Burge, one of the greatest fighters of the day and admitted to be a very shrewd judge, stepped over to shake me by the hand and said, "You will be a world champion one day." My backers made a mint of money over the fight and as a mark of appreciation presented me with a gold watch.'

As well they might. However, next on TK's list was something considerably larger – a gold belt.

KID LEWIS AND ALEC LAMBERT.

6 The Lonsdale Belt

'Perhaps the atmosphere had an exhilarating effect on me, as I felt like a fighting cock and was brimful of confidence.'

TK

The featherweight title had been the undisputed property of Driscoll since 1910, although he had claimed it since 1906. The first Lonsdale Belt for the weight was also his to keep with three successful defences of the title behind him. Thus, the winner of the newly minted belt would stand in direct line of succession to a fighter already regarded as one of the all-time greats.

Driscoll was the perfect combination: a stylist who had managed to please both the boxing purists and those who simply wanted to see a good fight. The constant comparison between the contenders and the departed hero, though understandable, had proved irksome, especially to TK. But as the big day approached, he could devote little thought to past heroes and how he might have measured up to them. He was on the brink, after just four years of professional boxing, of becoming a champion himself. 'I again made Whetstone my headquarters under the care of Dai Dollings. He was a very strict, conscientious trainer and, much as we all admired him, he had us all scared. He never spared himself when training a boxer and was a great believer in hard work. After meals he would take me on the road to cover an average of 12 to 16 miles a day, walking and running. It was stiff work and frequently the call of bed was the sweetest music of the day for me. He rounded me off fit for the fight of my life though there were some anxious times concerning my weight, but I managed to pull 9 st. exactly.

'After the weigh-in I had a good meal, a ten-minute walk and then to bed where I slept soundly until Dai woke me for a rub down, after which I felt good enough to go fifty rounds.

'Lambert looked very fit in the ring, whereas I was told I looked as usual pale and drawn. This may have influenced the betting which made Alec the slight favourite. Aschel Joseph was once again in my corner.'

Making the weight had been one of the talking points of the contest. It was now being suggested that TK was really a lightweight – he was already tall for a featherweight and was growing taller all the time. The question of whether he would suffer unduly taking off the stipulated poundage was influential in the ante-post betting, and the contrasting appearances of the two men, Lambert looking fit and well, TK looking pale and drawn ('very close to a wreck' according to the *Boxing*'s reporter) suggested that TK would find it harder to stay the distance.

The contest opened tentatively, with Lambert holding back, content apparently to let TK come rushing in impetuously. TK obliged, making the first move, and was avoided by Lambert who attempted to counter, only to find that he was well out of range, 'whereupon he [Lewis] started to slam that right for the head just as we all expected he would'.

However, the reporter conceded, 'He agreeably disappointed us, both then and later. Never once did he lose his head throughout the contest and when Lambert came in with a left to the face, Lewis pulled back, steadied up and retaliated with a similar punch.'

The two settled down for a long strategic battle with both fighters having periods of dominance, winning two, three rounds each at a time, Lambert seeming the stronger in the first period but TK, remaining cool and collected, using his longer reach and greater height and at times superior mobility to move away out of any trouble.

After ten rounds had passed, the fight began to move towards a definite conclusion. At first it seemed that Lambert was on the brink of overrunning TK: 'Rounds nine and ten had been Lambert's when good left-hand work aided by some stiff right-hand crosses plus some painful close work seemed to hurt Lewis, who had little in reply. Lewis came up slowly and obviously tired for the eleventh. He was ahead on points but a victory for Alec began to show over the horizon. It failed to arrive and even started to sink back again as Alec was seen to slacken speed even faster than Lewis.'

As the eleventh proceeded it was clear that Lambert was wilting. The twelfth went to TK and when Lambert forced things in the thirteenth, 'he took nearly all the remaining energy out of himself'.

Now it was simply a matter of physical power. They were both still connecting with rights and lefts, but TK's punches were the more telling, and at the end of the fifteenth a blow was struck that turned the contest completely.

Lambert was apparently doing quite well, 'until a hard and splendidly if somewhat luckily planted right to the jaw sent him flat to the boards just on the gong'.

From then on Lambert performed as though he had lead weights in his boots and gloves. He was chased about the ring in the sixteenth and just survived, but in the opening exchanges of the seventeenth a clever feint and draw by TK and a fierce right to the jaw sent Lambert on his face to the boards for the count of nine. 'He was plainly wool-gathering when he rose and Lewis, with victory well and clearly in sight, went wild for the first time.'

Lambert tottered and lurched about the ring until a right clip found his chin. 'It wasn't what could be called a really hard punch, but it sufficed to finish the contest. His knees gave in – and he lurched forward again on to his face. Whereupon Mr Douglas promptly intervened. Waving Lewis to his corner he proclaimed him the new featherweight champion of Great Britain and Lonsdale Belt holder.'

After the fight, TK scotched rumours that he had been weakened by reducing his weight. In a letter to *Boxing* he wrote: 'I have never felt so strong in all my life. I went carefully from the start because I wanted to win that belt in the first place and because he is a most awkward man in the second. But I felt sure I was going to win all the time and you can take it from me that while he may be a clever boxer he won't create a boom in red chalk to write up his doings as a fighter.'

Boxing was certainly won over by TK's performance: 'Hitherto the somewhat erratic Kid has usually been regarded as a boxer who was always liable to get rattled at short notice. Fast on his feet perhaps and, as a result, apt to be over-lavish with his footwork displays. Fond of using his right hand and ready to slam it out for all it could be possibly worth even at any price. But if this has been his usual practice, his championship form was removed to polar distance.'

And yet, the doubts lingered on. *Boxing* concluded: 'Is the Kid a worthy heir to all Driscoll's glories? Well, perhaps he isn't yet. Even his best friend must regretfully confess that the Kid has many rows to hoe before he can open out a real path to the heights on which Jim the Great reigned supreme. But the Kid is a comer. . .'

A week later, however, *Boxing*'s editor was moved to admit that it was inevitable that TK would be criticized in comparison to Jim Driscoll rather than on his relative form against potential and existing featherweight rivals. But the criticisms, he felt, were unfair to TK for the simple reason that Driscoll, when he was TK's age, had done nothing at all as a fighter: 'The Driscoll we all knew and admired was a man of twenty-five. Thus, it is a fairer and sounder standard to judge Lewis on the things he has done and the manner in which he has done them and on this form his future looks distinctly promising, to put the matter in the mildest words one can find.'

What had surprised the writer most, however, had been TK's strength: 'We had been told some most harrowing tales of the tortures Lewis had undergone in his efforts to make the weight and had rather anticipated the vision of an ethereal form, wasted by suffering and staggering under the gigantic burden of East End ambitions, pride, hopes and fears. But in the ring itself, though Lewis looked to be rather badly drawn, he certainly carried himself like a man in far better condition than his rival. Lambert didn't look so pinched, but he was almost sluggish at times in his movements and, save on the one occasion referred to, boxed throughout with a total absence of fire.

'And here we fancy we may deal with the department in which Lewis shone best in our eyes. References of all sorts have been made by other critics to his brilliant and magnificently directed left, to his fierce and nerve-shaking right and to other alleged or imaginary attributes. But so far we have yet to come across any public appreciation of his strategy or generalship. And in this contest, if Lewis revealed anything at all, he displayed the possession of a boxing brain of no mean order.'

So, with a certain grudging admiration, the official organ of British boxing finally accepted Kid Lewis as a worthy champion. In the East End, inevitably, there were no such reservations at all – and a few days after the title fight TK made a triumphant return to his old stamping ground, the Judean Club. 'The members of this East End rendezvous manifested their appreciation of having reared in their midst another champion when Kid Lewis, the new featherweight title-bearer, put in an appearance on Sunday afternoon. The crowd simply stood up and cheered and stamped until the rafters of the old building shook. It was indeed a happy moment for the ex-Judeanite who stood in the ring blushing like a young schoolgirl at her first party. . . It will be remembered it was at this club that Kid Lewis took his first lessons . . . and it was not to be wondered at that in the estimation of Judeanites he was their champion.'

The ghost of Driscoll, however, lingered on. On 22 November *Boxing* announced a challenge: 'A well-known sportsman and prominent member of the NSC has asked us to obtain Driscoll's consent to the following challenge, viz, that he will box Kid Lewis over the twenty-round championship course for the title in which case he (the said sportsman) would be willing to offer Kid Lewis a sporting wager of £1,000 to £500 on the result.'

Surely, *Boxing* opined, TK and his backers would jump at the chance of getting good money, 'and plenty of it' at 2–1. It went on to state that the contest, if it could be arranged, 'would surely be the big sensation of the season, hardly ranking second even to the forthcoming Wells–Carpentier match due for 8 December'.

Praise indeed, for Wells and Carpentier were now firmly established as boxing's matinée idols, at that moment attracting all the attention of a boxing-crazy populace.

For a while, however, TK was kept busy cashing in on his own newfound celebrity: appearing in adverts alongside men such as Freddie Welsh, Digger Stanley and Johnny Summers (advertising gloves), and appearing on several music-hall stages: 'As a consequence of becoming a champion I strutted my little hour on the stage of the music-hall.' But it was not an experience he enjoyed. He wrote some years later: 'Frankly I am not in love with the stage. First, it is a money-eating game; expenses are frightfully heavy because the average person is under the impression that music-hall artists are all Harry Lauders from the salary point of view and charge accordingly. When I look at some of my recent hotel bills I get cramp in my pocket.

'And the tips. It's an old saying that civility costs nothing. My experience is to the contrary – as it is the dearest thing in this country. The work is hard too. It is no joke working two halls and two houses at each. Give me a twenty-round contest any time. It is far easier – because you are in control, you decide what to do, especially if you can put your opponent away quickly – and it's not nearly so expensive. You can take it from me that the life of the music-hall pro is not all beer and skittles.'

And coming from one as generous, not to say profligate, with his money as TK, such a statement is surprising.

As the weeks progressed, and as his time away from the training camp and the ring lengthened, the rumours of a Driscoll fight seemed more and more attractive. Sam Shear certainly could see the advantages of the idea. When asked if he could manage to raise the £500 as backing for TK, Shear declared: 'Sure, why, he could find £1,000 any time he was asked. "If you want to win a race, the first thing you want is a good horse and the next is a good rider," said Mr Shear. "Well, I have a good horse in my boy and I am his rider," he added. "So it's up to Jim Driscoll." '

In fact, Shear would soon be unseated.

But Driscoll never took the final decisive step. He announced that he was interested but that it would take him two months to get into shape before he could begin proper training. He was almost thirty-three. TK was just seventeen. By Christmas 1913 it was clear that the match was not on. TK had mixed feelings: 'It was tempting up to a point, but I am glad that nothing came of it. To have met Jim in the ring would have been a grand experience, but the idea of fighting him was not to my liking. I preferred to think of him as a brilliant boxer of another era rather than my own and it has always annoyed me to think that his so-called friends enticed him into making that disastrous comeback against Charles Ledoux some six years later.'

The Driscoll non-contest was to be TK's last involvement with Sam Shear. Harry Morris, a promoter who was about to take over the running of Premierland from the bankrupt Harry Jacobs (ruined by gambling debts) induced TK to break with Shear, who promptly took them to court and sued for breach of contract. TK recalled: 'I did not enjoy appearing in court, it was a fight in which I had to defend myself with words. I only knew one way to fight and I couldn't do that in court. There were rumours that Shear had fixed some of the jury and, when they found in favour of Shear, I felt I had been hit in the solar plexus. It took my breath away when the referee – or in this instance the judge – came to my rescue. He overruled the jury and gave me the verdict. I am sure my luck changed from that day, for I felt on top of the world, free and on my way.'

Thus, as the new year of 1914 dawned, TK was once again facing a future dramatically transformed. By the end of 1914 he would have travelled almost the circumference of the world – a world also in the process of a dramatic, not to say terrible, transformation of its own.

7 Champion of Europe

'I put the trophy round my waist before I left the dressing room . . . when I peeled off the robe to put on the gloves a great burst of applause went up as the fans spotted the Lonsdale Belt.'

TK

On 5 January 1914 TK stepped up to face George Buswell at a packed Ring, Blackfriars. The fight was of little importance to him – just another payday, and a loosener for a more strenuous battle to come. He duly KO'd Buswell in two rounds. Yet it was a significant occasion in that, for the first time, it was noticed how TK was attempting to cultivatc an 'image'.

Boxing was passing through a fashionable, glamorous phase, Carpentier being the inspiration, and its top exponents felt obliged to produce more than simply blood and guts. Yet in the possibly more difficult realm of public relations TK was regularly outshone, even by men as lowly as Buswell: 'The Fulham youth's dressing gown was almost worth the price of admission [wrote a Boxing reporter] and he received a splendid response as he entered the ring garbed in one of Selfridge's latest creations.'

TK's gown was also impressive ('a sky-blue confection'), but Buswell upstaged him with a threatrical bow to the clamouring audience, 'even transcending the attempt of the Kid, whose footlight experience should have assisted him very materially in the cultivation of elegance'.

TK was a young man growing up in a hurry, not naturally given to artificial performance; his appearances on stage, though endearing, were hardly dramatically successful. He looked his best, of course, when in the ring, where he was a natural performer and rapidly becoming one of the ring's great artists. Outside it, he was sometimes awkward and embarrassed – and who could blame him? Just after the Buswell fight, a picture of him appeared in the press sitting on a hunter and decked out in full hunting gear. Now what was a nice East End Jewish boy doing out hunting with the Hertfordshire gentry?

Mercifully, the clowning and posing were to cease in early 1914 with the announcement that TK was contracted to face Frenchman Paul Til – for the European featherweight title.

The European title had last been held, inevitably, by Jim Driscoll. In June 1912 he had defeated Jean Poesy over twelve rounds – though as this match had also been billed as a world title fight (a title not recognized by anyone else, certainly not by Johnny Kilbane, the American who was the official title holder) there was some doubt as to Driscoll's European claim.

The match with Til caused a certain amount of grumbling within the French Boxing Federation. As Til was not the French champion at the weight, how could the fight be for a European title, it was asked? The British press immediately countered by pointing out that Carpentier, who between the years 1911 and 1914 had been European champion at welter, middle light-heavy and heavyweight, had often failed to hold the equivalent French title as well. But such arguments were strictly for rival journalists. TK, in his début as a sports writer, declared: 'Til, I reckon, is quite the best featherweight in France whether he is or is not the official champion.'

He also put his finger on why the bout had immediately captured public interest: 'It is about time, I should say, that an English champion beat a French one, isn't it? That was my first thought when this match with Til was put to me.'

Georges Carpentier had certainly caused a great deal of soul-searching among British boxers and their fans. Since 1911 he had regularly beaten the best Britain could put in front of him: Jack Goldswain, Arthur Evernden, Sid Burns, Young Joseph and, more recently in the fight of the season, glamour-boy and White Hope Bombardier Billy Wells, in one round! Along with Charles Ledoux, the man who had defeated Digger Stanley for the European bantamweight championship in 1912, Carpentier had been demonstrating French fistic superiority for too long: suddenly, TK was a British hope – at a time when patriotism was approaching feverish heights.

Paul Til, in fact, could boast a draw with Carpentier – achieved admittedly back in 1909 – but he was rated a 'tough morsel' by *Boxing* who predicted he would give TK his most strenuous test to date. TK certainly seemed aware that he was stepping up a class and was taking no chances: 'I have taken the precaution of securing Fred Jacks as a sparring partner and Jacks has fought Til and knows all about him. Then I have got Gus Venn as well who used to be one of Fred Welsh's sparring partners and I am getting along fine at the "Malt and Hops" in Brighton where I am suited down to the ground. I shall be fit and well and am confident that I shall make the weight all right without weakening myself in any way. . .I have got Alec Goodman, my old and first trainer, back with me and I am fairly satisfied that I am about as good as I could hope to be at the present moment.'

The occasion was to be yet another East End jamboree. Premierland had just been reopened by promoter Jack Callaghan and though the first bill had boasted Young Cohen and Joe Beckett as top-liners, the first European championship to have been held outside the NSC for many years was undoubtedly going to be the highlight of the East End season.

TK recalled: 'Tickets sold like hot cakes from the date of the announcement and how the promoters must have longed for rubber walls! It was a Monday night special and occasioned my return to the East End ring.'

When TK made his entrance wearing his Lonsdale Belt the house went wild with enthusiasm: on his home ground, his showman's touch was always sure.

Til could not have remained unaffected by the rampant enthusiasm of the crowd. Indeed, *Boxing*'s correspondent noted: 'Til was worried. In the first place the crowd was up against him – very demonstrably so. There were local sentiments and all the pride of London's Jewry. Sentiments and a pride which the referee unwittingly cultivated.'

The referee, from the very first minute, began shouting at Til (from the outside of the ring, of course, as was the custom then), whenever the latter attempted to move in close and work to the body – one of his apparent strengths. Referee Keen's behaviour, according to *Boxing*, typified the Englishman's idea of how to communicate with a foreigner: if you shout loudly enough, he will understand. But of course, Til was simply confused: 'The stentorian eloquence worried poor Paul pretty badly. He was obviously quite uncertain as to the things, actions, etc. which the referee expected and was prepared to allow.'

However, nothing should be allowed to detract from TK's performance that night. There was never a moment when Til appeared able to impose himself, never a period when he could put together more than two punches at a time: 'By the fourth round, Til was growing perplexed. The Kid was far quicker on his feet and Til was beginning to feel that the referee's admonitions were irksome. He spread his arms wide and actually turned round to talk to the presiding official, obviously under the impression that the gentleman was dying for a conversation. Lewis, who attended strictly to business throughout, promptly admonished him for so doing with left and right hooks to the jaw which jarred Paul badly. The Frenchman cast a look of indignant reproach at Mr Keen and was uppercut and thumped for so doing. . .'

The crowd laughed; the referee shouted louder; Til grew more and more despondent.

By the twelfth he was almost defeated, 'and was getting it all ways: body-jabs, right hooks and uppercuts. . .' and suddenly, after Til had made an attempt to hold in order to gain some respite, the referee disqualified him.

'Will you please tell me why the referee stopped me? I was not on the floor, and I was not holding. I was doing nothing. I did not understand Mr Keen,' complained the unfortunate Til afterwards.

But TK was happy enough. He had proved himself a worthy champion, albeit in a disappointing contest – a champion worthy enough to earn plaudits from the man who had for so long cast a shadow over his career – Jim Driscoll: 'Lewis is a very good boy indeed, better than I had been led to believe and I am not surprised that he has proved to be the best of the featherweights . . . the man who beats Lewis will have to be a regular top-liner. . .'

Thus blessed, TK immediately laid out his future plans: 'I am champion of England and champion of Europe – the first English featherweight champion of Europe, in fact – so all I have to win now is the championship of the world,' which seemed logical enough!

TK now had some hard choices to make, however. Ever since winning the British championship it had been suggested that he might travel abroad in search of more lucrative engagements. Alec Goodman had left for Australia before the Lambert fight and was now back. Ever the happy wanderer, he was keen to take TK off on his travels once again.

For, although world titles were occasionally fought for in Great Britain, by 1914 the Americans possessed almost all the titles – and to persuade a US fighter to come to Europe to defend a title was becoming a difficult business. TK declared he was after world featherweight champion Johnny Kilbane – yet Kilbane had never, and would never, fight outside the USA. And there were others whom he considered were now his natural ringmates: Leach Cross, Jewish/American feather/lightweight; Johnny Dundee; Joe

Shugrue; Willie Richie, world lightweight champion. He would have to go to them if he wanted a chance at a title.

Not that there would have been any difficulty fixing him up with lucrative contests in Great Britain. The French featherweight champion De Ponthieu was anxious to avenge the Til defeat. A Welsh promoter was already setting up the match for which TK was guaranteed £250. He was offered, and accepted, £200 for another Premierland contest – and stopped Harry Berry in three rounds; then, four days later, stopped Ted Saunders in six rounds. A match with Owen Moran was floated again, but the Welshman's demands were apparently as high and as prohibitive as ever – and the NSC in the shape of Peggy Bettinson was attempting to persuade featherweight contender Jerry Delaney into a match with TK.

However, cutting through all the speculation and purse offers came a cable from Australian promoter 'Snowy' Baker. Five fights at top money against prominent Australian and American fighters – it was an offer, TK recalled, that had its origins in a conversation he had had with Australian lightweight champion Hughie Mehegan almost a year earlier.

Mehegan had challenged Freddie Welsh for the latter's British Empire lightweight title at the NSC in December 1912. A few weeks later, Mehegan had visited Premierland to watch some fights and had fallen into the company of local boxers and managers, TK among them: 'I shall never forget that night . . . we had gathered in a little place at the top of Back Church Lane. I forget for a moment the chief fight of the night at Premierland, but it was all over and, as I say, we were drinking the cup that cheers. That is, with the exception of myself. I was sipping hot lemonade and cloves. I was a great admirer of Mehegan so you can guess how proud I was when he singled me out and told those about him that I should be a "good 'un".

Mehegan had returned to Australia and had mentioned to promoter Baker what a prospect TK was, and how he would draw the crowds. The subsequent offer could not have arrived at a more perfect moment.

Though a difficult decision to make, given his attachment to home, he was after all, approaching twenty-one. He had saved no money from his many fights; whatever he earned he handed over to the family. He had no independent life, no house of his own – he simply lived from training camp to hotel and thence back home again. Therefore, the chance to break free for a while to travel the world in search of fame and fortune must have been a compelling factor in making up his mind.

With the offer of fights came two tickets, one for himself and one for Alec. Thus, after two more fights (and two more knockouts) to raise some ready cash, he handed over the residue to his mother, packed his bags and sailed away, taking with him his Lonsdale Belt, and leaving behind not a few aggrieved promoters.

8 The Australian Adventure

'Go on as you are and you'll be a World Champion one day.'

Hughie Mehegan to TK

TK's Australian adventure, though it lasted no more than five months, proved to be a perfect introduction to the harsher, tougher world of champion-class fighting he would soon encounter in the United States.

He met and beat four of the world's best lightweights, learnt new techniques and tricks from each as well as from a boxing legend – Larry Foley – and he would also experience some of the more cut-throat business methods of international promoters such as 'Snowy' Baker, methods he would have to contend with for many a year to come.

But, at first, as he settled down on board ship it must have seemed as if he had entered a dream-world. After years of fighting and training month upon month he faced weeks of blissful inactivity – with nothing more strenuous to do than watch the waves roll by.

But sitting still was anathema to TK and before long he discovered numerous outlets for his restless, nervous, boyish energy. Life on board ship, in fact, proved one long fascination for him; he declared years later that every single day brought something new and interesting.

To begin with, everyone he met seemed determined to shake his hand and take a look at the Lonsdale Belt. Every night there seemed to be a party and he claimed he went to every one! In addition, he was fast acquiring a taste for gambling and found many of the seamen only too ready to let him join their gambling schools.

In later years this passion was to cost him much of the money he won in the ring and, on long sea voyages (in the 1920s he became virtually a commuter across the Atlantic), he invariably found an outlet for his gambling enthusiasm.

Cyril Mills, of Bertram Mills fame, recalled seeing TK lose £700 on a single throw of dice (a considerable sum for a 'mere boxer' in the 1920s). But for now he gambled with small change, extracting as much excitement from winning shillings and pence as he would much later when a relative fortune depended on the turn of a card. Because, as with most gamblers, the money was unimportant. It was a means to an end. In fact, he took to gambling in the same way as he took to boxing – naturally, thinking he could win at one as easily as he did at the other. There were similarities, he claimed. Boxing was essentially a gamble too: you won some and you lost some and there would always be the chance of another throw, another bout. The money earned was there to be used until it ran out, and then he would earn some more.

Alec Goodman, however, had been on long sea journeys before and, mindful of how easily and quickly a boxer lost condition, he prevailed upon the ship's engineer to set up a ring on deck so that TK could work off some of his excess energy. There were plenty of willing seamen, apparently, ready to chance their arm in order to be able to boast that they had sparred with a champion.

But it was mixing with people from beyond his own closely defined, strictly confined East End world that made that first journey such an exhilarating experience for him.

At Fremantle, the classic actress Ellen Terry joined the ship and TK was soon captivated by her. Later, on being introduced, she asked to see the famous Belt – and he never forgot how much he sweated with embarrassment as she chatted to him about his work and his life – she even took down his mother's recipe for chopped liver, a Jewish speciality!

He would always say that his real education in life began with meeting Ellen Terry, for she came to embody all his highly romantic desires in a woman; and where women were concerned, he was certainly a romantic. Her manners, gestures, the way she spoke – everything about her fascinated him. For years afterwards he sent her recipes he thought she might like. . .

On arrival in Sydney, however, the idyllic dream world ended abruptly – much, one imagines, to Alec's relief. For within forty-eight hours of going ashore, TK found himself stepping into the ring to face a truly world-rated opponent.

At first, however, it appeared there would be plenty of time to settle in and sightsee: 'We were taken to our training camp at Coogee and stayed at the Pacific Hotel. It was a Thursday when we arrived and by a happy coincidence a matinée show was being held at the stadium which consisted of four fights and a work-out by the principal boxers of the forthcoming Saturday show. After I had been introduced from the ring I met a number of British boys who invited me to a party after the show. Then I watched Herb McCoy and Milburn Sailor – the main bout opponents for Saturday – go through their exhibition, being particularly interested in them because I knew they were potential opponents.'

That night he attended the party: 'And what a party! When Sydney folk throw a party you can rest assured there are no half measures about it. Food and drink galore, bright boys, charming vivacious girls, the gathering went with a swing until nine o'clock the next morning. Fortunately, I do not drink, but I really enjoyed the company although Alec and I were tired when we got back to the hotel. . .'

Waiting for him was a message. He had to call the Baker Stadium immediately. Milburn Sailor had gone down with lumbago and TK was offered the chance to step into the ring with McCoy. He agreed immediately.

It was a golden opportunity similar to the one he had seized that night way back in 1911 when Fred Halsband had needed a last-minute opponent. TK never turned down such offers, despite the odds. 'Wasting no time I got into sweaters and went off for a five-mile walk.'

The boxing fraternity back at the hotel (a collection of British and American boxers plus numerous journalists) thought him foolish. McCoy might no longer be the Australian champion, having lost the title recently to Hughie Mehegan, but he was still a championship contender, much travelled and respected in the United States. The Milburn Sailor fight had been billed as his 'comeback' chance. TK was unmoved: 'I knew I was fit when I landed and Alec was convinced that I was good enough for McCoy so we carried on without a care in the world.'

In his favour was the fact that fighting at catch-weights was tolerated to a much greater extent than in Great Britain; as a last-minute replacement, he was thus allowed to come in at about 9 st. 11 lb. – two pounds above the lightweight limit and considerably above his normal featherweight poundage. But he had realized on the sea voyage that making featherweight was no longer possible for him. Hence the bitter-sweet mixture of exhilaration and regret he felt whenever he brought out the beloved Lonsdale Belt to show someone. He knew he would never be able to win it outright as Driscoll had done – eventually he would have to hand the belt back.

As he entered the ring for the McCoy fight he was – traditionally now it seemed – the betting underdog. Twenty rounds later he had pulled off a sensational victory.

Australian boxing writer W.F. Corbett, a notoriously hard man to please, had been mightily impressed: 'We have not for a long time seen a speedier boxer than Kid Lewis and we have not seen more than a few faster ones. He made all the use he could of the twenty square feet of space allotted for the contest and at that was never really running away. He hit from every angle and he hit from every position with either weapon. . . Lewis jumped and literally leaped in at times and occasionally rose two or three inches from the floor when jabbing a punch to neck or to head. . . He was frequently a kangaroo act and McCoy was clearly bewildered.'

McCoy, short, deep-chested and dogged, stood up to it all but he could never get close enough, often enough, to do much damage. Lewis, however, 'would bang away right and left to the head with power and speed that had the object of those intentions sorely puzzled, and time after time straight lefts drove McCoy's head back with such a jerk that his hair spread out and backward as his neck bent to the rear. . .'

At times TK was dazzling, 'whirling about McCoy and punching like some electrical appliance let loose'.

TK was literally an overnight sensation – the start of a brief, exhilarating honeymoon with Australia and Australians.

Almost immediately, promoter Baker matched TK with Hughie Mehegan, Australian lightweight champion, for a fortnight hence, and TK and Alec, plus Young Warner and Ted Broadribb's son, settled into a rented bungalow close by Chiddy Ryan's gym at Coogee, not far from Bondi beach.

Life must have seemed grand for TK during those sun-filled Australian days. 'Come and have a bite with us,' was the invitation he sent out to the Australian press and rival boxers, and the house-guests ranged from visiting US boxers, such as Young Shugrue, Tommy Lee and Bobby Moore who had also rented a bungalow further up the beach at North Bondi, to music-hall artists such as Harry Lauder and Ada Reeve, then appearing at Sydney music-halls. And once TK had posted off his purse money to his mother back in London, he had no responsibilities, no worries: just training, swimming, pretty girls, happy parties – and learning the fascinating intricacies of his trade.

Among the boxers, however, a special camaraderie swiftly developed and friendships were established that were to last many years.

The Americans, in particular, took to TK, their admiration for his boxing skill being matched, it seemed, by their concern for his welfare in the murky world of boxing politics. TK was honest, too honest, for his own good, it seemed, and his open generous nature inspired in some of the toughest nuts among the American boys a desire to warn him, advise him, educate him. When it was suggested that America might offer TK a bright future, men like Milburn Sailor and Jimmy Clabby were quick to suggest likely men who might manage him. TK had been unwilling to accept that a manager might be necessary; he was soon to learn that in America a manager was a necessity.

Australia was then a good place in which to learn. Peggy Bettinson once claimed that it was Australia that had been responsible for the Americans learning the true craft of the prize ring. The great boxing master Jem Mace had started a boxing school in Australia where he had taught Larry Foley all he knew; Foley had become a teacher and among his pupils were Peter Jackson, Fitzsimmons, Young Griffo. Peter Jackson had then established himself as a teacher in San Francisco, to be followed by other Foley pupils, and they had taught the Americans. Thus TK made sure that he met Foley – indeed they became friends: 'That clever pupil of the old fellow's put me wise to many things about Mace. He told me that Mace kept him retreating, advancing and balancing on his feet for a whole week before allowing him to take up the first position in boxing. What do you know about that!'

TK's education was not always to be so pleasant and painless, however. Against Hughie Mehegan – who greeted him during the pre-fight preliminaries by recalling their meeting back in 1912 – TK learned what it was like to be repeatedly hit in the kidneys, a punch then banned in Britain. The *Sydney Sun* correspondent noted: 'Not for many a day have we seen the kidney punch so much in evidence. Every time the pair got close together Mehegan's right pounded the region under the left lung heavily. . . There was no speed in the delivery, but there was weight and calculation and to such purpose that by-and-by a large and deep red splurge spread over the place; yet Lewis never even winced till late in the battle and then he was seen twisting as if endeavouring to avoid the wallop which he appeared unable to escape in any other way. . .'

Though TK did well when standing back from Mehegan, the wily and experienced Australian was more adept than McCoy had been at cutting down the ring and getting in at close quarters. It was an awkward and untidy fight with Mehegan constantly boring

in, hitting to the body, and TK dancing, flicking out back-handed
stinging punches, sometimes resorting to illegally wrestling Mehegan
to the floor when caught up on the ropes. W.F. Corbett professed
himself unhappy with the result – a points win for TK – but he
conceded it had been close. In total contrast, a report appeared in
Boxing some weeks later under the headline, 'Lewis beats Mehegan
all the way'!

However, his third fight in six weeks – against top-ranked Joe
Shugrue – found Corbett once again reaching for the superlatives.

It was the perfect fight, matching as it did two contrasting stylists,
and produced a contest that Corbett declared would give the boxing
boom a good, solid fillip. Shugrue, tough, fast and adept at in-
fighting (which was just as well, as he was going blind) brought out
the best in TK, who had been prepared for the hardest fight of his
career: 'For Shugrue had beaten Owen Moran in seven rounds, had
stopped Herb McCoy, then king of the Australian lightweights, had
stopped Benny Leonard in four rounds and won a points decision
over the famous Pal Moore, the boxer who was credited with having
out-pointed the great Jim Driscoll.'

TK was determined to prevent Shugrue getting too close too often;
'Mind you, I mixed it with him occasionally because I badly wanted
to learn this phase of the game. . . How Joe's eyes did brighten up
on the few occasions I ventured to rough it with him. The wily
fellow actually gave me encouragement as I feel sure he didn't
go all out during the first few rounds we had breast to breast
with each other. But I saw the red light the last time I let him
have his own way, so to speak. I was picking up points quite
nicely thank you and kidding myself that this in-fighting stuff
was quite easy when suddenly a punch came from nowhere and
landed on my chin. For a moment I saw a million lights and then
a spasm of darkness. This was relieved again by more points of
light which danced and twinkled bewilderingly before my eyes.
And then I heard Alec's voice as if in a dream growling, "Break
away, Gersh!" '

From then on TK kept clear of Mr Shugrue's close fist-work,
ignoring the older man's appeals to 'have just one more little slam
up close'.

At the end he had secured a satisfying points win, a win that would
boost his status around the world and, for a time, ironically bring to
a halt his rapid upward progress.

In fact, the Shugrue fight marked the end of the Australian honeymoon. After losing a return to McCoy two weeks after the Shugrue fight, TK incurred Baker's wrath by complaining to newspapers back in England that he had been robbed. The idea had been put into his head by local reporters who had revealed to a dumbfounded TK after the fight that the referee had been McCoy's brother-in-law!

Baker, affronted that TK, or anyone else for that matter, should question the way he ran things, 'punished' TK by arranging his next fight against relatively unknown Bobby Moore, the fight to take place in a small Melbourne stadium which guaranteed TK would receive a small purse.

TK obediently took the fight, but was once again shocked to discover he was being swindled and out-smarted, this time where his winner's purse was concerned. Under the impression (fostered by the stadium manager) that weighing in at ringside was unnecessary he had simply turned up to fight at the appointed hour. No one said a word about it until paying-out time, when TK found that he was £100 short. He was being fined for not weighing-in. It was time, TK decided, to return home. 'I was deadly serious in this decision and cabled home to Ted Broadribb asking him to take over my management and requesting him to try his utmost to get me a contest with Freddie Welsh for the world lightweight title.' Welsh, much to TK's chagrin, had managed to entice Willie Richie to England and had taken the title in July.)

But somehow, TK never did board the liner headed for England. In September *Boxing* carried a small paragraph headed, 'The Mystery of Kid Lewis. Where Is Kid Lewis? This is the one outstanding puzzle of the day,' it began. Expected home on the SS *Orsova*, it seemed there were rumours that he was, in fact, en route for the USA. . .

PART TWO
The Smashing, Dashing, Crashing Kid

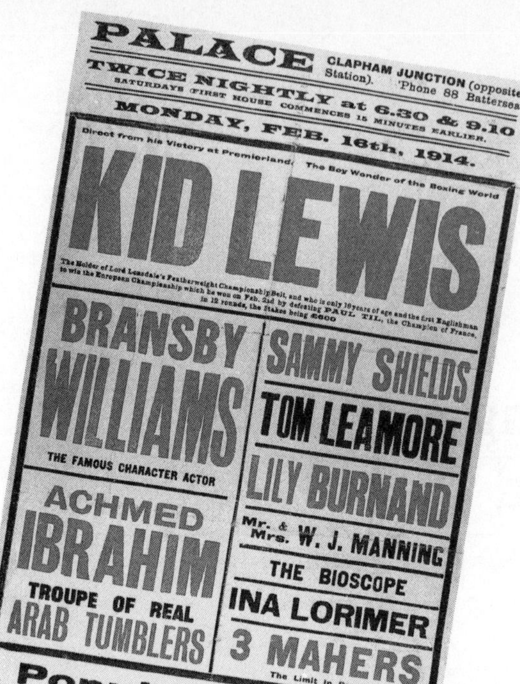

TOM ARNOLD presents

MAE WEST
in
'DIAMOND LIL'
By MAE WEST

CAST in order of appearance :

Skinny Schultz	MAI BACON
Frances Donovan	DIANA BILLINGS
Flo	PAMELA BEVAN
Kitty	HONORINE CATTO
Steve	J. McCARDLE
Bill the Barman	TED (KID) LEWIS
Pat Whalen (a Pianist)	BERT WALLER
Jim	MARK BAKARIAN
Woman	ELISE SENIOR
Maggie Murphy	ANNE ARNANE
Girl in automobile	BERYL OSTLERE
Man on tandem	RAY BROWN
Girl on tandem	JOYCE PATON
Dan Flynn	FRANCIS DE WOLFF
Kane	DANNY GREEN
Gus Jordan	DAVID DAVIES
Sally	JEAN McDONALD
Rita Christina	NOELE GORDON
Pablo Juarez	BRUNO BARNABE
Mike the Coachman	VICTOR HAGAN
Bessie	MARGARET STALLARD
Polly	BERYL OSTLERE
Violet	GINA CACHIA
Gloria	BARBARA TODD
DIAMOND LIL	MAE WEST
Captain Cummings	RICHARD BAILEY
Pete the Dope	ROLAND D. WHITE
Police Officer Doheney	BARRY O'NEILL
Jacobson	DANNY GREEN
Chick Clark	HAL GOULD

Toughs, Society Ladies & Gentlemen, Police, etc.

9 Early Days in the USA

'I was a young reporter in New York. I was talking to Ted in Grupps Gym as he changed, when he handed me his diamond pin and ring for safe-keeping! Can you imagine! Being trusted by the great Kid Lewis? I was thrilled!'
Harry Levene

The decision to sail to America rather than back home had been taken, typically, on the spur of the moment. There was also, according to TK, something a little fishy about the method of decision: 'Alec remarked that although Baker had provided our return tickets for England he could not object if we returned via America. I wasn't too enthusiastic about the suggestion and so Alec said, "Let's toss for it – heads, England; tails, America." The shilling came down tails.' TK was later to wonder whether the coin that had been used was a double-tailed one!

Once the decision had been taken, however, there was to be no turning back. And with the news that he was heading for San Francisco, his friends among the USA boxers were quick with advice regarding to prospective managers.

Jimmy Clabby, who was to sail back with them, was adamant that TK needed a manager who would have the power to push his interests, and he suggested they contact one man in particular: Charlie Harvey, in New York. Harvey, Clabby claimed, looked after his boxers and would be the perfect man to handle TK. An exchange of cables suggested that Harvey was interested and so TK took his leave of Australia.

He was never to return and he left with mixed feelings. He had met with nothing but kindness from individual Australians ('Snowy' Baker apart) and the freedom and friendliness of the new land had made a deep impression.

Yet, on landing in San Francisco some four weeks later, it seemed that TK had found another open, friendly and generous land.

They were met in San Francisco by Charlie Harvey's West Coast agent James J. Croffoth (a great guy, according to TK) who escorted them to their hotel. Croffoth could not have been more helpful or generous, handing over a roll of dollars which he said they could repay once TK had started to fight.

For four days, TK and Alec toured San Francisco, the City of the Golden Gate. Everything interested TK, especially the Chinese quarter which had been entirely rebuilt after the earthquake and fire of 1906, eight years earlier. The following year the Great International Exhibition was to be held to celebrate the opening of the Panama Canal in 1914 and the buildings, entirely contemporary, were in the process of being erected. With memories of the municipal corruption which followed the earthquake, the people of San Francisco had only one topic of conversation: who was going to make the most dollars out of the graft which they presumed to be inevitable? TK, in his innocence, was amazed that, far from being shocked at the idea that politicians could be bribed to grant concessions, the man-in-the-street looked upon this as one of the accepted facts of life.

After four days, a little sickened by the dishonesty and vice paraded on every street corner, TK and Alec took the Santa Fe express to New York. Four days later they were in Charlie Harvey's office in the Bowery. Charlie Harvey was busy, but they were welcomed by his Man Friday who introduced himself as Jimmy 'Jay Jay' Johnston. Though his was a humble job, it soon became apparent that Johnston knew everything there was to know about the boxing game. He quickly explained that, for the time being, he would be fronting for all practical arrangements as Charlie Harvey still had a few months to run as member of the New York Boxing Commission and, during his term of office, he was not allowed to act as a manager. Though an unpleasant surprise to TK, both he and Alec were quite satisfied to go along with Johnston.

However, as TK was to comment, 'Our partnership reversed that old adage, a good manager makes a good fighter. Where Johnston and I were concerned, it was a good fighter making a good manager.'

One thing Jay Jay did do almost immediately, however, was to alter TK's name. Jay Jay disliked the epithet 'Kid'. When he asked TK what his real name was, Gershon, he didn't like that either. What, he asked, was the English equivalent. Gerry, TK suggested. No good. Joe Kid Lewis? Awful. What about Edward? TK remembered suggesting. 'Ed, Teddy, Ted – Ted Kid Lewis. I like it,' Jay Jay concluded. 'That's a name I can work with. Ted Kid Lewis.' And that was that.

Johnston invariably smiled even when the smile did not spread to his gimlet eyes. Here was a shrewd man, or a sharp man, depending on whether he was on your side or not. In the years that TK was to know him, Jimmy Johnston acquired considerable fame and become known as the 'Boy Bandit'. 'Jimmy took us in hand at once and then began a tour of the newspaper offices, so exacting that by the time we had reached the last one we were thoroughly worn out and were glad to stay in our Broadway hotel for the remainder of the day.

'Next morning Jimmy took us to meet Harvey at 1402 Broadway – his office for many years – the walls of which were a veritable gallery of fight pictures. I got quite a kick out of examining them, and one stood out in my memory for years afterwards: Owen Moran *v* Ad Wolgast for the world lightweight championship which took place in San Francisco in 1911 and which Wolgast won in the thirteenth round.

'Harvey proved a charming man with whom it was impossible not to feel at ease from the moment one met him. We got to know each other intimately and during the whole time I was under his wing we never had a written contract. His word was his bond – or so I thought at the time.'

At first, however, the American fight writers viewed TK with considerable misgiving. He moved well in training but they had seen all that before. Most of the British boxers who had raised optimism in their training sessions had proved 'daisies' in the reality of a fight. Most of them were what the Americans termed 'fancy dicks' – boxers who had skill but little punch and even less aggression. In fact, 'spoilers'. It seemed to them that the British still looked upon boxing as the 'noble art of self-defence', whereas the American fight fan wanted blood, excitement and knockouts.

After some weeks of inactivity, TK grew tired and not a little restless. It had been almost three months since he had fought; Harvey therefore decided that the expense of a training camp was a worthwhile investment. TK and Alec were dispatched to Dai Hawkins's camp at Westchester, near New York.

TK was delighted to get back into the ring again, even though he was not training for a specific date. Once again, inactivity had added to his weight and he was over 10 st. At five foot eight and a half he was too short for the classic welterweight. During his campaigning in the States he became so adept at shedding or adding poundage that some of the sports writers dubbed him the 'India rubber Man'.

'For a month or more they kept me hanging about making matches and then calling them off until I hardly knew where I was. They told me I was to fight Jack Britton on 12 October, but he cried off after he had been told what they thought of me in London.

'Then Joe Mandot was offered fifteen hundred dollars to fight me, but he remarked that he could get that money for fighting mugs, so what did he want me for? It was a very nice compliment but it did not get me a fight.

'Leach Cross was another who passed me up and even a match between me and Ad Wolgast, the former world's lightweight champion, came to naught.

'Eventually Phil Bloom of Brooklyn was found as an opponent, in a ten-round no-decision bout. We shared the top place of the bill with a fight between Mike Gibbons, one of America's greatest middleweights, and Young Mike Donovan.'

Determined to prove his aggression, TK went out fighting from the first bell. In fact, he tried to change his style completely. But Bloom was experienced – an awkward fighter who could make himself seem all arms and legs and who liked to drag his opponent into clinches and rough him up inside.

Thus, although TK tried to keep up a non-stop onslaught, Bloom was able to avoid him with comparative ease. At the end of the third round Jimmy Johnston came to the corner and, slapping TK lightly across the face, said, 'I thought you said you could box! That's what I read. Why don't you box now?'

TK took the instruction, though intending to try boxing for only a round. But as soon as he began to use his skill, sending that long left with unfailing accuracy to Bloom's face and body, there was only one man in the contest. By the last bell there was no doubt that, if a points decision could have been awarded, it would have gone to TK (this was the period when only 'newspaper decisions' were allowed in many states). As TK explained it: 'In those days, all contests in New York were under the Frawley Law which had just been passed permitting boxing contests, as such, but prohibiting decisions. Before that date when a promoter wanted to stage a fight he had to fix up with some gymnastic club, and make the fighters members of this. It would then be advertised that there would be exhibition contests between members of the club and all the spectators had to be members. No referees' verdicts could be given, but they were fights right enough. Still the system did not work well and so Senator Frawley brought in a law to be worked by a commission.

'Fights were legalized, but decisions were still disallowed and all contestants, whether they were fighting at weight or at catch-weight, had to go to scale at ringside. There would be plenty of betting on the results, which were worked this way: those who wanted to bet would agree to have their wages decided by the newspapers. They would pick out three or so and would pay out on the verdicts given by the newspaper critics.

'It was good for the pressmen, you can bet. Every well-known critic would have a panel or a box, if you like, in his report of the fight and would print: "In my opinion So-and-So won", and the bets would be paid out on the majority of such verdicts. You can guess that some of these press critics made a nice bit for themselves.'

The sports writers admitted the next day that Lewis had clearly won, but they were hesitant in assessing his true ability. Bat Masterton, one of the most famous of American boxing journalists, wrote: 'Ted Kid Lewis, the much-touted British lightweight, cannot be truthfully called a wonder on this showing. The Englishman was disappointing, but it was his first fight in this country and he might not have been quite himself.'

But Charlie Harvey and Jimmy Johnston congratulated themselves on having a boy fighting for them who, they were sure, would reach the top – and become a sure-fire money earner.

Thus, a second contest was quickly arranged for TK at the National Athletic Club in Philadelphia against Young Jack O'Brien, the brother of the great light-heavyweight.

TK was a good 9 lb. lighter than his opponent, yet was awarded a unanimous decision by the following morning's papers. Within a week, he was in the same ring, giving away 14 lb. to Willie Moore, the brother of Pal Moore. Again, though a no-decision fight, the reporters next day adjudged TK the winner.

Four days after this contest, TK had coffee with Freddie Welsh, the man he had been challenging ever since Welsh had won the world lightweight title the previous year.

Here was the opportunity, he thought, to get a tilt at the world crown, but the shrewd Welshman simply shook his head sympathetically. 'No, Ted, it doesn't make sense. We're both British. They won't pay as much to see us here as they would do in England. You'll have to wait. When I defend my title in America, it will be against a Yank. That's common sense. We're not in this for the glory – it's the money that counts.'

Though TK argued hotly, Welsh remained adamant. He would fight him when and where they were able to draw the most money. Any other arrangement would be, to his way of looking at things, unprofessional. So TK had to remain patient, not an easy task for, once again, even run-of-the-mill contests had dried up.

Each morning TK would leave the hotel before breakfast to buy a newspaper, joking with the paperboy on the corner, giving him advice on how best to sell his papers, admitting that he himself had once been 'in the trade'. But his heart was not in such trivial conversation, for he felt he owed his country so much for having given him the chance to raise himself out of his poor environment and now that Britain was fighting the First World War, he wanted to help. His family were in London, bombed daily by Zeppelins (news had just reached him that his beloved Judean Club had been reduced to rubble – not a quarter of a mile from his family home). Yet when he visited the British Embassy, officials assured him that he could do more for his country in America that he could by going home.

Many American towns had large German populations and were extremely anti-British. If he could win popularity for the English with his fists, he would be doing something to overcome that hatred. Reluctantly, he agreed to stay on, but increasingly his thoughts were turning to London and his home in the East End.

It might have been easier to accept the British Embassy argument if he had been fighting regularly, but it seemed that few American boxers showed any desire to get into the ring with him. He fretted, therefore, showing little patience with his manager's excuses, daily ringing up to demand to know whether any fight deals had been settled. Harvey and Johnston appreciated that they might eventually lose their potential meal ticket if they could not offer him regular work, but their only solution was to change TK's training camp and bring him into the brotherhood of other fighters with whom he could box during the day and talk boxing during the evenings.

Alec and TK were, therefore, moved to Staten Island where they found themselves with Leach Cross, Ad Wolgast, Frank Moran – the Pittsburgh fighter with the much-vaunted punch named 'Mary Ann' – Johnny Kilbane, Billy Papke and Jack Britton. But although he enjoyed the company of other boxers there was no substitute for real action.

Weeks passed without any firm news of a contest and TK began to believe there was a conspiracy to freeze him out of the American ring. He decided not to rely on his managers alone – he would write to the papers, demanding to know if American fighters were afraid of him!

However, if TK's letter did not attract the attention of promoters or fighters, it certainly interested a certain Mr Freeman Bernstein who, in February 1915, visited TK's hotel with a proposition.

Box with the Gloves the British Champions use.

We offer them on Easy Payment Terms.

" Excellent Gloves in Every Way " . . .	Bombardier BILLY WELLS.
" The best made and neatest finished I have ever used "	FREDDIE WELSH.
" Cannot be beaten "	JOHNNIE SUMMERS.
" I have always used them "	KID LEWIS.
" Excellent Gloves in every respect " . . .	DIGGER STANLEY.

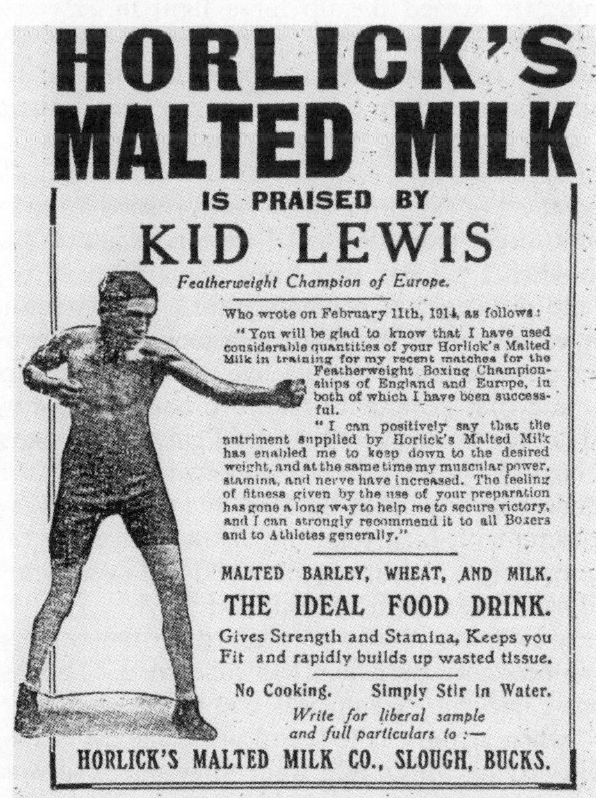

10 The Havana Interlude

'This man could really tell the tale, and I wasn't the only
boxer to whom he told it.'

TK

Freeman Bernstein was an 'entrepreneur', a fixer, a con-man,
according to whom one talked. TK must have been tailor-made
for the smooth-talking Bernstein, although it seemed at first that
Bernstein was merely offering TK the chance to earn some money
in the ring. 'He signed me up for a fight in Havana, Cuba. I
was to fight one Frankie Mack, a lightweight from Boston, and
we were to go on, either as a supporting bout to the world's
heavyweight championship contest between Jess Willard and Jack
Johnson, or for some introductory promotion which would get the
Cubans interested.'

The vagueness of the proposition was brushed aside by TK and
Alec: 'Don't forget that Alec and I were getting real short on the
dollars, so when I tell you that I saw a guarantee of £2,000, plus
expenses and privileges of percentage for a twenty-round contest,
I just jumped to sign it. Mr Bernstein took me to his own home,
telling Alec and me that we could live there more cheaply than at
any hotel, and that experience ought to have put me wise. I was
young and not too clever, perhaps, and I got enough signals to warn
me that I ought to break the contract I had signed, but there were
all those dollars staring me in the face, and anyway I was going into
a training camp with Jack Johnson, acknowledged to be about the
greatest heavyweight champion the world had ever seen, so I guess
you would have fallen for it as easily as I did.'

However, so many things seemed to be not quite what they
appeared to be where Bernstein was concerned: 'This "shmoozer"
with whom I had got tied up was one tough guy. He was never
"at home" when anyone called, and when the caller looked like a
government official who might want to get more satisfaction than
that bald statement, he would dodge into another room and there

climb out of the window. Still, there was the fight ahead, and he held me to it with the bill he presented for bed and food at his house.'

Once under way, however, it appeared that boxing was not the only enterprise Bernstein was involved in: 'We were to go to Cuba, and he did book us through, but we had to travel with a circus which he was sending out to the island under the management of one of his brothers.

'This circus was some venture. We got to Cuba with them, and they opened up at Havana. No one was on wages. When the takings were reckoned up, and it could be happily discovered that there would be something left over after paying for the animals' food, then, but only then, the human performers would get a trifle, but not otherwise. As a result most of them were half-starved. I saw the promoters and managed to borrow some money out of the purse I was to get, and so was able to buy these people some food. Two or three of them were without boots and shoes till I bought some for them.'

Already TK's money was slipping inexorably away. On top of that, bad luck seemed to dog the tour from the start and when things went wrong, Mr Bernstein was conspicuous by his absence: 'Their worst bit of luck came when their star acrobat had a bad accident and the show had to close. The American Consul did what he could, but Mr Bernstein could not be located. He was too wise to show up, yet he managed to touch the promoters for some of my money. He was one experience, believe me.'

Once in Havana, however, TK was at last able to turn his mind to the matter in hand – boxing. He was now moving among some of the greatest fighters in boxing history. 'Jess Willard had started in to train, and presently Jack Johnson arrived. Jack has had his enemies and his critics, but he was never close-fisted, and as he had more money than I had, he was able to help out the circus crowd until the American Consul shipped them back to the States.'

TK now had the opportunity to observe at close hand possibly the greatest of all boxers – certainly the most charismatic and controversial in boxing history. And TK came to a surprising conclusion about the forthcoming title fight: 'Johnson wasn't too popular in Cuba, not even with the people of his own colour. Somehow or other they resented the presence of his white wife, who was, of course, equally unpopular with the white Cubans and the Americans. He didn't seem to mind and was generally in good spirits, although he had come to Cuba to lose his title. That had been arranged beforehand. All Europe was at war, so Jack could not get any fights and he could not enter the States without going to prison. So they got to him, promising that if he lost to Willard he would be allowed to return to Chicago and that the charge of transporting a woman over a state line would be dropped.

'That looked good to Jack, who wanted to get back to his mother and his people, and who also wanted to have a chance of making some money. Yet, as you know, he wasn't able to dodge the warrant. In the end, he went back and went to prison for a year. So he might just as well have kept hold of his title. Jess Willard could never have beaten him if the fight had been on the level.'

Whether TK was correct or not, boxing historians refuse to come to any firm conclusions – and probably never will. However, for TK there came an opportunity he was to regard as the highlight of his career thus far: 'I joined Jack's camp, but I only boxed with him once. It was no use my trying to hit him. He was the most wonderful defensive fighter who ever put a glove on. So he was no assistance to me, whatever I may have been to him. Funnily enough, although Johnson knew he had to lose, he did put in some fairly hard training. It had been agreed that the fight had to last twenty-six rounds, so Jack had to be fairly fit. He went on the road and I went with him; but Jack wasn't wanting to strain himself to any extent. I would leave him on the road to cover my distance, and then return to the camp, and would pass Jack plugging along. He had had to pull up for rests every few hundred yards.'

Although TK's fight with Frankie Mack took place before the big fight, TK was forced to wait until the Johnson fight was over to see if he would receive any money. Jack Curley, who along with one Dick Klegin, was promoting the heavyweight title fight, was asked by TK to hold his purse of $2,000 – not a wise move as it turned out: 'In the end I was lucky to finish with $200 as there wasn't any money left over when Johnson was paid! They were broke to the world. I guess the hotel keepers and a lot of Havana tradesmen remember that Johnson–Willard business, seeing that most of the Americans who were handling the business end made hurried dives for the boat. Someone, by the way, did book Dick Klegin's passage, but the "Jewish Ambassador" did not know this and hid in a coal bunker till the ship left for the States.'

TK joined the scramble to get out of Cuba as he was afraid that if he stayed he would end up penniless. But in his haste, he forgot his precious Lonsdale Belt: 'I had left this at a jeweller's shop on exhibition in the window, and I only remembered it just as the boat was leaving. So I sent a cable to Leo Flynn, asking him to collect it for me. That looked all right, but when Flynn got to New York, he told me that the jeweller had handed over the belt to someone who had called for it with a note signed "Ted Lewis".

'That was bad enough, but there was worse to come. When I got to New York I found a cable from Mr Bettinson asking me to return the belt, as I could not defend it now that I had grown out of the featherweight class. You can guess how I felt. I could not tell him I had lost it. All I could do was to go to the police and hope for the best.'

Thus ended TK's Cuban fiasco. TK and Alec chased Bernstein but to no avail. There was no money to be had; it was a salutary lesson.

Empty-handed and saddened by the loss of his precious belt, TK retraced his steps to JJ's office.

Old friends who have come together again—in spirit, and who will shortly do so in flesh: Jack Greenstock, Zalig Goodman, and Kid Lewis.

11 Chasing Titles

The Havana fiasco had been an independent move on TK's part, born out of the frustration of inaction – but Harvey was unforgiving. 'He asked us how we had made out and though I tried to hide it, I couldn't conceal from him the fact that we had been swindled. However, he seemed to have found out that we had been promised $2,000. "We get a cut of that," he said, referring to the fact that Johnston and he were still our managers. I was dumbfounded, but what could I do? Not only were we broke, we now *owed* money! And no amount of arguing could convince him that we had not received at least some of the cash. All he would agree to was a regular deduction from future purses. . .'

As compensation, however, Harvey arranged a fight for TK almost immediately, against Jack Britton at the 135th Street Athletic Club. It was to be a no-decision fight, of course, but it had exciting implications. Although Freddie Welsh had refused to defend his lightweight title against TK, the welterweight championship was still unclaimed. Since Mike Sullivan had given up the title to campaign as a middleweight, there had been numerous pretenders to the throne, all of whom had been subsequently defeated except Jimmy Clabby, who had had to give up for weight problems.

The managers of Harry Lewis, Ray Bronson, Matt Wells and Mike Glover had all argued persuasively without being able to convince anyone as to their respective boys' right to the title. But to the enlightened onlooker it appeared that Jack Britton had the strongest claim and, if TK could defeat him, he must come into any championship eliminator.

At worst, a victory would mean more fights and higher purses.

Jack Britton was eight years older than TK and far more experienced. Indeed, the battle with TK would be Britton's 150th contest and to date he had only lost six decisions. He was two and a half inches taller than TK and a natural welterweight. He had fought Packy McFarland and Phil Bloom and defeated Mike Glover, Pal Moore and Soldier Bartfield, all star performers. In the ring he looked awkward, but many experts regarded him as being – Jack Johnson excepted – the most skilful boxer of the day. He was a 'thinking' fighter who would change his style as circumstances demanded. He would seldom repeat a mistake and boxing was to him as much a mental challenge as a physical one.

His manager was 'Dumb' Dan Morgan who had earned his nickname not by keeping his mouth shut but by talking so loquaciously that everyone else became dumb when he was in full spate.

TK knew that to stand a chance against Britton he had to be in the finest condition and he retired for a week to the monastic life of the training camp.

Britton, born of Irish-American parents (his real name was William J. Breslin) was guaranteed strong New York support whenever he fought in the city.

TK decided that as Britton had been fighting for so long he was likely to be used to the typical bustling American fighting style which allowed Britton to stand off and make the best advantage of his classic left hand. So TK decided to forget his efforts to beat the Americans at their own game – at least for this contest – and to try to outspeed and outbox his experienced opponent.

The first contest between the two was not one of their most exciting. Britton boxed well but he had never met TK's style before and, for the first time, found himself up against a faster man. At the end of the contest, before leaving the ring, Britton crossed over to TK's corner: " 'I guess you knew too much for me tonight, Kid, but maybe we'll meet some other time," he said. How right he was!'

TK waited to read the morning papers before cabling home. A clear majority of reporters awarded a close fight to the English boy.

Two weeks later TK fought local New York boy Harry Lenny, a tough, hard-punching opponent, and once again the morning papers were unanimous in their verdict – TK could cable home the word 'Victory' once again, along with a portion of his purse. However, at the bottom of one report he noticed an item announcing that Britton had agreed to two contests in Ohio. TK had thought that Britton's next contest would be a return with himself for the disputed welterweight championship, but if Britton was off to Ohio such a contest must, be concluded, be at least two months off.

In his disappointment, his thoughts turned again to home and a swift return. 'I was beginning to hanker for a sight of the Old Country, my family, and maybe I could help a bit with the war. Alec, of course, did not want to know. He was happy in the States and, besides, the money was here. I booked passage on the Cunarder *Lusitania* which was due to leave New York in five days' time.

'The next day, however, an offer came for a fight in Montreal and as I had never been to Canada and always wanted to go there I decided to cancel my booking, much to Alec's delight, and make the trip. I was matched with an Irishman named Johnny Lore in a ten rounds no-decision affair and the scheduled date was 16 April.

'What a lucky break I had! The *Lusitania* sailed without me and she was torpedoed off the Irish coast by a German submarine, an incident that did much to bring America into the war.

'I beat my opponent in Montreal and must have created a good impression there. . .'

Indeed the Montreal fans demanded that TK stay on for a second contest, so a fortnight later he was again in action, this time against Johnny Lustig, an American who had been campaigning in Canada most successfully. It was another unanimous verdict for TK: 'There was plenty of work for me in Canada and when I learned that Freddie Welsh was due to arrive I immediately put myself forward as an opponent. I knew I could easily reduce myself to lightweight if he would meet me under championship conditions and to my delight the match was fixed up.'

Unfortunately, no one had told Welsh, 'and when Freddie turned up he refused to give me a fight'.

Welsh reiterated his reasons, given some months earlier, i.e. the match made no financial sense. 'It was quite obvious that nothing would induce him to change his mind so I refused further offers to fight in Canada and returned to New York hoping by that time Jack Britton had put in an appearance.'

Once again, TK was out of luck. However, as if Dame Fortune was giving him a sign, his long-lost Lonsdale Belt was suddenly found. TK recalled: 'We had wirelessed some friends in Havana to retrieve the trophy and bring it back to New York.

'Weeks passed, and I was terribly uneasy because we had received no word about it. To make matters worse, as I had outgrown the featherweight division I had been requested by the National

Sporting Club to return the Belt to one of their representatives who would call on me in New York.

'It was in an unenviable frame of mind that I met this person, and there was no course open to me but to tell him the truth. He suggested that we inform the police.

'Mr Bettinson kept cabling and I was getting more uncomfortable every day. At last the police got on the track of the belt. The man who had pinched it had pawned it in Cuba and I had to borrow the money to pay this loan and get the belt back, but that was a relief.'

On 9 June, he met Kid Graves of Nebraska and won a clear newspaper decision over one of the self-styled champions who had based his claims on two no-decision contests with Britton and similar bouts with Jack O'Brien and Soldier Bartfield. They fought at the St Nicholas Rink, New York, and this time Charlie Harvey took over TK's management, as the 'Boy Bandit' Johnston was promoting the tournament.

Two weeks later, TK again topped the bill at the Rink, this time against Johnny Marto, a local fighter. By now Johnston, a most persuasive man who would have made an excellent advertising agent, was thumping the large drum on Ted's behalf. Johnston challenged the world. He dared every lightweight and welterweight in the country to face the 'Smashing, Crashing, Bashing Cockney Kid'. He also proclaimed TK was so confident of his ability to defeat whoever accepted the challenge that he would fight for a percentage of the gate on a winner-takes-all basis.

TK was confident but he saw no reason for fighting for nothing and he taxed Johnston on his generosity on his behalf. The little man brushed his objections aside: 'You fight, I talk. Get that straight. Have I asked you to fight for nothing? Have I? You know I haven't. What I tell the press guys and what I tell you are two different things. Now get out of my office and train – that's your job. Leave the talking – and thinking – to me. I know more about it and do it better.'

TK obeyed the order. Johnston was proved right.

Johnny Marto was tough, but not in Ted's class, and he was footsore and bleeding from nose and mouth before the end of the contest. TK was unmarked – which was just as well, because two days later he faced Mike Mazie, another popular New Yorker, at Brown's Far Rockaway, a boxing club. Again, it was an easy victory.

His next opponent, however, was a very different proposition. Charlie White was a class performer who had been born in Liverpool

but had done all his fighting in the States. The Liverpudlian
had become known as 'Left-hook Charlie', a nickname earned
by eighteen knock-outs in the last two years. The fact of the
no-decision rule had little effect where he was concerned, for few
of his opponents heard the last bell. In 1915 he had already knocked
out five opponents within six weeks and his sensational progress had
only been halted by Freddie Welsh – who had received a divided
decision from the press, and Milburn Sailor, who had also managed
a draw.

White was a natural lightweight and without consulting TK,
Johnston had contracted for him to meet White at 9 st. 7 1b.
But TK, since fighting welters, had allowed his weight to increase
and now turned the scales at 10 st. (140 1b.). Alec grumbled and
argued but there was nothing for it. In two weeks TK trained down
to the requisite poundage and from then onward Johnston loudly
proclaimed the ability of 'his boy' to come in at any weight from
light to middle. This may have been no more than mere newspaper
braggadocio but TK certainly found he could control his weight far
more effectively and without loss of power than most other fighters.

White might have been born in Liverpool, but the New Yorkers
looked upon him as one of their own and his record of twenty-seven
knockouts made him a clear favourite in the betting: 'It was a
"capacity" house and I had the pleasing knowledge that in the
gallery were some five hundred English fight fans, many of whom
I knew personally. There was a further incident before we entered
the ring when three suffragettes endeavoured to make themselves
heard, but they were quickly ejected.

'One particular friend, Johnny Ford, was in my corner in all my
American fights. He was a great guy. He did not act as a second but
he kept the time and would always tip off Alec Goodman for the last
fifteen seconds. Incidentally, he was a wonderful dancer, the Fred
Astaire of his day.

'My English friends had some tuneful doggerel which they
chanted throughout the fight. It went:

> "What's the matter with Lewis?
> He's all right.
> Who's he going to lick tonight?
> Charlie White!"

'Hardly an effort which would gain the post of Poet Laureate,
but it was sufficient to annoy Charlie who began to talk to me as

we fought, probably in an endeavour to upset my confidence. But in this he was unsuccessful.'

Once again, it was TK who did the boxing and Charlie White who did the chasing. TK knew that his opponent's left hook was his main artillery. With this in mind he had decided to keep his right hand up high and to touch his right cheek occasionally to be sure that the right hand was there. He kept rigidly to this while circling to the left, drawing White after him and on to short rights to the body, which were fast becoming a feature of his work.

After two rounds of assessing his opponent, however, he switched tactics, attacking with fast vicious lefts to the head. Several times White landed with the full force of his left hook, but TK was able to block these blows as if they were of no account.

White was not used to having his best punches brushed aside as if they did not exist. He became wild and, in so doing, he left himself open. TK moved in and out with such speed that the New Yorker appeared slow and lumbering. During the interval between the fifth and sixth rounds an Irishman sitting at ringside exhorted TK to 'murder the Jewish bum!'

Alec, in the process of wiping TK's face with the sponge, shouted out to him, 'But Lewis is a Jew, too!'

The Irishman stood up in disgust. 'They're both sheenies?' He threw his programme into the ring. 'Then xxxx the both of them,' and he strode out of the hall.

He was alone in not enjoying the contest, however. The rest of the crowd were loving it, and the English contingent roared their approval when, in the last round, TK floored White with a straight right to the jaw. Once again, there was no dispute as to the winner.

Two weeks after beating White, TK was matched with Mike Glover, a leading middleweight title contender, the fight to take place in Boston. The fight was made at 10 st. 15 lb. over the weight he had had to make against White, and preparations were intense, as victory in this contest would be extremely important to TK. Although he had been winning 'newspaper-decisions' regularly since arriving in the States, this was his first contest in a town which permitted the referee to give the decision and he could not delude himself as to Mike Glover's ability. He would be a tough opponent. A former claimant of the welterweight crown through his victory over Britain's Matt Wells, Mike Glover had suffered a rare defeat six weeks earlier at the fists of Jack Britton. He was a fully fledged welterweight and would outweigh TK by over eight pounds. TK was fighting as a substitute for Soldier Bartfield; and although fighting so regularly meant that he was always reasonably fit, there is a vast difference between that and being trained for an actual contest, when Alec would have had him reach the peak of condition on that very evening.

Despite Glover's record, TK was confident that on his present form he could win, and win quickly. But the Boston fight fans thought otherwise and made the local boy a two-to-one favourite.

The contest had aroused much excitement, which increased as money poured in on both boxers. Every seat at the Atlas Athletic Club was occupied and the standing room was packed.

TK knew the odds against him were based on Glover fighting before his own crowd and that, as a proven puncher, his opponent's extra weight should allow him mastery at in-fighting. For this reason, TK decided on a policy of speed. He would try to rattle his opponent by his elusiveness. From the first round he never allowed the Irish-American to set himself for a big punch, and when Glover did throw his straight right, it was invariably out of range. This angered Glover and, as the contest progressed, his attacks became more and more savage. But savagery is the enemy of control and the wilder he became, the wider were his misses. Meanwhile, TK was scoring points with his left, varying this attack every now and then with a swift left-hook to the body, a shift of weight, and the same fist hooked upwards to the jaw. The press christened this the 'loop-the-loop' punch, but years later the selfsame combination, when used by world lightweight champion Ike Williams, would be renamed the 'bolo' punch.

At the end, TK had won handsomely – it was his first undisputed decision and marked a turning-point. By the end of the month he would be stepping into the ring again in Boston, only the stakes would be immeasurably higher. . .

12 World Champion at Last

'Put your money where your mouth is – it's big enough!'
Jimmy 'Jay Jay' Johnson to Dan Morgan

TK had been in the USA for nine months and for much of that time he had been struggling against the odds to make some kind of impression on the US boxing scene. As he took two more decisions from Kid Curley and Fighting Zunner in mid August 1915 in Buffalo, it must have seemed that the uphill task would continue indefinitely.

But his constant nagging at Johnston, his determination to succeed in a bid for a world title – in particular the world lightweight title – eventually paid off. Johnston, largely through TK's efforts, was rapidly becoming a power in the American boxing scene. Indeed he had acquired a new nickname and was now commonly known as 'Three Js'. 'I worried Jimmy about getting me another contest in Boston where verdicts could be rendered and eventually he got me on the phone and announced in great glee that he had brought off my heart's desire – a twelve-round contest with Jack Britton – to a decision and for the welterweight title'

However, Johnston was too shrewd a manager not to appreciate the interest which could be built up in a contest between two boxers who had demolished every other welterweight of class. So he announced, to everyone's bemusement, that the match was to be made at 135 lb. – the lightweight limit!

'When Jimmy clinched the fight he stipulated that the weight should be 135 lb., and although I had been boxing some ten pounds above this weight, I could make 9 st. 9 lb, without any trouble when I set my mind to it with, of course, the scientific aid of Alec Goodman.

'We were to box twelve rounds to a decision for the welterweight title, and by sticking out for the lightweight poundage Jimmy had two pieces of strategy in mind: firstly, he knew that I could make the weight without harmful effect, whereas it would be a strain for

Britton, and secondly, he imagined that victory at the lightweight limit would force Freddy Welsh into a defence of his championship as well.

'The Welsh Wizard had side-stepped both Britton and myself and without any doubt we stood out as his foremost challengers with me slightly more to the forefront because of my newspaper verdict over the New Yorker. It was my manager's idea that public opinion would force Welsh into a title fight and I made up my mind that nothing would stop me from scoring a decisive victory over my Boston opponent.'

The arguments then began between Johnston and Britton's manager, the far from 'Dumb' Dan Morgan: 'You can imagine what it was like when the two managers got together for the purpose of discussing the details of our proposed match. Both Britton and I went out of town and just sat quiet and waited to be recalled for action. . .'

By the time the boxers climbed through the ropes arguments concerning the stakes, the referee and the judges had raged and finally been settled. Patsy Haley would referee with two prominent Boston sportsmen acting as judges. But the managerial altercations had left Ted tense and anxious to get on with the fighting. 'Dumb' Dan had not finished yet, however: 'Hardly had my gloves been tied on when Britton strolled over to my corner and complained that he was dissatisfied with the gloves he had been given. Although brand new and the best money could buy, they did not suit him and for some unknown reason he decided that mine were better.

'Immediately, Morgan and Johnston started at one another's throats, but in order to get down to business I ordered Alec to untie the gloves and pass them over to Britton, who went grinning to his corner very pleased with himself at having scored over me. . .

'To add to my troubles Morgan next took exception to the way my hands were bandaged. . . I was fast getting irritated, but the gloves were soon adjusted and I sat waiting for the bell to ring. I thought of that old saying about, "He who laughs last" etc. and made up my mind that Master Jack was going to feel my punches with added venom behind them.

'No sooner had the bell started and we came out to commence battle when Jack suddenly dropped his hands and went to his corner!'

'He refused to continue the fight as I was wearing a gumshield. . .

'To say that I saw red is to put it mildly. At first I was tempted to claim the bout on the grounds that my opponent had lost by forfeiture, but that would have gained me nothing. The bell rang again; this time the referee ordered me to my corner and directed that I should take out my mouthpiece. To this I strongly objected, saying there was nothing in the rules that had any bearing on the subject and that, in any case, I had conceded enough to Britton in one day.

'While the wrangling was going on one of my seconds got infuriated with "Dumb" Dan and let fly with a left hook. Fortunately, it missed his chin and landed on his chest but that was the signal for a general mêlée to begin, whereupon there was a lot of pushing and barging about while the fans were howling, cheering and hissing, the whole combining into a bedlam of racket that could be heard far outside the building.

'Matters were fast approaching a crisis when I suddenly became icy cold and realized that we were merely playing into Britton's hands.

'Pulling out my gumshield I flung it at Jack's feet and yelled, "All right, let the fight start", an action that was greeted with a cheer from the fans and one that did me a power of good throughout the contest, for they were with me to a man.'

Eventually the ring was cleared again and the bell rang for the second time. After what had transpired, it was not altogether surprising that the fight turned out to be one of the most vicious that TK had ever fought. In the first round his anger made him impetuous and he suffered for it, being dropped momentarily by a short right. But by the time the bell sent them back to their corners, he was attacking furiously once again.

As round gave way to round, the pace grew, if anything, hotter. Britton was an extremely experienced pro and knew every trick, legal and illegal. If TK wore a gumshield, it must be because his mouth was vulnerable, so Britton was not above using his head in the clinches. By the eleventh round TK had outpunched and outfought Britton, and he had the satisfaction of sending the Irish-American to the canvas for a count of six. At the final bell, the referee and the judges wasted no time totting up the points: each one of them found for Ted Kid Lewis, the new world welterweight champion.

Morgan started to complain, shouting that the officials were bought and that his boy had been robbed. There was only one answer to this and with the fans yelling their appreciation of what several sportswriters described as 'the fiercest contest ever fought in Boston', a rematch was made for three weeks later. For this second decision contest, negotiations were considerably simpler because of

TK's victory. He was the champion and Britton the challenger. If Morgan wanted a return, then he would have to agree to all of Jay Jay's terms.

Three weeks later, the principals met again at the ringside for the weigh-in. Britton was first on the scales, weighing 9 st. 10 lb. – 136 lb. – well below his best weight, but Jay Jay had stipulated this to be the limit.

This time Morgan made no complaint when the decision was announced in Lewis's favour. He had won far more easily than on their last contest, even though Britton had learned a way of avoiding TK's short body blows, by standing almost sideways on to his opponent, leaving only a shoulder to be seen, and using his eyes to feint; a strategy he used with great skill. TK had also profited from the first contest, and used a combination punch of straight left, followed by a left hook, with excellent effect. Twice Britton was floored and this time the crowd – a record 6,500 – were brought to their feet, not by the viciousness of the battle, but by the skill of both boxers.

A legacy of the Britton fights was to be the continuing controversy over TK's use of the gum-shield. In the USA during these early years it was not in universal use – in fact, TK was something of an innovator. He could have been much more than that – if he and Jack Marks, his dentist back in London, had realized what they had been developing over the years, they might well have become millionaires. TK recalled: 'I was sitting in Jack's dentist chair, with a mould in my mouth as he was taking an impression, and I asked him if he could make me something like it, but smaller, that I could wear in the ring. He said he didn't see why not. At that time boxers were putting orange or lemon peel between their lips and teeth to protect them. Well, I made about six to eight visits for fittings, all the while trying them out in the gym. Finally one worked and that's how the gumshield was born.'

It was due to TK's trials, tribulations, tenacity and perseverance that the use of the gumshield became recognized throughout the boxing world. If not the co-inventor of the shield, he was certainly the promoter – a pity Marks and Lewis never registered a patent!

With two decisive victories over Britton, the offers of contests poured in, with the purses increasing dramatically. TK was now instantly recognized wherever he went in New York and he would have been immensely happy to bask in his fame had it not been for the grim news of war. British soldiers were dying by the thousands

TK, 1911

Solomon and Leah Mendeloff

TK, Elsie and Morton Lewis, 1931

TK and Elsie with their first grandchild, Marsha, 1944

Albert Hall, 1923. TK loses a 20 round decision to Augie Ratner

Holland Park, 1922. TK stopped Frankie Burns in the 11th round
for the Empire middleweight title

Albert Hall, 1921. TK versus Boy McCormick (light-heavyweight
champion). TK won in the 14th round

Jack Britton

Mike O'Dowd

Willie Richie

Benny Leonard

Charlie White

Battling Ort

Mike Gibbons

Soldier Bartfield

Alec Goodman and TK, 1912

TK and Jack Britton when TK won the
World Welterweight title and belt, 1915

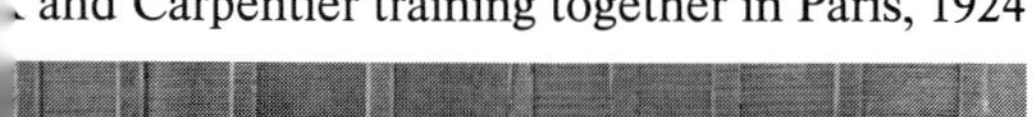

 and Carpentier training together in Paris, 1924

TK with his backer, Ernie Mogford, 1914
TK wears his new Lonsdale Belt

Albert Hall, 1920. TK stopped Johnny Basham in the 19th round for the
welterweight title

in the mud of the Western front, while the landings in Salonika were not proving nearly as successful as had been hoped. However, American opinion was swinging increasingly towards the Allies and, already angered by the sinking of the *Lusitania*, they were horrified by the news of the execution in Brussels of the British nurse, Edith Cavell.

Furthermore, TK's immense popularity had one great advantage, in that it allowed him considerable choice of opponents. Three weeks after the Britton fight he beat Willie Moore in Philadelphia over six rounds; eight days later that he was back in Brooklyn, which had now adopted him as its own, to KO experienced French-American Joe Mandot; seven days after that he met Milburn Sailor whom he reduced to a shuffling, forlorn figure in the very first round; and three weeks later he was in the ring against Jimmy Duffy of Lockport, New York. Though reputedly a tough fighter and a hard puncher, TK KO'd Duffy in one round. Charlie White, the Liverpool-born battler who had fought TK in July, sent him a telegram: 'One rounders my copyright. Don't infringe.'

TK was amused and replied: 'Copyright! I've been carrying it about for weeks, waiting to slip it to you.'

Such intense action had to produce a reaction of some sort: 'Exactly seven days after the Duffy victory was a return with Mike Glover, although it was not according to plan.

'I forget who it was Johnston had signed for me to meet, but he could not put in an appearance and Mike Glover was brought in as a substitute. Luckily the match was made at 155 lb., so the title wasn't at stake. . .I felt sluggish and off-colour. It was extremely hard to get going and it was not before the tenth round that I really woke up. I made a great effort then to reduce his points lead and although I won the last three rounds, the referee's verdict had to go to Glover and rightly so.

'Naturally I was disappointed at the result. It was my first defeat in 22 American contests and as I imagined a setback to my ambitions.

'Jimmy was not perturbed in the least, however, nor did he apparently think I was being overworked.' TK was then booked by the apparently insatiable Johnston for Madison Square Garden – a famous arena of which he had just managed to become matchmaker. But this time Johnston was doing more than hustle TK into yet another payday: 'Three Jays had surpassed himself this time by getting me matched with Willie Ritchie in a no-decision contest

over ten rounds, billed as for the welterweight championship of
the world. We had to make 142 lb. and no one took exception to
the match as a championship affair for the simple reason that there
had not been a universally recognized welter title-holder for many
years until I beat Britton four months earlier.'

At the ringside weighing in TK was the lighter man by 4
lb., touching the scales at 139½ lb, and though he had been
in America for just over twelve months and had participated
in 22 contests and boxed 231 rounds, TK professed himself as
eager about this contest as about any other bout in his whole
career: 'I knew that if I won I should have powerful backing
behind me in my championship claims and I resolved to win
the bout by the widest possible margin. I knew there was little
hope of knocking out such a wily old bird as the Californian,
for he had won the world's lightweight title from Ad Wolgast
and defended it against the best in the universe until outpointed
by Freddie Welsh.

'For ten rounds we put up a battle that had the crowd
thrilled not only at the pace but at the versatility of the fistic
exchanges. We went at each other like a pair of wild-cats,
but never for a moment did I lose faith in my ability to
win. . .

'The first two rounds were mine by a wide margin; Willie put on
a tremendous spurt in the third and had me a trifle wild in some
of my deliveries. He peppered me with lefts and rights and the
fans got extremely excited as it seemed that the tide of battle was
turning.

'My seconds were yelling "Zie Klug, Zie Klug" which means "Be
clever" and I certainly had to pull out all I knew to prevent myself
from being overwhelmed. Fortunately, he was taking a great deal
out of himself as I found out when we came up for the fourth, for
then I got back into my true form and, piling on the pace, hit him
with all I possessed.

'I made great play on his face with jabs, hooks, uppercuts, and
crosses until his features were just a swollen mass. I closed both his
eyes, raised lumps on his cheeks, brought his lips up like balloons
and spread his nose all over his face. . .

'When I think back on that scrap I realize what a game opponent
I had that night. No matter how much I battered him Willie was
always coming back for more and never once did he waver . . .
several times I had him rocking. He would waver and reel but there
was never a chance that he would go down or even go on the retreat.'

And at the end, there could be no other verdict: 'They credited me with winning eight of the ten rounds and every newspaper the next day acclaimed me as a worthy holder of the world's welterweight title.'

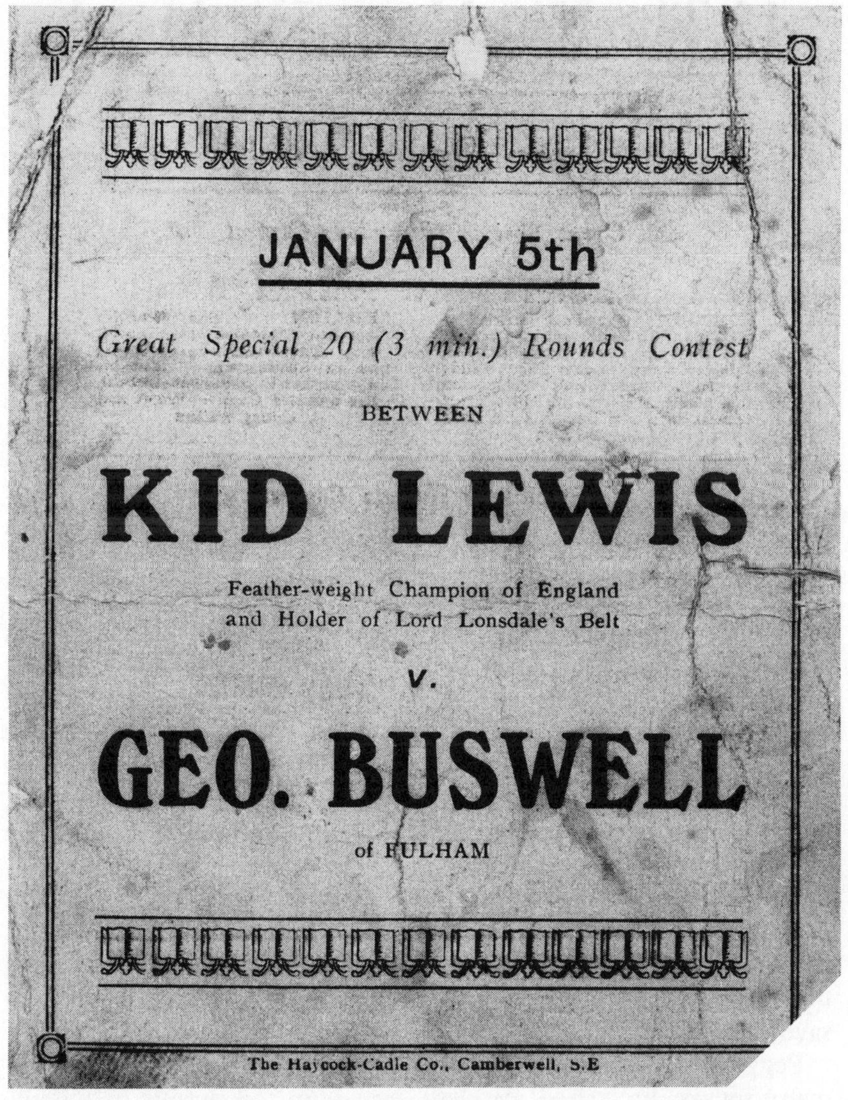

13 The Kid Meets His Match

It had been a hard battle for TK to win acceptance in the States. TK
was, after all, not twenty-one until October 1915, and although he
had a strong theatrical element in his character, he could not bring
himself to boast and threaten and ballyhoo as was the habit in the
boxing world at the time (and remains so today): 'Jimmy Johnston
told me to go out and get pinched for speeding! It was a good way
to get publicity on the cheap and he told me not to worry about
it, that all publicity was good just as long as they spelled my name
right. . . .'

But TK had also to counter the unenviable reputation created by
the abject performances of British boxers touring American rings
seeking easy money. At first, his style of fighting, though impressing
the American fight fans with its speed, did not particularly appeal
to their boxing taste, as they had been reared on the concept
of ferocity before skill. But, almost automatically, and certainly
subconsciously, TK had adopted the American all-action style,
whilst retaining his boxing skill and speed. Now he could be
guaranteed to fill any hall, whoever his opponent might be. TK
openly relished his newfound popularity, and would find pleasure
in walking along Broadway, enjoying being stopped every few yards
by some fight fan anxious to shake his hand. It would have been
unnatural for a youth of his age and background not to have
savoured the lionizing to which he was now subjected.

Peggy Bettinson of the National Sporting Club wrote of TK, 'In
many senses, he is free, careless, easy-going, generous to a fault.
"Chicken today – feathers tomorrow" – that, I feel, is his abiding
rule in life, for he was never given to swagger. Even when his
pockets bulged with money he was never offensive.' That was
something he lived up to for the rest of his life.

TK never became swollen-headed. Indeed, he remained far more modest than his trainer, for Alec took much of the credit for TK's victories upon himself and was clearly disappointed if the fight fans did not ask for his autograph as well. In fact, TK had become something of a philosopher, though he would not have recognized the fact himself. Alec's little conceits amused rather than irritated him. Yet his was a complex nature, for while he could recognize Alec's vanities, he was unable to see the clearly apparent faults and vices of others. So he was always an easy, gullible subject for the most bare-faced confidence trickster.

'I found many of my admirers all wanting to do something for me or, should I say, for themselves. But I was too young at the time to pick out the good men from the con-men. When they smiled and shook my hand and patted me on the back, they all seemed good guys. I think I was a prime target for most con-men.'

TK was now getting the taste of 'Clothes make the man' and was fast becoming a smart dresser. Friends used to take him to the tailor's to be measured for $200 to $300 suits, whcn it was $5 to the pound. Then to the shirt-makers and hatters. 'It was many years later that I learned that they would have paid and supplied the suits and shirts free to have photographs of me wearing their outfits for publicity. But I really didn't mind; it made you feel good when you were dressed well.'

TK always had problems with shoes, having to get them stretched in the right places because of bunions and hammer toes on both feet. One of his so-called friends suggested that his feet would look better if he had his shoes made to measure and would take him to be measured if he was interested. 'Take me, was the operative word, to the shoemaker. There were wooden lasts hanging all over the workshop, with famous names attached, all different sizes and shapes. I was impressed. My feet were measured from every angle and drawn on brown paper. My friend didn't give the shoemaker a chance to tell me the cost. I wasn't concerned, as money was now rolling in. He said he would go back and get the figures later and we left. The next day, Johnny Connolly (I shall never forget his name) arrived, said he had just come from the shoemaker and that it would cost $1,500 to make the last and the first pair of shoes and, because they would have my last, I could order as many as I wanted at $250 a pair. I was dumbfounded! I think it was the first time in my life that I remember saying, "No! No, I'll carry on buying these and make them last." I couldn't resist saying that. He tried and said maybe he could get the price down a little. I was annoyed and told him to forget it. About a week later, the shoemaker came up to Grupp's gym and asked why I hadn't gone back for further measurements for him to finish the last. I told him in no uncertain terms what I thought of his prices. He stood motionless, as if I had hit him, then he came to. "*What*, how much?" he shouted, and then it all came out. (It seemed that the shoemaker was getting 10 per cent and Connolly, the con-man, was getting 90 per cent as the agent.) "Sure I'm expensive, we are the best." And two weeks later I had my first made-to-measure shoes. The last cost $100, and the shoes $40 a pair. He made my shoes for another eight years until he went out of business some time in 1923. I was to learn the hard way throughout my life, but usually after I had paid – I never did really learn.'

However, there were more pleasant sides to being a sporting celebrity in New York, not the least of them being the increased opportunity to socialize that TK now had, not something he was ever completely at ease doing but he enjoyed it, nevertheless. In fact, in early September, just after the first Britton fight that saw him acclaimed as world welterweight champion he received an invitation that was to change the course of his life.

He and Alec were having lunch when a three-man committee of former Englishmen living in New York approached TK asking if he would be their guest of honour at a gala evening for their London Social Club, on 18 September. They wanted him to open the ball, lead the grand march and make a speech. He would meet a lot of his old friends and make some new ones. TK was a little apprehensive, but Jack Goldsmith, the club secretary, was very persuasive, and TK finally agreed and promised to be there. 'When the invitations arrived for Alec and me to attend the London Social Club dance, and although I had a pretty good wardrobe by now, it meant I needed a dinner jacket. We went along to the tailor's and got fitted up. I enjoyed doing that. It was my first, and I bought Alec one as well. I think he made a deal to bring his back and change it for a lounge suit! Gee, he was tight, he'd never let an opportunity go by, but I guess he must have known what he was doing.

'September 18 1915, that's a date I shall never forget. Alec and I were dressed to kill. If only the folks could see me now, I thought.'

At the Casino, TK was received by the president and introduced to most of the prominent members and made very welcome, but he was ill-at-ease on such social occasions, and in spite of being dressed to kill, he was still very much the East End boy and found it hard to relax entirely. What worried him most was the idea of having to open the dancing. Although he could dance reasonably well by now, dancing for one's own amusement and opening the ball before a crowd of several hundred were entirely different things from acknowledging crowds from the safety of the ring. The club secretary, Jack Goldsmith, was a busy little man, whose stay in the States had led him to cultivate his English characteristics, until he had become a caricature of an Englishman. As he outlined the evening's arrangements, TK heard him out until he came to opening the dancing. 'I asked, Jack, where's my dancing partner? "She's not here yet," he said. I felt a bit relieved and muttered to myself, "Thank God", thinking I might still get out of it. Goldsmith continued, "Don't worry, I'm expecting her any minute now, and I can tell you she's a charming girl. She works for a friend of mine as a model in his showrooms. He'll be bringing her himself." And he patted me on the shoulder. "I'm sure you'll like her." '

They were joined by other people, wanting to know all about his fights. TK and Alec were kept busy answering their questions. 'About half an hour later, as we were preparing to take our places, my eyes turned towards the staircase, and at the top I saw what was to me a wonderful vision. A girl dressed in white, which blended beautifully with her smooth, warm, southern complexion, was making her way to the dance floor.'

She was petite and dark-haired with a high forehead and a wide, generous mouth. Her eyes were deep brown and her skin was extremely white. Her every movement announced her vivacity and love for life. She was dressed in white satin with a single rope of coral around her neck. As she walked down the steps, you could feel her shyness. After all, this was a big occasion for an eighteen-year-old girl. Her escort felt her nervousness. He squeezed her hand, looked down at her and smiled. She looked up and, as some of her confidence returned, she smiled back. TK recalled: 'Somehow I sensed that I was intimately concerned in the whole matter, and my joy knew no bounds when I discovered this was Elsie, the lady with whom I was to dance. My conscience smote me when I thought that I had mentally muttered "Thank God" on learning that she had not arrived a short while earlier.'

He forgot the people he was talking to – he was in love. Jack Goldsmith watched TK with mounting pleasure; his judgement had been right. He grabbed TK's arm. 'Come on over, I'll introduce you.' Goldsmith effected the introductions. 'I should like you to meet Ted Kid Lewis. This is Elsie . . . Elsie Schneider.' Both Elsie and TK nodded with embarrassment. 'And this is my good friend, Dave Segal.'

TK had eyes only for Elsie. He took Segal's hand and shook it, with a quick glance of acknowledgement, then looked back at Elsie. Segal attempted to apologize, 'I'm sorry we were late. We had trouble getting a cab.' He was too much of a gentleman to say that he waited over half an hour while Elsie changed her dress four times before deciding what she should wear for the occasion. But it would all have been wasted on TK. He was on 'Cloud Nine', in a dream.

Goldsmith intervened as he grabbed Segal's arm, saying to him, 'Why don't we get things moving?'and to Elsie and TK, 'While you two get to know each other.' And Goldsmith and Segal walked away.

There they were, left standing facing each other, Elsie Schneider, just turned eighteen and Ted Kid Lewis, still not quite twenty-one. Little did they know that this was to become the most successful matchmaking job of Goldsmith's life. They could feel everyone's eyes on them. TK regained his confidence. After all, he was here to open the ball, and wasn't she the best-looking girl in the hall? 'We're going to open the ball.' Elsie nodded and managed to say, 'Yes, I know.' At that moment there was a loud roll of drums, followed by a crash of cymbals. They were saved by the bell. 'Ladies and Gentlemen,' the master of ceremonies called out, and there followed the usual introductions, until 'Mr Ted Kid Lewis, the new welterweight champion of the world, and his lady, Miss Elsie Schneider, will now open the ball.'

As everyone applauded, TK became all smiles. He took Elsie's hand, walked her to the centre of the dance floor and, as the band struck up, he gently put his arm around her waist, and they waltzed slowly around the floor. He made sure there was daylight between them. He was afraid to get too close. And he was extra careful where he put his right hand. He said to himself, 'This is one girl whom I don't want to get the wrong impression.' He was truly knocked out.

'You're a very good dancer.'

Elsie replied shyly, 'You are light on your feet.'

He smiled. He knew what to answer. 'In my game, you have to be – fast as well.' She returned his smile.

When the dance was over, they stopped in the middle of the floor and before they could move, they were surrounded by well-wishers of both sexes. As the band struck up again, one lady made a quick grab for TK and Elsie was asked to dance by Gus Bland. For the next hour they were both dancing, but not with each other. TK spent that hour dancing but his mind was not on his partners. He was walking on their feet and they loved it. All the single ladies were making a beeline for him, but TK was oblivious to them all. He had eyes only for Elsie – when he could see her. Eventually, he manoeuvred his latest partner near to Elsie and, as the band stopped, thanked his partner – then turned quickly to Elsie. 'This is our dance, I think.' Elsie smiled and nodded. She was afraid to speak too much because she had a slight stammer. The next time they met – and she was sure they would meet – she would somehow overcome her impediment.

The band stopped for refreshments. TK reluctantly escorted Elsie back to Dave Segal's table and thanked her for the dance. Elsie felt flustered and at a loss as to what to do, when Dave came to her rescue and offered to get her some refreshments. In the meantime, TK was surrounded once again, and became separated from Elsie. When the band started up, TK made a beeline for Elsie's table, but was beaten to the punch. It seemed to TK that everybody wanted to dance with Elsie, and it took another five or six dances before TK got a look in. They didn't leave the floor for the next half an hour. 'I don't think I gave her a chance to say anything, I told her my whole life story, where I came from, my family, my ambitions, I never stopped, I must have been in dreamland. It was only years later that she told me she would like to have spoken, but was afraid because of her stammer. Yet I never ever noticed her stammering – I suppose love is blind.'

The music stopped and as they returned, Elsie looked at her watch, and looked at TK. 'Do you have to go?'

Elsie nodded. 'Yes, there's an early show tomorrow and it's getting late.' She extended her hand. TK quickly clasped it in his.

'Thank you for the dances. I hope to see you again, soon.'

Elsie smiled. 'Yes, I hope so.' People started crowding around TK again, as Elsie left on the arm of Dave Segal, much to TK's chagrin, until she reached the top of the stairs, where she turned, caught TK's eye, smiled and waved goodbye. All TK could do was wave in frustration, as he was hemmed in in the middle of his admirers. The dance finally ended as the band played 'God Save the King', to the accompaniment of handshakes all round, and TK and Alec departed. Outside, TK stopped. 'I haven't got her phone number,' and started to go back. Alec stopped him. 'You can get it from Jack Goldsmith tomorrow.' He hailed a taxi. They jumped in and drove away.

The next morning TK called Goldsmith, thanked him for a wonderful evening and, by the way, did he have Elsie's phone number? 'Jack was delighted to hear of my interest, you could almost hear him humming, "Matchmaker, Matchmaker", but unfortunately he didn't have her home number. I was crestfallen, but cheered up when he said, "But I do have the number where she works." I called during the lunch hour, so as not to interrupt her working hours. She was out to lunch.'

He called again at 4 pm, only to be told the show finished at 3.30 pm and all the models had gone. Just then he remembered, 'Is Mr Dave Segal there? Tell him Ted Kid Lewis would like to speak to him.' Segal took the phone, hoped TK had had an enjoyable evening and what could he do for him?

TK was lost for words and just blurted out 'Could you let me have Elsie's home phone number?' and held his breath.

'Certainly, I'm sure she wouldn't mind.'

Later that day, TK called Elsie at home. 'I got your number from Dave Segal, I hope you don't mind my calling you at home.'

There was a long pause. 'It's nice to hear from you so soon.'

TK became excited; after all, it was the first time TK ever wanted to date a girl seriously. 'What are you doing tonight? I thought we might have an evening out, there's a show in town called "Hit The Trail Holiday", Fred Niblo's in it, he's a friend of mine and we could have dinner afterwards – how about it?'

There was another pause before she answered. He didn't realize that Elsie was fighting to control her stammer.

'Perhaps another night . . . I promised my friend Ada we'd both wash our hair tonight.'

TK was not going to be put off. 'That's no problem, wash your hair another night, and bring Ada with you. I'll call the theatre and book three tickets,' he said, giving her no chance to answer.

Elsie commented years later, 'I was so flustered when he called. We weren't washing our hair, I was too excited and I made it up. The truth was, Ada and I were trying on some new clothes.' In fact, Elsie was delighted to be seeing him so soon and that Ada would be able to give her moral support and perhaps help her out in case her stammer returned.

'I'll pick you both up in an hour, okay?' Another pause, which must have seemed a lifetime to TK.

'Yes, we'll be ready.' And TK hung up. He was on 'Cloud Nine', until he made a grab for the telephone again. He had forgotten to ask her address.

So Ted Kid Lewis took his dream girl and her friend Ada to the theatre. Fortunately Ada enjoyed the show, for so engrossed were Elsie and TK with each other that neither addressed a remark to her. Dinner followed the show with TK and Ada doing all the talking, and with Elsie chiming in every now and then. He drove them home and plucked up courage to kiss Elsie goodnight on the cheek and, to cover any embarrassment, he kissed Ada as well. Both Elsie and TK knew that their lives would be intertwined from then on.

All of a sudden it was hard for TK to turn his mind back to boxing. Keeping in shape meant he normally had little time to relax; he fought so regularly that he was either just recovering from a bout or just about to step into the ring for the next one. With no distractions, this tempo could be maintained with little trouble – but now he had Elsie, and this was going to cause Charlie Harvey, Alec Goodman *et al* considerable problems.

Typical was TK's response to the news that he would be defending his world title against Britton not long after he had started seeing Elsie regularly.

Johnston wanted to get TK out of town. 'I've made arrangements for you to start work tomorrow at the Catskills training camp.' TK, however, objected, saying he could do just as well at Grupp's in mid-town New York (and thus of course close to Elsie. . .) Love was clearly filling the young man's mind to the exclusion of all else and his handlers feared it would weaken his concentration for the job in hand. Thus, Johnston was insistent and supported by Alec. 'No, the air will do you good, there's plenty of good boys there to spar with and you gotta be in tip-top shape for this one. You and Alec leave tonight.'

TK was a little put out. 'Okay, I'll go up, but not tonight. We'll leave in the morning,' and both Johnston and Alec had to be satisfied, knowing they could only push TK so far.

TK called Elsie at work, to explain he was going out of town for a week, and that he would like to see her before he left in the morning. Would she and Ada have dinner with him that evening? But she was sorry – she had a date for that evening and was unable to break it. Okay, he would call her from the training camp and perhaps she could spend a little time with him after the fight. She would love to and wished him luck. TK spent a miserable evening, having dinner with Alec. TK trained hard and his many calls to Elsie helped to relax his thoughts. Alec got him in great shape and TK defeated Britton comfortably on points, with the newspapers confirming him undisputed welterweight champion of the world.

The following morning TK, as promised, called Elsie at work. 'I won last night, have you read the papers?' There was a pause.

'Yes, but are . . .?'

But TK didn't let her finish the sentence. He was so excited to be speaking to her. 'They say I'm undisputed world champion.'

'But are you . . . hurt?' At last Elsie managed to finish her sentence.

'Hurt?' TK was so surprised and delighted that she took such an interest. 'Hurt? Of course not, not a mark, and that's more than I can say about Britton.'

One thing TK took a long time to understand, however, was that Elsie had a number of admirers and that he would have to overcome the competition. Many years later, Elsie said, 'TK couldn't understand that I had to turn him down sometimes, because I had another date. I kept breaking them, but couldn't do it all the time. I was also being dated by Tex McCloud. He did a vaudeville act, like Will Rogers, spinning a rope with a girl jumping through it, while he told jokes. Well, one evening I was getting ready to go out with Tex, when TK dropped in, wanting to take me out. I tried to explain that Tex was picking me up, but he wouldn't take no for an answer, so I left my sister Anna to explain to Tex. He was rather put out and wanted to know who this guy was who had taken his girl out. When Anna told him it was Ted Kid Lewis, he calmed down, and said, "That's different then". We all became good friends after that.'

Many years later, when Tex was in London to play at the London Palladium, he needed a replacement girl for his act, and TK introduced him to Binnie Barnes who worked with Tex for some time before breaking into the movies. It was during the three-month period between 28 September after defeating Britton for the title, and his contest on 28 December against Willie Richie, that TK started his courtship in earnest, and he gradually saw off all his so-called opponents for Elsie's hand, either by getting Elsie to break her dates or make excuses that she was already going out.

Elsie was beginning to enjoy the attention she was receiving from TK. During the same period TK had to train, keep fit and travel out of town, to take on five strenuous opponents who wanted his scalp, prior to the Richie fight.

It was a few days after beating Mike Glover, in fact, that Elsie invited TK home to meet her mother. Naturally, TK was nervous and ill at ease, but the warmth of her family's welcome soon helped him to relax, and her brothers, Joe, who was a film salesman for Universal Pictures, and Harry, an accountant, were both fight fans, so TK was encouraged to talk about his sport. Elsie's sisters, Rose and Anna, were there, and friend Ada, who was accepted as one of the family, and who was to be their lifelong friend. The next evening, he visited Elsie's family again, and the night after that. Although he had known her for only a month, he knew their future lay together.

One evening, sitting alone with Elsie's mother, TK was endeavouring to ask permission to marry Elsie, but his words did not convey what he was trying to say. Mrs Celly Schneider, a small woman – an older version of Elsie in looks who for the last thirteen years since her husband's death had had to bring up five children – and who knew the value of having a partner. Her one aim in life was to see her children happily married with families of their own. She smiled and helped Ted to complete his sentence. So clearly was their young love evident that Mrs Schneider had already accepted the situation. She had no misgivings about her daughter's future despite the brevity of their acquaintance.

TK and Elsie wanted to get married immediately, but on this question Mrs Schneider was firm. As a mother she could appreciate how Mrs Mendeloff would feel if she were to hear by letter that her eldest son had married a girl of whom she knew nothing. His family should meet Elsie before their wedding. They should be present on such a joyful occasion. TK felt embarrassed that he had had to be reminded of his duty. He suggested that Elsie and he should go to England and be married there, but Elsie wanted Joe to give her away. Once again Mrs Schneider came to the rescue and solved their predicament by suggesting that TK should bring his family over to America. What a magnificent holiday it would be for the Mendeloffs away from the restrictive life and hardships of the war.

Thus, TK wrote to his father, saying that he intended settling in the States, truly the land of opportunity. He went on: 'How long will it take you to make arrangements and bring the family over here to live? It would be a new life for us all and, besides, I want you all to be present at my wedding. I am enclosing a picture of my girl, Elsie. You'll all love her as I do. Write and tell me when you can be ready and when you have arranged a passage. I'll then cable you the money. You'll have nothing to worry about when you get here. I'm earning plenty of money.'

TK met Elsie after work, took her to dinner and presented her with a diamond engagement ring. Elsie commented years later, 'TK sat me down. He was very excited, ordered the meal, then took my hand and said, "I've a surprise for you", and put the ring on my finger. Then he said, "Now we are properly engaged." The ring and the speed with which he gave it to me and that we were engaged, took my breath away. He told me he had written home and told his family to come over for the wedding. We finished dinner and rushed home so we could tell my mother that we were engaged and that TK had written home for his family to come over as there was going to be a wedding.'

Mrs Schneider was delighted with the news and suggested that they wait for the family to arrive before arranging a date for the wedding. In the meantime, they should look for suitable accommodation, not only for the Mendeloff family, but also for themselves to set up their first home. TK became a regular visitor to the Schneider home, and was treated like one of the family. And a few weeks later, there came a letter informing him that seven passages had been booked and that his father, mother, three sisters and two brothers were to arrive in New York on 22 January 1916.

The ticket for the dance at which TK met Elsie.

14 The Title Slips Away

'Only a lightweight is he? Give me heavies in future.'
Mike Gibbons

Unbelievable as it might seem today, TK was back in the ring just four days after beating Willie Richie, this time in Buffalo against Kayo Brennan, an iron-tough Dutchman. The Dutchman was 10 lb. heavier and knew how to make every ounce count. By the end of ten rounds, TK was slowing up and visibly leg-weary, and the following morning most of the press voted the contest a draw, with the others nominating Lewis the winner.

TK was dissatisfied with himself in every way. He had been fully trained and yet the usual co-ordination had been missing and he hadn't fought with his accustomed relish. No doubt having two hard contests in four days contributed to his lackadaisical performance, but he was depressed at disappointing the Buffalo fans, who had cheered him so enthusiastically after his two earlier contests. Back in New York, he was complaining to Alec, wondering whether he should change his training schedule in view of the fact that he had been contracted for another two contests within the next two weeks, when there was a knock at the door.

It was a deputation of Harlem fight fans. Ted Kid Lewis had settled in the Harlem area of New York shortly after arriving in the city. In those days Harlem was a good residential area, and by now the people of Harlem considered him to be one of them. He had just defended his title against Willie Richie; the Harlemites evidently thought that in so doing he had brought renown to their precinct, and they had come to express their appreciation.

'You see, Ted, we just don't know how to tell you what you mean to us. Geez, when we saw you put the skids under Willie, we just didn't believe it. A Harlem boy! Our champion!' TK tried to answer but the leader of the deputation, Harry Mortimer, motioned him to silence. 'It ain't just our wishes we bring. Here, Jumbo!'

Jumbo, an enormous black sparring partner of TK's, edged

forward with a large box. He held it gingerly as though it contained porcelain. 'Give it to him!'

TK took the box from Jumbo's hands and opened it. Inside was a large silver loving cup, inscribed, 'To Ted Kid Lewis – the Greatest. From his Brooklyn pals.'

The tears welled up in TK's eyes and that sentimentality which was never far beneath the surface rose up in him and, instead of the speech he would like to have made, he could only murmur, 'Gee, thanks.'

It was Alec who stepped into the breach and said, 'This will make a wonderful wedding present for Ted.' Then TK sent for drinks and a merry party ensued, TK feeling that he was really accepted at last and was now one of the locals.

The incident had the effect of lifting his spirits, sending him back into the gymnasium with a renewed enthusiasm. The next morning found him sparring with Grupp of Grupp's gym – an old-timer of thirteen stone who could not be kept out of the ring although his active days were long past.

Ten days later TK exacted revenge on Mike Glover for the latter's earlier victory over him, beating him easily on points over twelve rounds. Four days later and another return bout saw him gain a no-decision newspaper verdict over Kid Graves, but it was a result that carried a penalty: he suffered severe laceration of the lips. Did he take time off to let them heal? 'Hardly had my split lips had a chance to heal when Jimmy had me on the train to Buffalo. It was an emergency, my fellow-countryman Matt Wells having had to call off a contest at the last moment. So I substituted for him. Can you imagine a world champion doing that today?'

And TK's opponent in this stand-in bout? None other than Jack Britton. But this time there were no managerial subterfuges – after the last fight's shenanigans, no one was in the mood. This time it was left to the fighters alone. TK even found himself sharing a dressing room with Britton and they established a friendship that day that was to last over sixteen more contests and many years beyond.

Britton was at his best in this, their fourth contest, and TK was prevented from adopting his usual attacking methods by a fear that the wounds on his mouth might be opened up. It was a no-decision contest, but TK freely admitted that Britton had been the better man on the night.

However, he had no time to brood on his display, for two days later his family arrived from England.

During, and in between, training, fighting and travelling in and out of New York, TK and Elsie with the help of Ada had managed to find a furnished apartment for TK's family in time for their arrival. TK's main worry was the publicity the U-boats were receiving in the press. Elsie, Ada and the Schneider family loved him for his concern; they were able to console TK with, 'It's a very big ship and will be well protected by the British Navy.' It seemed this worry outside the ring made him fight harder inside.

The big day came, however, and the family arrived. Elsie commented years later, 'TK was like a jack-in-the-box, he kept jumping up and down until he spotted them on the deck, shouting to me and everybody near, "There they are, there they are!" I never saw him so excited. He ran forward as they all trooped down the companion way, hugging them all in turn. Then he ushered them towards Alec and me. They were all stony-faced. I suppose landing in a foreign land, with strange faces all around, only recognizing Alec and maybe me from my picture, must have been an ordeal for them, but it was more so for me.

'TK introduced me: "This is Elsie, the girl I am going to marry." You could have cut the atmosphere with a knife. I felt their eyes penetrate right through me. I didn't know where to look, but then Alec broke the ice as he stepped forward and shook hands all round. I tried to put on my best smile, until his sister Dolly came forward. I remember her words well, "Why, Gershon, she's beautiful," then she put her arms around me and kissed me on both cheeks. Everybody else just shook hands. TK then got busy with the immigration officers, the porters and in no time we were on our way. I shall never forget their faces when "The Gang of Seven" as I used to call them, were shown around the apartment, or how TK felt. He was so embarrassed, I didn't dare say I found it for them. I didn't know what they expected, it was very nice, large and had four bedrooms, and TK said in comparison to what they had in London, it was great; however, they unpacked and eventually agreed it was comfortable. But TK was so upset.'

Since leaving England, TK had lived a full life and had gained in experience – had matured. He was moving now in a different society, and he had forgotten the one he had left just a few short years before. Though he bore a deep affection for his family, he nevertheless could not help but feel a certain sinking feeling within him as he recognized, once again, his father's inability to receive good fortune with any humility. Even though he understood that

Solomon's avarice and impatience were deeply rooted in early hardship, he could not but feel disappointed and embarrassed in front of Elsie.

Though TK could have done with a holiday at that point, in order to listen to the local East End gossip, hear about the war and about missing comrades, Johnston had other plans. He declared that it would be in TK's interests not to get too rusty, not to get too involved in family life when he was struggling to stay at the top of the boxing world.

He had, therefore, arranged six more contests for TK spaced over the next twenty-five days! There was very little risk of rustiness occurring with a programme like that. And so TK was forced to leave the family – not entirely without a certain feeling of relief. Having supplied them all with sufficient ready cash with which to amuse themselves, he left them in the hands of poor Elsie, who was no match for the Mendeloff family's cunning ways, and returned to the task of training: shadow-boxing, sparring, bag-punching, miles and miles of road-work. With seven members of the Mendeloff family, a future wife, a trainer, two managers, various bagmen and sparring partners and who knows who else to support, it took him all his energy and effort to just keep ahead of the next bill. . .

In spite of the various injuries he was now picking up, in particular a sore right hand, there was to be no respite. First on the list was Marty Farrell in Philadelphia, followed by Soldier Bartfield in Buffalo. Within a week, he defended his title against his old pal Britton again, at the Broadway Sporting Club, followed a week later by Jimmy Duffy. Three days after that, Harry Trendall, and five days after that, in New Orleans, he climbed into the ring and successfully defended his title against Harry Stone. Four thousand people saw him win every round, though because of his damaged right hand he could never quite finish Stone off . . . but he was still the champion.

Johnston, with the rustle of dollars now almost deafening him, was all set to arrange yet another series of fights when TK finally put his foot down. In fifty-nine days he had fought ten contests and one hundred and five rounds. He had rarely been able to see his family or, more important, Elsie, for more than a few days and he was worn out mentally and physically. He demanded a six-week break; he wanted to plan his marriage.

Johnston grudgingly conceded at first, but ultimately he could not be denied. After two weeks, he telephoned TK to say that he had signed a most important contract – a twenty-round decision contest to defend the title against Jack Britton. TK had no option but to shelve his wedding plans and resume the routine of training.

Though he seemed on top form against Jack Able in a warm-up contest five days before the Britton fight, in the championship bout itself his tactics were sadly awry. Having recovered from the right-hand injury that had dogged him for some months, he concentrated on trying to KO Britton, reasoning that he could allow the Irish-American to score points if, by landing one good right hand, he could finish the contest. By the end of the fifteenth round, however, Britton was a mile ahead on points.

'Box him, Teddy, box him!' Johnston exhorted from the corner, but it was too late. Though he won the last few rounds against a tiring Britton, he had no complaints when referee Dick Burke crossed the ring to raise Britton's hand. . . 'Well, I had held my world title for a few days short of seven months. I was considerably down-hearted as can be imagined, but the thought of my forthcoming marriage was a great consolation; moreover I retained the handsome silver loving cup which the party of friends in Harlem had presented me with after my triumph over Richie.

'The loss of my title took the wind out of my family's sails. They became very worried, with no champion and getting married to boot. I could have laughed at the situation, if it hadn't been me. Elsie was more upset about my cut lip and bruised hand than losing the championship. We weren't married yet, but I think she had hopes I would retire and go into business.'

But this was no foundation for getting married. TK had no intentions of retiring. He had reached the top of his profession once and wanted to get back quickly. He badgered Johnston to get him Mike Gibbons, but Johnston thought he was too big for TK. 'I saw him fight Packy McFarland for a lot of money, and I could have licked the both of them.'

'Tell it to the press,' Johnston replied. TK did, only to be scoffed at. Nevertheless, TK persisted. He knew Johnston's weakness. Not only was he TK's manager, he was also the matchmaker at Madison Square Garden. The thought of filling the Garden and his manager's share of TK's purse overcame his crocodile tears at Gibbons being too big for TK. Johnston made the match at 11 st. (today's junior middleweight) – quite a handicap for TK, as his natural fighting weight was only a little over the lightweight limit. 'I wanted the fight so I had no complaints.' But there was a storm of protest in the newspapers at so unequal a match. To give so much weight to a man, who was acknowledged to be the greatest middleweight in America at that time, was considered little less than suicide. 'This opinion was shared by most boxing fans, in fact, several people went so far as to visit my mother, asking her to persuade me not to go through with it.'

However, the fight was set for 18 May 1916 at the Garden. 'It left me eighteen days to get in shape. I needed to win this badly.' This meant early to bed and early to rise, road-work every morning and working out in the gym every day. Elsie, still only eighteen, was left to help look after the Mendeloffs with the help of her brothers.

Amongst the celebrities who visited TK in training was the man who was to become the Czar of American boxing, Nat Fleischer. TK, in answer to Fleischer's questions, said that he was confident. Fleischer smiled. 'I've already been to see Mike and after the stinkeroo he and Packy MacFarland put up, he says nothing short of knocking you out will satisfy him.'

TK grinned at the boxing writer from the massage table. 'You know, Nat, I'm not going to the Garden to please Gibbons.'

'Well, so far the betting boys have made him the top guy by a mile.'

'Have they? They've been wrong before. I've sorta got used to being the outsider.'

'There's one other thing, Ted. You mayn't be so popular as usual with the crowd.'

TK frowned. 'Everyone's treated me fine since I came out here and they found out I could fight.'

'It's not that.' Nat Fleischer patted the boxer's shoulder. 'Mike's an Irish boy, and Limeys aren't too popular with the Irish at the moment.'

'Well, I don't know anything about that. . .' TK paused a moment. 'But whatever we did I'm sure we had to do.' He would always be quick to resent any criticism of his country.

'I know that.' Fleischer paused. 'I'm just telling you to be ready for a bit of malarkey from the crowd. Don't let it upset you. But then, I'm sure you won't.'

The boxers presented a strong contrast as they met in the middle of the ring for their instructions from the referee. Mike Gibbons was three and a half inches taller than TK and looked even heavier than the 15 lb. difference between them. Hair *en brosse* and with a snub Irish nose, he had heavy, powerful shoulders, narrow hips and light legs – in fact, the ideal build for a boxer. Those who had been shouting the odds quietened, as a glance at the contestants revealed that every advantage lay with the American. When the racket rose again, there were few takers for TK despite increased odds.

In the first few seconds of the contest, TK appreciated his supporters' misgivings. Mike Gibbons might be the Dancing Master, but he could punch as hard as any middleweight then fighting. When TK landed with a really heavy right which would have dropped any welterweight, Gibbons only grinned and moved forward to attack.

Back in the corner, Alec chided TK. 'Treat him as just another fighter, Gersh. Don't get overawed . . . but keep a close eye on him. He's an artful dodger, bloody clever!' In the next round, TK began to use his speed, showing that he could not only dance as well as Gibbons but was actually faster. Just before the bell, he suddenly stopped back-pedalling and jumped in with a hard right, landing on Gibbons's cheekbone, splitting the skin.

'Seeing the damage did me a world of good. I stepped up the attack, even though it had been pretty fast up to then, and in another couple of rounds had the satisfaction of seeing what both Alec and I had been hoping, Mike showing signs of "bellows to mend". Mike fought back desperately in the seventh round, with a right-hand smash to my nose, and it poured blood like a tap. That round was not so good for me, we thought that Mike might have gained a lot of lost ground.

' "Move fast and keep up the pressure, he's running out of gas," were Alec's last words as he sponged the blood from my nose when the bell sounded for round eight.'

And speed it up was just what TK did; he kept up a persistent stream of lefts shooting to the Irishman's face, so that in the interval, Alec was able to say, 'We're in the home straight, go in and win, he's yours for the taking. And remember I've two weeks' wages on you.'

TK recalled, 'It made me smile. Alec risking his money was remarkable, he never spent a penny by mistake, and as I left the stool, I told him not to worry, the money was in the bag.'

And to ensure there were no mistakes, TK took complete control and dominated the last two rounds. The majority of the press found for Ted Kid Lewis and Alec collected his winnings. Years later, writing in the *Ring*, Nat Fleischer commented: 'Lewis actually outpointed the St Paul Phantom and those who had come to cheer Mike to victory turned to cheer the cocky Britisher instead. When the bout was over, Gibbons was bleeding from several cuts about the face, and his wind was none too good. Lewis left the ring without a scratch. There had been some Irish boos when Ted climbed through the ropes, but nobody appreciates true fighting qualities more than the Irish, and the New York Irish rose to cheer him in the end. He had won the American support for his cause and thereafter they flocked to his bouts because they knew what kind of action to expect.'

Six days later, Ted fought again in Dayton, Ohio, knocking out Eddie Moha on 24 May in the thirteenth round.

For the first time since November 1914, and it was now 1916, Johnston did not have anything lined up, so TK thought he would take time off so that he could court Elsie in earnest. But his mother's sister, whom the family had not seen for many years, lived in Philadelphia, and TK was persuaded to take the Mendeloffs on a visit. Elsie was unable to take time off and understood TK's situation.

TK told Johnston of his plans, that he was taking his mother and father to Philly to see family, and would be driving up in his new red open Stutz car. Johnston cautioned TK about driving too fast, for he was worried lest his charge might be injured and so he would lose his biggest dollar-earner. 'But take a vacation, a real holiday – you sure earned it.' Nevertheless, the Mendeloffs had not been in Philadelphia for more than two days when the inevitable telegram arrived, summoning TK urgently back to New York. He feigned displeasure for his mother's sake, but inwardly he was pleased, as he would rather be visiting Elsie than relations he had never met before. The Mendeloffs returned to New York, thus ending TK's first-ever vacation.

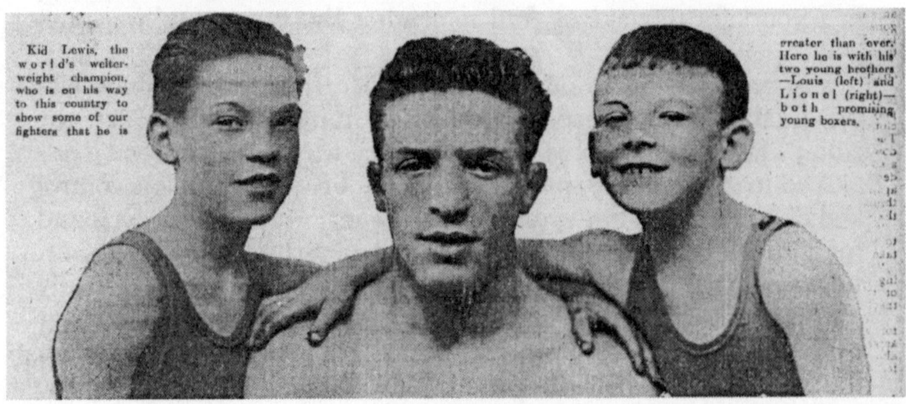

15 The Kid Gets Hooked

Charlie Harvey and Johnston, anticipating that TK might be upset, quickly outlined their offer of work in Buenos Aires. Not fewer than three fights with a ten grand guarantee for each one and a good percentage: five grand up front and the rest after each fight, plus first-class return tickets.

'It sounded good to me and then Jay Jay piled on the sales talk.' Johnston got into gear, he didn't realize that TK was sold on the idea. Billy Gibson, who managed Benny Leonard and subsequently Gene Tunney, was organizing the trip on behalf of an Argentine Count, who wanted Gibson to bring fourteen or fifteen top-line names to put boxing on in a big way in the Argentine. The names included Sam McVey, Sam Langford, Harry Wills, Joe Jeanette, Augie Ratner and many others. TK's first bout was to be against Albert Badoud, the European welterweight champion.

It seemed to TK that the trip offered him a change of scenery and perhaps subconsciously a chance to get away from the constant worry of his family. However, he told Johnston, 'I've got to talk it over with Elsie and see what she thinks.' Elsie could see that he wanted to go, that it would give him a rest from his family and at the same time enable him to pick up some (as TK put it) easy money. She would, of course, miss him, but was sure the trip would do him good. The Mendeloffs, however, tried to talk him out of it, but his mind was made up and he told Johnston to sign up.

They sailed on the SS *Vatari* and the party was met by Willie Gould, an expatriate Englishman who spoke Spanish fluently. The boxers were installed in a training camp at Vincente Lopez, about fifteen miles from Buenos Aires, where they settled down to work.

'Augie Ratner and I trained and sparred together and were good friends. We had two fights together in later years and may have had some disputes, that's the fight game, but there is very rarely bad blood between fighters.'

After a week's training, however, the bad news broke. The promoters overlooked the fact that boxing had been banned in Buenos Aires and all contracts were off! 'It was pretty plain that we should not get our money. We couldn't find the "Count" who was to give us our return tickets before we were to leave. We began to worry, I didn't know how long my money would last and for that matter neither did the other boys. Gould tried to find the promoters to get us an advance and our tickets, but without success. So he managed to arrange a couple of fights to earn some ready money, at an out-of-town venue. The first of these fights [between Sam Langford and Harry Wills] turned out to be the last, however. The local fans hadn't seen any big-name fighters, but they weren't mugs, and before Wills and Langford had boxed three rounds they were getting boos and hisses – not kisses from the fans. It looked like there was going to be a riot. However, they put on a good show for the fourth and last round, Gould grabbed the money and we all left town quietly. He tried to get something moving, but after another couple of weeks, the writing was on the wall and our money had almost run out. Eventually, Billy Gibson, realizing the position, sent tickets and we all returned home from yet another foreign fiasco, with a lot of wisdom, but no money.'

The fiasco did not end there, because TK's first visit on arriving back in New York – even before going home – was to his manager's office. He had to learn how he stood financially in order to be able to face his father's inevitable probing, and not to appear to Elsie as irresponsible. Yes, Harvey had collected the first $5,000, but he had got into trouble and had to borrow it. However, he promised TK he would deduct it from his manager's share over the next few fights. There was nothing to be done, TK told himself. He decided to say no more for the moment. He turned to Johnston, the 'Boy Bandit'.

'By the way, Jay Jay, I hope you got the dents on my car's mudguards fixed, like I asked you. Where did you take it, I'd like to pick it up now?' There was a moment's silence. This time it was Johnston's turn to look embarrassed. TK recalled, 'He figured that as I was going to be away for about four months, and as there was a lot of work to be done and garage rent to be paid, that it would be a good idea to sell it, and that I could buy a new one when I came back. I asked if he had got paid, and he said yes. Where was the money, then? He really squirmed. "I had to use it, Ted, I was in a hole, of course we'll pay you back, won't we Charlie? We'll see that you don't lose a cent. You know that. Would Charlie or I cheat on you? Would we? You know we wouldn't."

'Well, I never got paid back. Somehow they talked me out of it and, as a matter of fact, I never even found out what he got for the car.'

He continued, 'All this was cheering news. I had been away for over three months, spent a lot of my own money, I might have been busy in the States and added several thousand dollars to my bank roll and the result . . . I didn't get paid for my car and I got "gypped" out of my guarantee, which had persuaded me to make the trip in the first place. They had taken a real liberty with me and, as you can imagine, I felt real mad about it all. Still, in the fight game you have to forget and forgive a whole lot. There was only one thing to be done and that was to get back into the ring, where I was my own boss, and try to make up for lost time.'

But first things first, there was music to be faced. TK called Elsie to say that he was back, and that he would stop over to see his folks and would see her that evening. Solomon Mendeloff had a great deal to say about the Argentine fiasco and even more about his manager's behaviour. It was the 'I told you so, I told you not to go', that TK found hard to take. They had been inefficient, they had kept the money from the car and the guarantee, and in his father's opinion, he should not only break his contract with them, but sue them in the courts.

It must have been like going from hell to heaven when TK visited Elsie at home. She listened to TK's story and sympathized with his problems, as did Mrs Schneider. TK felt at home with Elsie's family, and he let his feelings out to Mrs Schneider. 'I think it's time that we got married and I would like to do it in the New Year.' Elsie was delighted, as were the others. Mrs Schneider commented, 'Have you asked your parents, and what did they say?'

TK replied, 'I shall tell them when we've set a date. It's not up to them, I know what we want to do.'

For over three months TK had not read an English or American newspaper and it wasn't until he returned from Argentina that he learned that Lord Kitchener had been drowned. Like all Englishmen at the time, he found this news a personal shock. Once again, TK visited the British Embassy, but the advice was the same: 'You are doing more good as an ambassador of sport here than you could by going home to do some office job. . . Besides, your feet would still keep you out of active service.'

If he couldn't fight for his country, at least he would fight in the ring. Besides, with his two managers having relieved him of his money, it was essential for him to fight, frequently and soon. Keeping the Mendeloff family and with a second establishment of his own soon to start, required a steady flow of dollars into his bank account. Luckily, the winter season had begun and top-class performers were in wide demand.

TK had been out of the ring for almost five months. In the Argentine, he had sparred regularly, but in a desultory manner, having no specific date to reach his peak. So he was out of condition, worried by the news, wanting to get married and short of money. But he would still fight anyone. In these circumstances, with his managers more interested in making a profit rather than in looking to his future, they would let him fight anybody. 'Johnston lost no time in getting me a match, although I had to smile when he called me up to say I would be fighting at the Armoury AA in Boston on 17 October. "Jack Britton, I suppose?" I knew the answer before I asked the question. It was our seventh meeting and the third in Boston, a place where a fighter could come time and again if he gave the crowd their money's-worth. If they didn't get satisfaction you wouldn't dare show your nose inside the city, let alone the door of the arena. . .

'Knowing my own limitations – the long lay-off, the two-way sea journey and the change of diet in Buenos Aires having taken much of the sparkle out of my boxing – I made up my mind to bundle into him from the beginning and either try to put him away or at least take him out of his stride. Putting on a swift attack I had Jack backing up while I stormed into him going all out for victory. I bothered and rocked him with successive left hooks in the first three rounds, but Britton was very fit and he was able to take my best shots without showing hurt.'

From the fourth round, Britton began to attack TK to the body at times dangerously close to the belt. . . 'I politely asked him to keep them up. He was killing my knees, but every time he countered one of my leads he seemed to land his swings lower than ever. These illegal blows soon began to slow me down and in the fifth he dropped one in so low that referee Conley stopped the fight and gave Britton a lecture.'

After this warning Britton was more careful with his punches, but the punishment had weakened TK and though he managed to mount an attack which had Britton hanging on in the tenth round he knew he was well behind on points. Whereas in the past he had been able to draw upon his remarkable powers of recuperation, his long lay-off left him – despite the fact that the fight was a championship affair – feeling almost disinterested in the result. He could raise no objection when the referee lifted Britton's hand at the end of the twelve rounds.

A week after his lack-lustre performance against Britton, TK was in action at the Coliseum, St Louis, for the promoters who rejoiced in the somewhat fanciful name of 'The Future City Athletic Club'. He won a clear-cut victory over Young Denny and, thus emboldened, he stepped up his preparations for a return title fight with Britton, training every day at Grupp's, boxing with men of weights from feather to light-heavy; polishing up his speed with the lighter men and practising his punching on the heavier.

He took only one day off from training as New York went mad during the Presidential election which resulted in Wilson being elected for a further term.

Back in Boston, TK met Britton and boxed better than on his last appearance there, but certainly not well enough to claim a victory. The referee declared the bout a draw and TK sighed with relief, for he had backed himself for $3,000. . .

Two more no-decision contests, both against Johnny Griffiths, ended the eventful year of 1916. Leaving aside the Argentine fiasco, he had fought nineteen times and lost only twice – each defeat at the hands of Britton. He had won five decision fights and had been awarded press verdicts in eleven contests fought under the no-decision rule. He wasn't altogether satisfied with his form but then, he had found his life out of the ring becoming increasingly complicated. The carefree days when it was just TK and Alec against the world were now long gone. He had responsibilities as well as ambitions.

Where the latter were concerned, he was confident that he could beat Britton the next time they met, even though one sportswriter had written that, on their present form, TK could go on trying to win the welterweight championship for the next ten years without endangering Britton's crown. If TK was not overpleased with himself, New York had taken him to its heart and, wherever he fought, he was assured of vociferous support from the people of Harlem.

It was an exciting period of history, with the Americans leaning more and more towards the Allies. Before Ted climbed through the ropes again, President Wilson demanded a clarification of the war aims of both sides and asserted that he deemed the Germans responsible for the war which was now costing thousands of lives daily. This statement naturally enhanced the popularity of the British still further. Now, when they walked down the street together, Elsie's eyes would sparkle with pride as drivers of passing cars lowered their windows to shout greetings to TK and complete strangers halted them in the street to shake his hand. In fact, TK decided it was time that he and Elsie married.

The Mendeloffs put up a strong rearguard action, but no matter how many subtle strokes they tried to pull, TK had made his mind up to get married. 'They kept saying to us, "Wait, what's the hurry, you're both young." This went on until just before Christmas, when Daddy finally said, "Let's go and get a marriage licence and to hell with everybody." '

Elsie filled in the application, putting 'Sketcher' where it asked for occupation, as that was one of the jobs she did for her firm. 'And when it came to TK's, I asked him what I should put down as his profession, and he said, "Cabinet-maker".'

Subconsciously, he must have still considered it was a good trade. Both families were then told that the couple were getting married in a register office on 15 January 1917. Solomon was very annoyed that he had not been asked first. Mrs Schneider knew how the two felt, but was delighted for them. However, to keep the peace, it was agreed to have a proper synagogue wedding a few weeks later and that the Schneiders should make it. The press were out in full force at the registrar's office together with the boxing fraternity, friends and both families, to witness the ceremony. And then it was off to Grand Central Station, to see TK and Elsie off to Buffalo for a two-week honeymoon at Niagara Falls. TK recalled, 'The weather was cold, we were well wrapped up and the hotel was great. We were having a great time, that is, for the first five days, until Johnston called. He thought he had better remind me, he said, that I was boxing Willie Beechner on 29 January and perhaps I should get in five or six days' training?'

Unbeknown to TK at the time, Johnston needed a top-of-the-bill substitute to replace Mike O'Dowd who had to pull out. Thus, the newly-weds spent the last week of their honeymoon in their new apartment at 25 St Nicholas Avenue, New York City, with TK on the road every morning and at Grupp's gym in the afternoons – no way to spend a honeymoon.

However, on 12 February 1917, the police were having trouble untangling the traffic outside the synagogue on the corner of 110 East 105th Street, New York City, as fight fans and friends waited outside to see the bride and groom arrive.

Inside the synagogue Gershon Mendeloff, now Ted Kid Lewis, stood under the 'chuppah', the ceremonial canopy used at Jewish weddings. 'There was I about to link up my future with the most wonderful woman in the world.' How he must have recalled his early days, dressed in his ragged clothes, battling against the 'goys', and then the sixpenny fights and a cup of tea at the Judean. And now, seven years later, he was in New York, immaculately dressed, money in the bank and practically the entire population of New York sports fans waiting to congratulate him on his marriage.

He could not believe his good fortune as he saw Elsie being led towards the chuppah on the arm of her brother Joe. 'I shall never forget, she looked the most beautiful bride in the world.' Rabbi Jacob Kowalsky performed the ceremony to the delight of the Schneider and Mendeloff families. The ritual glass was placed on the floor and, as TK shattered it, there was the usual sigh of pleasure from the congregation, as they cried out 'Mozoltoff'. This is a Jewish tradition, meant to bring good luck to the young couple, that their happiness should last the same number of years as there are splinters of glass. And the floor was patterned with glass slivers. 'My dad paid the new Mrs Lewis a fitting compliment when he remarked to me, "Brains you must have, that such a fine maid should marry you. You don't want a dowry with a girl like that." I'm not sure, but I think he was trying to tell me that he had made a financial sacrifice.'

16 The Title Regained

'I had a hard row to hoe before I could get a chance to regain the title. But Britton was the piper and I had to dance to his tune.'

TK

Ted's first contest of 1917, when he was twenty-three years of age, was at the new Palace Sporting Club in Brooklyn, an arena recently opened by Jimmy Johnston who in three years had forced himself into the position of being one of the most influential people in the American fighting world. His opponent was Willie Beechner, a tough East-sider who gave TK little more than a work-out, which was just as well, as TK had had to break his honeymoon in order to take the fight.

Two days later he was booked to fight again, this time in Providence, Rhode Island, against Sam Robideaux of Philadelphia. TK won on points over fifteen easy rounds.

Every day brought news of ships sunk, Allied and neutral, some even hospital ships. In a matter of weeks the *Caledonia* had gone to the ocean bed, as had HMS *Cornwall* and the *Laurentic*. Germany no longer made any pretence of recognizing neutrality and arrogantly proclaimed: 'Unrestricted U-boat warfare'. Daily the war was drawing closer to America and citizens of German origin no longer cheered news of the Kaiser's victories. On 3 February 1917 the President announced that the United States of America was severing diplomatic relations with Germany.

With America now on the brink of war, TK continued to fight: Kid Graves, Johnny Griffiths, Willie Moore, and a no-decision title defence against Jack Britton; then Jim Coffey, Billy Weeks, Johnny Griffiths and Jimmy O'Hagen. All were successfully dealt with. When Elsie woke TK with the news that America had entered the war at last he wasted no time and went to enlist; despite his flat feet, he was accepted into the American army. But there was more frustration. Instead of rushing him to a training camp, as he had expected – and hoped – they sent him home, telling him that they would let him know when they were ready to use his services. 'In the meantime Jay Jay kept me busy with three no-decision fights: Jack Britton in Toronto, Joe Egan in Boston and, two days later, Mike O'Dowd in New York.'

In the course of time he found himself in uniform as a 2nd lieutenant but, like the British, the American authorities considered that he could do more good in America than overseas and he was asked to box exhibitions regularly at army camps to entertain the soldiers. He threw himself enthusiastically into his work, though he still considered it a poor way of trying to defeat the Germans. On several occasions he applied to be sent out as a fighting man, but on each occasion they soothed his complaints and assured him he would be doing his best, both for his old country and the country which had adopted him, by staying in the States and boxing. However, he never realized that when he joined the US Army he might automatically become an American citizen. So much was happening, and so quickly.

On 28 May, however, a turn of boxing events spurred him into making some decisive moves regarding the welterweight championship. Freddie Welsh, so long pursued by TK, was beaten by Benny Leonard in New York, knocked out in the ninth round of a no-decision ten-rounder. TK was bitter, but determined to press his own claim – but Leonard would have nothing to do with a Lewis challenge. Thus, TK made up his mind that, come what might, he would regain the welterweight title from Jack Britton: 'I told Jimmy Johnston that I was not interested in any other opponents and that he would have to get me Britton for the title or I would get him myself.'

Goaded into action, Johnston swiftly arranged a deal: TK was to box Britton ten rounds no-decision in St Louis on 6 June and a further ten rounds no-decision in New York eight days later. If he came through those two with newspaper verdicts, the Dayton, Ohio, promoters were prepared to put Britton and TK on over the twenty-round championship course to a decision with the title at stake. 'Well, I got over the first hurdle with flying colours, getting a unanimous vote at the end of ten hot rounds at the Future City AC at St Louis. The consensus of opinion of the ringside critics was that I had outpointed the champion and only the fact that it was a no-decision bout saved the title from changing hands.'

Their second contest eight days later was more even, with TK winning the first three rounds, Britton the next four and TK taking the last three by a shade. It was close, but good enough for the Dayton promoters.

The championship fight instantly caught the public's imagination. 'Dumb' Dan Morgan and Jay Jay began issuing threatening statements to the press, building up the impression that there was deadly enmity between the camps. Both Britton and TK were amused at their managers' antics and were happy to leave the 'banging of the drum' to 'Dumb' Dan and Jay Jay while concentrating on their own preparations.

The fight night was a glittering occasion. Every man who was anyone in Dayton was there and far more women than was usual at a boxing tournament. For TK, there seemed to be a tenseness about the atmosphere that he had never experienced before: 'As I stood there shuffling my feet in the resin and pounding one glove into the palm of the other, I made a vow that everyone in England would have some pleasant reading in the sports pages the following day. Here was my chance to make up for Freddie Welsh's defeat.'

In the other corner, 'Dumb' Dan was arguing violently with Jay Jay, who was insisting that Britton show him his gloves again, yelling that Britton had gained relief once before by conveniently splitting the padding when things were turning against him. 'Dumb' Dan, bristling with resentment, was appealing to the crowd to witness the fairness of his boy and how Jay Jay should be suspended for 'the good of the game'.

Alec rubbed TK's shoulders, not that such a massage did any physical good, but that it might reassure him that, though he was fighting for the crown against an American in America, he still had loyal support.

Although for the last eleven days, since fighting in New York, TK's entire concentration had been on the contest, now the moment of truth had come, his mind was on his Harlem home. How Elsie, who was afraid to see him fight, would be sitting at home, knitting, trying to keep her mind off the contest, and yet all the time waiting for the telephone to ring, and praying her man would not be hurt.

His father, Solomon, would be waiting outside the building. He could not now bear to watch his son fight, but wanted to be close to him just the same.

Jack Britton gave TK a friendly nod and the seconds swept the gowns from their men's shoulders. The bell rang again and Ted Kid Lewis from London's East End turned to face Jack Britton, the Irish-American, for the undisputed championship of the world.

Both boxers were well aware of the importance of the occasion and each began by weighing up his opponent as if they were meeting for the first time. Would the Englishman depend on his big punch and tigerish aggression? Would Britton try to make it a boxing match? Like two poker players testing each other out, neither of them wanted to declare his hand too early. This was their thirteenth battle, and one that must prove unlucky for one of them.

Somehow the crowd didn't show any disapproval of the uneventful first round in which only a few light blows were struck. They could sense the mental battle taking place in the ring, which is every bit as important as a trial of physical strength. Both men tried light left leads, usually out of distance. Neither stepped in with any real assertiveness. 'Back in the corner Alec asked me, "How's it going?"

' "He's waiting for me. And I'm not falling first," I replied. "This time, I'll call the tune. I think he's going to try and fight close in, and that suits me." '

The bell brought them up in the centre of the ring again. TK flicked forward his left and Britton failed to stop it landing. Then another. Britton moved into attack, showing by the way he carried his guard that he expected the usual Ted Kid Lewis counter-attack. But TK moved out of distance and again led with his left from his thigh, catching Britton with a light straight left, and then a much harder following left hook. This time it was Britton who moved backwards. This wasn't the smashing battle of two men determined to knock each other unconscious, but a battle of wit and boxing skill. This was a duel, not an assault.

At the end of the round, Alec massaged TK's stomach muscles. 'That went real lovely. It was your round by a mile.'

TK grunted. 'It's too early yet. I'll bet Jack's got lots up his sleeve. But we'll stick to the same routine.'

The next five rounds were even, with neither boxer able to win ascendancy. In the eighth, TK opened out, though still keeping the fight at long range. Once again his footwork was too swift for Britton who nodded his admiration when TK scored with three crisp, straight lefts without reply.

TK had now taken two rounds, and Britton, a shrewd judge of a contest, had no intention of allowing TK to sneak ahead so far on points that he'd be forced to stage a grandstand finish to win. So, in the eighth, Britton attacked, concentrating on the body and crowding TK, so that he was forced to fight back instead of maintaining the long-range battle. Britton took this round clearly.

Now it was TK's turn to take the initiative but Britton, though outboxed, scored well towards the end of the round to make it even.

The next three rounds went to TK's skill, whilst Britton took the thirteenth. TK reasserted his authority in the next two.

Britton now realized he was well behind with only five rounds to go. But try as he might in the sixteenth, he could not get close enough to hammer his attack home to TK's ribs.

Desperately, and with great courage, he did his utmost to turn the fight in his favour and for the next two rounds kept TK too busy defending himself to launch any attack of his own. Now both men were nearing exhaustion, but once again TK found some source of energy and had the crowd cheering as he fought back in the nineteenth.

As they shaped up for the last round, Britton's corner were shouting to him that he must knock Lewis out to win. Britton threw away all caution and tore into his English opponent, throwing punches from all angles. One hook caught TK on the jaw, sending him sprawling to the canvas, but it was a matter of lost balance rather than the force of the blow, and he was up without taking a count. At the final bell, the two men were flailing away at each other with both hands.

Lou Bauman had no need to tot up the points. He walked straight across the ring and held up TK's hand. Alec, with a shout, lifted TK high in the air, whilst Jay Jay threw his arms around his neck, and caught the eye of those ringsiders actively connected with the sport as if to say, 'This is the boy to fill your halls'.

TK couldn't disguise – nor did he need to – his intense excitement. Now he could cable to the National Sporting Club, reporting his victory and signing it: 'Ted Kid Lewis, undisputed Champion of the World'. 'I caught sight of Britton on the edge of a crowd of well-wishers, waiting to congratulate me. Thrusting Alec aside, I held out my hand.

'Bad luck, Jack.'

'Nope, you won. I've got no beef,' he replied.

'But I'll give you your revenge, I promise you.'

'I knew you would, and make the most of that title, Ted,' he said. 'I'll take it back one day.'

'Maybe you will,' I smiled, as the promoters came forward to present me with an imposing – if not particularly expensive – winner's belt. Alec went to adjust it round my waist after the presentation but I said, "No, I take the cash. The belt goes to my father. As long as there's a hallmark on the metal, of course!" '

17 The Birth of a Son

'I couldn't hold my gloves up. I didn't know what was
wrong – until I got the cable – I was a father!'
TK to Morton

When TK and Alec returned next day to a reception that awaited
them from friends and family, TK found Elsie overjoyed to see that
his face was not marked. Tears poured down her cheeks with pride.
It was wonderful: she was married, her husband was world champion
once again, in his chosen profession – and she was well on her way
to becoming a mother. TK and Elsie were both emotional and it is
easily understood how close happiness is to sorrow, and that pride
can cause the tear ducts to work as easily as sadness. It was quite a
homecoming.

Today, people would be surprised if a champion fought more than
once a year because the income tax would make it unprofitable to
fight twice a year for championship purses. Yet in 1917 TK was back
in the ring within nine days of securing the title. Not only that, but
his new title was at stake.

Looking back over the years, TK would always say that actual
fighting was the best way to keep in tip-top condition. In fact, his
words were, 'It was easier to fight than train.' TK thrived on regular
fights. After all, it was the only thing he could do and do well, and one
can confidently assume that Jimmy Johnston was happy to cash in on
TK's readiness to face any man, regardless of weight or reputation,
at a couple of days' notice.

His first defence was on Independence Day, 4 July 1917, a no-
decision bout against Johnny Griffiths in Akron. Four weeks later
he took on Jimmy O'Hagen in Saratoga and in less than a fortnight
was back in the ring to defeat Irish-American middleweight Mike
O'Dowd – giving away 20 1b! O'Dowd's heavy body punching told
on TK but he gained a close no-decision verdict. However, eleven
days later, O'Dowd had his revenge, scoring a twelve-round points
victory over TK in Boston. The contest was summed up by one

boxing scribe, who wrote: 'Lewis is nothing more than a good-size lightweight. O'Dowd is a big middleweight. Why does Lewis take him on? What can he gain from such matches? No one denies Lewis's ability to take on men heavier than himself, but to challenge a top class middleweight like O'Dowd seems just plumb crazy. Not that anything anyone says will have the remotest effect on the champ. This is one Limey who would take on Goliath himself if he was fighting over here now.'

Incredibly, three days after this hard contest at New York's St Nicholas Rink, TK defended his title against European Albert Badoud. Badoud suffered the consequences of the O'Dowd defeat – TK, annoyed and anxious to assert his authority once again, knocked Badoud out in one round!

TK recalled: 'Naturally, Jimmy Johnston claimed the European title for me after my sensational one-round win and to show his appreciation he sent me off to Buffalo to meet another "easy" one in Soldier Bartfield with whom I had already had a lively time in the same city.'

Soldier Bartfield, whom TK had met in a no-decision contest some nineteen months earlier, was not the greatest boxer TK would meet, but he was certainly one of the toughest, and though TK dropped him in the fifth round, the Soldier bounced to his feet, disdaining to take a count. However, TK got the no-decision newspaper verdict. Eight days later, in Rochester, TK scored another unanimous decision over him. By now, the fights were coming fast and furious.

Three days after the Bartfield fight it was Jimmy O'Hagen again, a poor fighter who was determined to stay the distance this time and who resorted to wrestling for most of the fight. But TK gave him a boxing lesson, and a rough time, to take the verdict. The following day (yes, the following day!) he was in action again, this time disposing of Italian Joe Gans. There followed a nine-day break, when TK gave Frankie Carbone 9½ lb. and beat him with a great deal to spare. TK was still under great pressure to continue earning money, enabling him to supply the Mendeloffs' ever-increasing demands. He did not have the heart to stop this terrific drain on his bank balance, but, more important, Elsie's pregnancy was fast approaching its end and there was the possibility that he might soon face his induction into the US army. 'I was pushing Jay Jay to arrange some local fights, so that I could stay in town and be near Elsie when the baby arrived, or get called up by the Army.'

The United States involvement in the war had now intensified and conscription was starting. 'Alec became very worried and, true to form, he was on the run again. He told me he was going to Mexico to train some baseball players. I tried to talk him out of it, but without success. It seemed he liked other people to do his fighting.'

Johnston, in the meantime, had arranged three fights in California. 'I told him I wanted to stay in town, he knew Elsie was pregnant and it was nearing her time.' But Johnston had already signed the contracts. Elsie, in fact, felt TK would be better out of the way and would go crazy waiting about for her to have the baby. She would cable him when it happened. Johnston explained: 'The offer is for three fights of four rounds each [as the Californian authorities only permitted four-round contests] with a guarantee of $3,000 per fight. Grab it, it's easy money.'

Easy money it may have looked, but his first opponent was Battling Ortega, a local hero of little skill, yet for TK it was still a difficult decision.

'I arranged for Manny Seaman to take Alec's place as trainer. Years later Scaman would supervise the conditioning of heavyweight champion Joe Louis.' But Seaman was a comparative stranger and TK felt intensely lonely as the train roared across the Kansas prairies. His training camp was at San Rafael, but the beauty of the bay held no attraction for him. Seaman confided to a friend that he had never handled a more morose or tetchy fighter. TK seemed to be living in a dream. He made no attempt to come to terms with the press, snapping out replies to their questions in a tone of voice which made it abundantly clear that they were only allowed into the camp on sufferance. The reporters who knew him realized that something must have caused this uncharacteristic change in approach, but the others wrote of him as a swollen-headed champion.

As the fight approached, local opinion suggested that TK would not be detained for long, however. The *San Francisco Examiner* told its readers: 'Stay around to shed a stray tear with the friends and fond relatives of one Battling Ortega. Prepare yourselves to gather up fragments and sections of this champion in the Emerville ring tonight. For Ted (Kid) Lewis is going to be turned loose against him and the sympathy valves have been thrown open.'

TK read the reports with wry satisfaction, but inside himself he was profoundly depressed. The only thing that could have stirred him out of his depression was good news from home, and thus far, the wires had stayed silent.

In such a state of mind, it is no wonder that TK found it hard to concentrate on his opponent as the bell sounded. Battling Ortega, a full twenty pounds heavier, was a tough fighter but one who would not have been expected to face a world champion.

Ortega, on the other hand, was apprehensive and almost respectful when the bell brought him face to face with the champion and he had good reason for his apprehension, for TK quickly cut loose with a rapid series of blows. Then, incredibly, the champion's hands dropped to his sides.

Ortega was cautious. He hadn't connected with a blow – could it be a trap? Tentatively he led with his left, and to his surprise, it landed. Another left cut through TK's guard, but still Ortega warned himself to be watchful. On the bell he threw a straight right which usually would have caused TK no trouble, but this time it landed clean on the champion's jaw, throwing him back on his heels!

In the corner, Seaman bent his head close so no one else should hear his words. 'Your hands gone?'

'No,' TK grunted.

'Then what's up?'

'I don't know. It seems like I'm carrying a couple of hundred-weight of lead about with me.'

'Well, pull yourself together. This boy can punch.'

TK tried to pull himself together but it was useless. His legs would not respond. He found it difficult to move.

Ortega, sensing that something was wrong, began to gain confidence. In the second round, he was still careful, but by the third, realizing that the champion had nothing to offer, he drove TK from one side of the ring to the other. In the fourth, TK managed to land with a flabby left hand but otherwise it was all Ortega, and TK was the most surprised man in the hall when the referee – no doubt impressed by his being the champion – awarded a draw.

As soon as Seaman had cut the bandages from his hands, TK dressed and left the arena, ignoring the youths waiting outside for his autograph. 'What could be wrong?' he asked himself. 'They gave it a draw, I couldn't understand, or remember a thing, that is until the morning when the telegrams arrived, which explained everything.'

He was waiting in the lobby of the Hotel Continental when he heard a pageboy shouting 'Ted Kid Lewis'. He took the cable from the boy's hand and tore open the envelope in a frenzy of fear. It was the traditional message: 'Elsie gave birth to a beautiful eight-pound baby boy. Both doing well stop. Don't worry. Love Flo.' TK had a son – he was a father.

Before he could go home to meet his son, he had two more contracts to fulfil, across the bay in San Francisco on 13 November with Johnny McCarthy, and 5 December back in Oakland with an opponent yet to be named. Jimmy Johnston had arrived in answer to an urgent summons from Manny Seaman but couldn't understand what all the trouble had been about, for, instead of the angry, morose fighter he'd been led to expect from Seaman's message, he found an almost complacent young fighter who, whilst reiterating constantly his wish to return home and be introduced to his son, was otherwise confident and friendly to all around him.

Johnston seconded TK in his contest with McCarthy who provided only token opposition.

Jay Jay asked, 'You know this Charlie Chaplin guy, don't you?'

'I certainly do.'

'Well, why don't you go to Hollywood and see him? He's getting ready to start on a new film. It'll be a change for you, and keep in fight training for the fight on the 5th.'

This idea appealed to TK and he and Manny Seaman took the train out of San Francisco. In Hollywood, Chaplin welcomed him warmly, and TK invited the comic genius to become his son's godfather. Charlie Chaplin accepted, and gave TK $500 to open the kid's bank account.

Hollywood was expensive and Johnston had paid TK only a small percentage of his purse for the Ortega and McCarthy contests. Soon TK was down to his last few dollars. But he wasn't worried, for already other Californian cities were vying for his services. But Fate, in the shape of a small-time promoter, Dick Klegin, intervened. 'He said he could fix up a fight for me in San Diego, with a guarantee of $5,000, and I said "Get to it".'

TK had to lend Klegin $100, however, in order that Klegin could first travel to San Diego – yet even this unhopeful start failed to warn TK that he was heading for yet another independent fiasco.

Two days later, Klegin wired, 'Everything Jake; you fight Monday'. TK packed his bags, after putting in two days' training, and left for San Diego on the Monday morning. TK was delighted and relished the thought of relating to Jay Jay how skilfully he had handled his affairs without his manager's advice.

'Dick always had to spread himself in great style. He had known that I should be bringing quite a crowd with me. We motored over. I went with Syd Chaplin and his wife Minnie in their car, and there were about twenty others with us also in cars. I might mention that

I drove our car myself which wasn't a right thing to do just before a fight but then I reckoned that I would certainly be able to get through four rounds all right, especially now my mind was clear and I was a father.'

The party arrived in San Diego and were met by Klegin who directed them to an hotel where he had booked rooms for them all. When they arrived they found that Klegin had booked eight suites of rooms, and stacked them all with the best wine and cigars. The staff were all bowing and scraping to Klegin, which convinced TK that the promoter had come into a fortune!

'Well, we left our luggage and went off to the fight club where Dick had reserved seats for all the party. There was a bout in progress as I passed through to the dressing rooms but I was not overjoyed to notice that the club was only half-full. This made me wonder where the money was to come from and I was now determined to see the promoter and to collect my guarantee of $5,000 before I went into the ring.'

By now the crowd was getting restive, calling out for Lewis, but TK was adamant – he would make no move until he had his money. The promoter of the contest, however, insisted that Lewis would be paid after the fight, although he intimated that the final amount might be significantly short of $5,000. 'I wanted to know what he meant. He fetched out a bundle of IOUs signed by Klegin. These totalled up to about $4,000.

'You can guess the shock. I didn't want to let the promoter down, but I wasn't going to be played for a sap so I went out to see Klegin. Dick was at one of the doors checking the takings. I asked him what he had done with the money. All I got was an assurance that he didn't know a thing about the IOUs and that it was all a "frame-up". So I just walked out of the building, got into one of the cars which we had left outside and went back to the hotel. I heard afterwards that there was a big row at the Club.'

In fact, Syd Chaplin was handed the task of getting up into the ring and explaining to an increasingly noisy crowd just what had happened. He failed to satisfy them, nor was the replacement boxer much compensation for missing out on seeing Ted Kid Lewis. Indeed, some of the crowd threatened to go and vent their anger on TK himself.

'I received this cheerful piece of news when the rest of our party got back to the hotel. I was warned that at least one of the crowd outside was armed with a "gat" and that there would probably be several other gunmen among the lot. That sounded cheerful!'

A character called One Round Hogan who was a member of the Lewis party – an ex-boxer now in the movies – complicated matters by offering to use his own gun on the crowd, but Minnie Chaplin, Syd's wife, persuaded everyone to calm down and stay put until morning. So they sat up until 5 am playing cards, before slipping out to motor back to Los Angeles.

The next morning, as day broke, TK and the Chaplins arrived back in Los Angeles and the headline of the first paper they bought proclaimed: 'World Champion Runs Away. Lewis Yellow!'

Evidently the story had received nation-wide publicity, for Jimmy Johnston, he learned, had already been ringing up all the likely hotels on the coast. When eventually his manager ran him to earth, TK received a verbal thrashing. The 5 December fight had been cancelled. TK was told to catch the next train back east.

Though resenting the abuse – which he realized was partially justified – the orders he accepted with alacrity. After all, they meant he would be going home to Elsie and would meet his son. 'So I bade farewell to all my friends and the train could not travel fast enough, as you can imagine.'

The moment when he first saw his boy was one TK never forgot; and in the years to follow, whenever he introduced Morton to anyone, it was always with the same words: 'This is my son.'

TK was now looking forward to spending time with his family. However the following week Jay Jay called: 'You're defending your title on 17 December.' TK was delighted – he could use the money – and came out an easy winner over twelve rounds against Bryan Downey in Columbus.

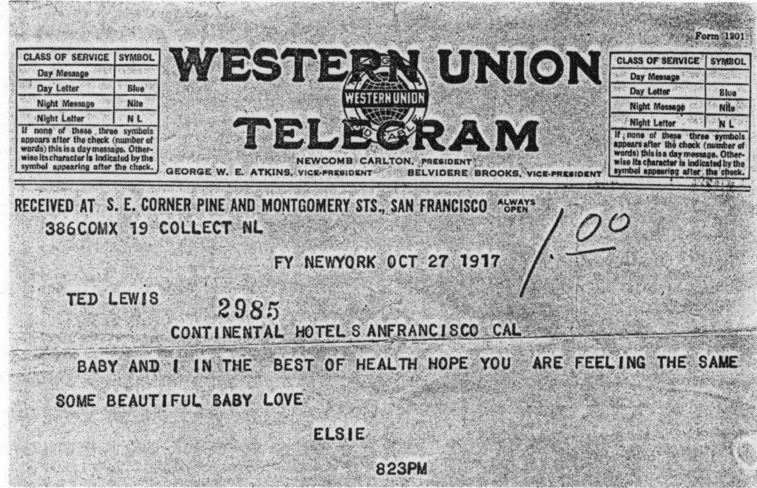

18 The End of an Era

Nineteen-seventeen had been a wonderful year for the twenty-four-year-old Englishman. He became a husband and father, he had fought twenty-nine times, and suffered only one defeat – that by Mike O'Dowd. He had regained his world title, the first time a British-born boxer had achieved such a feat, a record which still stands today.

The following year began in similarly victorious style, with two satisfying wins over old adversary Soldier Bartfield. TK then proceeded to KO Johnny Tillman and Jimmy Duffy in rounds six and one respectively. The following week he fought his sixth contest and got the verdict over Soldier Bartfield. The next night he was again in action against a coloured welterweight, Willie Langford, on a 'Black versus White' bill, scoring an easy points victory. The week after he was fighting yet again, against his old friendly enemy, Jack Britton. This was their fourteenth meeting and their first since he had deprived Britton of his title. As usual, it was a close battle with TK just about edging it. Ten days later TK took a ten-round decision over Joe Eagan, then, two weeks later, he had his fifteenth outing with Jack Britton. This time the press were unable to find for either man.

In the meantime Johnston accepted a challenge from Johnny Tillman for TK's title. The bout was to be held on 17 May in Tillman's home town of Denver. It was a twenty-round contest and TK clearly outboxed his rival for the first six rounds. In the seventh, Tillman threw all defence to the winds and mounted a non-stop attack which TK just managed to contain. By the fourteenth, the experts realized that with his early points advantage, TK must be so far in front that Tillman could win only by a KO. Evidently someone in Tillman's corner apprised him of the fact, for the Denver fighter, to the delight of the crowd of three thousand, rushed TK to the ropes and landed a heavy right hook. For a moment, TK's knees wobbled and then he was back in the contest, throwing punches so fast that many spectators declared it was impossible to count them. From this round to the last bell, the crowd were on their feet as the two boxers fiercely punched away without thought of defence. The referee's decision in Lewis's favour brought no complaint from Tillman or his supporters. The record book shows this was TK's sixteenth successful defence of his world welterweight title and twenty-fifth world title bout.

Reports from the Western Front were becoming alarming. The list of casualties was growing daily and when a tournament in aid of the Red Cross was scheduled for 24 May at Madison Square Garden TK, along with many other top boxers, offered his services free. TK later recalled that he would remember that night as long as he lived: 'The old Garden was decorated with flags, hundreds of fashionably dressed women were round the ringside and almost everyone of importance on Broadway was there. Dozens of pretty girls dressed as nurses collected a large sum. In fact, as a result of the tourney over 154,000 dollars was handed over to the Red Cross.'

Augie Ratner, Battling Levinsky, Lew Tendler, Gunboat Smith, Harry Greb and Johnny Dundee were among the prominent fighters who were on the bill with Britton and TK. The Lewis-Britton clash – their sixteenth – was the final bout of the evening. One might have imagined that after so many contests, and with the knowledge that they would eventually meet for the title, both men would fight with greater care, especially as the contest was over only six rounds. But TK was determined that, even though he was fighting for nothing, and it was only seven days after the Tillman contest, he would treat the fans to a display which would prove beyond all doubt that he was the rightful king of his weight. From the first bell, he flew at Britton, and in the fourth round caught his rival with a left hook, sending him crashing to the boards. Britton had never been knocked off his feet since he had been KO'd by Steve Kinney in 1905, his first year of fighting, and he had had close on two hundred contests.

Britton managed to scramble to his feet by the count of eight, but had to hang on desperately for the last two rounds to avoid a second KO on his record. After the fight, Jimmy Johnston told Dan Morgan: 'Ted is more delighted by sinking your lad on his backside than if he had a purse of thousands. And I reckon what he's done once, he can do again.'

Dan Morgan, his face red with anger, snarled back: 'It was just a lucky punch. Next time he'll be willing to mix it. Then Jack'll nail him. And whatever you scream about, we'll claim the title.'

The result of the managers' argument was that the two rivals were booked to fight again – for the seventeenth time – a month later. Once more the contest was only six rounds. This time neither man was able to establish any mastery.

Five days later, TK was again in action, this time in Boston. He had been much disturbed to hear that his two managers had fallen out and that in future his affairs were to be handled solely by Johnston. Although Charlie Harvey had cheated him after his South American escapade, TK still had complete faith in him as a manager. However, as usual, he didn't argue, but shrugged his shoulders and accepted the 'Boy Bandit' as his mentor. There was a weight clause in the contract for the contest with Tommy Robson at the Boston Armoury. TK easily made the weight, but Tommy Robson was so much overweight that it was useless even suggesting he should sweat off the extra poundage. But TK waved aside all suggestion of claim.

Using his extra weight, Robson forced TK on to the defensive and the contest was extremely close, though the judges and referee all awarded the verdict to TK. The boxers readily agreed to return.

But before this could take place, TK was faced with Johnny Griffiths for the seventh time. TK showed remarkable confidence in agreeing to fight Griffiths in his home town, and on Independence Day, when it was likely that every advantage would be shown to the American challenger. The arena, of course, was sold out.

Once again, Griffiths put up a great battle but the press were in no doubt as to the winner and still champion.

The match received little attention for the American newspapers had other more vital matters to report. First they had used all their most colourful adjectives to describe the valour of their American 'doughboys' who had swept the Huns back and taken Vaux. The mood had been one of exhilaration. But it was followed by reports of vicious fighting, culminating in the French and Americans opening the summer offensive. Once again there were the tragic lists of those dead, wounded and captured. Confidence sagged until, once again, came news of victory as the Allies crossed the River Marne.

Once more the impact of the news brought TK to argue with his manager that it was time he ceased to pay lip service to the theory of being an American soldier and started being trained for active service. The 'Boy Bandit' had to call on all his oratory guile to persuade TK against any 'unwise', if patriotic, action. Johnston was critically in debt, and amongst his main creditors was TK. And TK as champion was his only chance of extricating himself from bankruptcy. If TK went to France as a soldier, Johnston would lose his only regular source of income.

TK listened to his blandishments in a surly mood. By his fists he had raised Jimmy Johnston to the top of the boxing world. He had financed his manager's gambling and in reward had been cheated out of his purses. Why should he consider Johnston's interests at such a time? Furthermore, he had set his heart on a contest with Benny Leonard. Leonard had won the lightweight title from Freddie Welsh and was publicly proclaimed as the greatest of all the living world champions. TK was intensely proud and resented this claim. The press were continually referring to him as a 'blown-up' lightweight. If he could trounce Leonard at catch-weights, there would be pressure for a title contest and he was confident he could reduce to 135 lb. If he succeeded, then the whole fistic world would accept Ted Kid Lewis, the London cockney, as the boxing Colossus of his day . . . in skill if not in poundage.

But there was a snag in such a contest. Leonard had extremely high principles. The 'Boy Bandit' had built up a reputation for being 'too clever by half'. Benny Leonard stated openly that though he would be only too pleased to test his skill against Lewis, he would not do so as long as the Britisher was handled by J.J. Johnston. TK began to think that Johnston, far from being his guide, was much more of a load on his back.

He agreed, however, not to apply for full-time army service until after the return contest with Tommy Robson.

This contest had been made at 147 lb. and TK made the weight without shedding any of his clothes. But Robson was a few ounces overweight. There was a weight forfeit clause in the contract.

'Don't worry, Tommy,' said TK. 'I won't claim it.'

Robson looked at him with an expression of contempt. 'That's a change. You were quick enough to claim your pound of flesh last time.'

'I don't get it!'

Robson laughed. 'You don't get it! But you did; you claimed every last cent when I was over before. So don't give me any of that sportsman kidding now.'

TK made no reply. He hadn't received any forfeit from their last contest. There could be only one answer. The 'Boy Bandit' had done another of his 'strokes', and had first claimed the weight forfeit . . . and then calmly pocketed it for himself.

TK won the contest with ease, but shrugged off his manager's congratulations.

A fortnight later TK went to Jersey City and had the best of an eight-round contest with Walter Mohr. Then he returned to New York. His first action after greeting Elsie and inspecting his son, Morton, was to call on Charlie Harvey. 'I've had enough of Johnston. He's done me forwards, sideways and backwards. I'm going to tell him to jump in the lake.'

Charlie Harvey smiled sympathetically. 'Yeah, I knew you'd get wise in time. The things that man would do. He sure lets down the whole sport.' This from a man of no higher principles might have irritated a more experienced person than TK. 'But what now? You can't look after yourself.' He paused. 'Now Ted, you put yourself in my hands again and we'll make a real killing.'

'I don't want a killing. But I'll tell you what I do want. I want one contest . . . against Benny Leonard. I want Leonard. Get him and you can handle me.'

Charlie Harvey beamed. 'Good. Have a three or four weeks' rest with the family and I'll be in touch.'

Two weeks later Harvey informed TK, 'Start training.'

Benny Leonard raised no objection when he learned TK had split with Johnston. However, he imposed certain conditions. Charlie Harvey went on, 'Firstly, he wants his own chief second, George Erzle, to be in your corner throughout the contest.' It was difficult to understand the reasons for this condition, for there had never been any suggestion that TK's great powers of stamina were engendered by drugs.

'Secondly, we must accept Leonard's nomination as referee.'

TK agreed to both conditions and the fight was promoted at the International League Ball Park, at Newark, New Jersey, over eight rounds on 23 September, at 10 st. 2 lb.

The fight aroused a great deal of partisanship in Harlem where both boxers resided. From 110th Street to 113th Street came TK's following, while from there to 116th Street everyone was rooting for Benny Leonard. On the corner of 116th Street stood a bakery which was popular with sportsmen and there they fashioned a cake in the shape of a coffin with the inscription, 'This is where Ted Lewis will rest after his fight with Leonard'. 'At the time I was in strict training at Lakewood, N.J., and did not see the confection, but it was resented by my staunch supporters and a number of "gang" fights resulted. In justice to Benny, let me add that he was in total ignorance of the affair and immediately he learnt of it he ordered the cake to be taken away.'

The contest caught the public imagination. There was heavier betting than on any contest in the decade, with the odds slightly on the native-born American. At the weigh-in, TK scaled 10 st. and Benny Leonard 9 st. 9¼ lb. This was TK's only contest in the States where he had a weight advantage. There was some suspicion, however, that Leonard's real weight had been concealed, though Leonard himself had no hand in this, being a fighter with an impeccable reputation for fair play. But Leonard's backers wanted, on all accounts, to safeguard their fighter's reputation and should he lose to Lewis, then it would be valuable to be able to draw attention to the contest being over the lightweight limit. Certainly, this accusation was given supporting evidence, for when the referee announced that at the weigh-in both men were inside the prescribed weight, this did not suit Leonard's manager. He refused to let the fight start until the actual weights had been announced.

This was a contest of dancing masters. Perhaps their mutual respect might have spoiled the fight from the spectators' point of view. As the gong finally rang, TK moved into an immediate attack and landed a smashing left hook which had Leonard momentarily swinging on the ropes. Leonard was a superb ring craftsman and danced his way out of trouble. But a great deal of his confidence had gone. TK did not go all out to follow up that first advantage because he knew he was facing one of the cleverest boxers ever to grace the boxing game. The fight developed into a duel with left leads and parries, with both boxers feinting, weaving, ducking, without a real solid punch being landed. It was truly a fight for the connoisseurs of boxing – one which would have been much more appreciated in England than in the States.

The gate was 32,000 dollars after tax deductions, and TK's purse was 10,000 dollars.

The following morning the press were undecided. The morning papers gave the decision in TK's favour, while the evening editions leaned toward Leonard. Benny was most disappointed as he really wanted to win in order to establish himself as a challenger for TK's welterweight title. Naturally Charlie Harvey wanted to angle for the return which he was confident would draw a record gate. But TK would not have it. The Allies were advancing in France and already people were talking tentatively of final victory. Elsie knew how deeply he resented being kept out of active service. 'You won't be happy until you're there,' she told him. 'God knows I don't want you to go, but I'd rather have you go than see the look in your eyes each morning when you read the news from over there.'

TK bent and kissed her. It was wonderful to him that he had someone to share his unhappiness with, and with whom he did not even have to speak of his inner feelings. Elsie was so close to him that he lost for the first time in his life the sense of having to rely solely on his own decisions, a sense which had grown in him through the injustices and cruelties of his East End youth.

The Leonard fight was to be TK's last in 1918. For a while, he would be in uniform – something he had wished for for the last four years.

'Charlie Harvey drove me to Washington. I contacted Dr Raycroft who was in charge and was greeted with open arms. This was on Friday. I was told to report to Camp Gordon, Atlanta, Georgia, on Monday, to Mike Gibbons, who was a captain in charge of boxing where I was immediately put on a course in company with quite a number of prominent fighters, including that grand guy Packy McFarland. The course finished, I was transferred to Camp Upton, New York, where I contracted yellow jaundice and was in bed when the Armistice was signed. The news proved too much for me, ill though I was. I defied all medical orders and went out to celebrate.'

Demobbed soon after the Armistice, TK took his family, accompanied by his sister Dolly and Charlie Harvey, for a holiday to the Adirondacks. Once again TK's luck seemed to be out as on arriving at their destination Elsie found it impossible to wake him. It was then discovered that TK was the victim of sleeping sickness and for three weeks Elsie was kept busy waking him up. On returning to New York TK consulted a specialist, and the prognosis was that it would be many months before the champion would climb through the ropes again. TK grunted on hearing this and resolved that he would give his physician the lie by recovering and fighting within a month. By mid December, he was in light training and demanding action.

Charlie Harvey had his doubts, but knew of old TK's determination, and he needed money – his family were squeezing him dry. He accepted a no-decision contest for 1 January with Brian Downey. TK fought throughout in a lack-lustre manner. He attributed this to ring-rustiness and a fortnight later was again in action, this time against George Rivet in Montreal. Once more he found himself boxing as if he was standing a yard away from himself, and taking only an academic interest in the proceedings. Now he knew it was something deeper than lack of practice causing his poor displays and he agreed to cancel another contest which had been arranged for the following week.

In training he recovered his spirits and began to spar more like his old self, with the result that Charlie Harvey contracted him to defend his title against Johnny Griffiths in Memphis.

While training for the Griffiths contest, TK was offered a further match with Jack Britton. Charlie Harvey was in two minds about accepting, but TK was once again full of optimism.

'Why not?' he demanded. 'I can take Jack whenever I want now. He'd have to knock me out to claim the title, and that he couldn't manage in a week of Sundays.' He waved Charlie Harvey's objections aside. 'I can handle Jack. Besides, I'm a hundred per cent OK now,' although in his heart he didn't really believe it.

His optimism was ill-founded, as his showing against Griffiths proved. True, he won on points, but he was made to work all the way and the newspapers only gave him the verdict by a shade.

Once more Elsie insisted on his going for another medical check-up. The doctor said he was not fit to fight, that he was 20 per cent anaemic and needed plenty of rest and nourishment to put his blood back in order.

'I'm not surprised,' TK told his manager. 'When I'm fighting, it seems as though I'm watching myself from outside the ropes. Jack will have to wait.'

Charlie Harvey drew on his cigar. 'You'll be OK. Go and grab thirty grand. It's a lot of money right now. You've gotta strike while the iron's hot. It's a no-decision bout, and if you lose, it will only be a newspaper verdict and that ain't worth a dime. He's gotta knock you out to take the title and, as you've always said, he couldn't put you down for count in a . . . as the Limeys say . . . in a week of Sundays.'

So Ted did not persist. He didn't want Charlie to call him yellow and, as they could both use the cash, against his better judgement he gave in and agreed to fight Britton a week later at Canton, Ohio.

It was a momentously foolish decision, one that he was to regret for many years to come.

It was clear to everyone that he was in no condition to fight – a newspaper columnist wrote a few days before the fateful contest,

'Ted (Kid) Lewis, the slashing, dashing, crashing, smashing English box-fighter, is just off a sick bed and wants chicken and plenty of it. Bully beef as an article of diet is an "also ran" so Ted wants Jack Britton, as what the pair will draw will purchase succulent roosters for many weeks to come. All the same, when I met the Englishman on Broadway a few days ago I told him that he was pursuing a shadow, and would probably drop his crown in the endeavour to get chicken. For he looked sick and his skin was the colour of a chinaman's.'

March the seventeenth arrived, and TK stepped up for the eighteenth time to meet Jack Britton for their thirteenth world title fight.

The contest started with TK boxing well inside himself for the first two rounds to conserve his energy. But by the third round he began to tire and looked as if he wanted to go to sleep. He spent the rest of the third, the fourth and fifth rounds attempting to outwit Britton. Seldom had TK been seen on the defensive. Britton now sensed that something was wrong. By the sixth round Britton was well ahead on points. His confidence was growing. He was throwing stiff punches and they were landing on target. In fact, it came as no surprise to the noisy fans when a strong left hook to the jaw dropped TK for a count of four. TK was in trouble.

'In ordinary circumstances the blow would have had no effect – I had taken dozens of lefts like that from Britton – but this time my weakened constitution and poor resistance caused the punch to have more than the usual effect.'

Up at the count of four, he was staggering, and reeled into the ropes for support. Britton swiftly followed him, whipping in another left hook and once more TK was on the canvas. He knew it would be fatal, however, for him to be counted out, for although it was a no-decision contest, Britton would be able to claim the title if he stopped TK – something Harvey and the rest of the camp had not even contemplated when pressing ahead with the match.

Thus TK pulled himself together and managed to get up, but before he could raise his arms in self-defence a swinging left sent him back down for the third time. He managed to rise again and hang on until the bell, but throughout the following two rounds he grew weaker and weaker, until survival began to look impossible. In the ninth round, TK was all in and fought more by instinct than anything else. Down he went again, and the next he knew he was being supported by Alec Goodman out of the ring. He had not been knocked out, however, he had simply collapsed. But Britton was now claiming the title. TK was no longer champion of the world.

'When I came to a full realization on the morning after my disastrous fight with Jack Britton – I was in a more or less comatose state all through the night – I was a sore man. I reckoned little of my bruised face and body but my inner most soul was racked with torment.

'Even the praise of the sports writers the next day failed to soothe me, but do you know that even my champion knocker, old "Bat" Masterton, was kind to me in my hour of defeat.'

Masterton wrote: 'Ex-champion Ted (Kid) Lewis will sure go down in boxing history as one of the gamest men to ever scrape his boxing boots in resin. His refusal to admit defeat when a helpless target for Jack Britton's punches stamps him with the guinea gold brand of pluck. Nothing will ever become him better than his behaviour in the hour of defeat.'

So, after regaining and holding the welterweight championship of the world for eighteen months, he had lost it for the second time to the man from whom he'd won it. The British press claimed, with some logic, that as neither of the contestants had weighed-in before the contest, he had not lost his title. But TK was never one to seek alibis and though he knew he should never have fought, he told the press in his dressing room, 'Jack won, and good luck to him. He'll be a great champion. . .' Then, a wry grin twisted the corners of his mouth. 'But tell him to look after the title . . . for I'll be back for it.'

WORLD'S CHAMP TO BOX!

Ted "Kid" Lewis vs "Kid" Carter

WELTERWEIGHT CHAMP   OF NEW YORK CITY

SIX ROUNDS

LIBERTY THEATRE

Wednesday Evening, January 29, 1919

Program Starts 7 p. m.   Camp Upton, N. Y.

Six other bouts between champions of Camp Upton and Camp Mills. Also moving pictures and lots of music. Proceeds to go to camp athletic fund. Civilians welcome

PRICES: Officers' Reserved Seats $1.00—Enlisted Men 25c.

ROYAL ALBERT HALL

FRIDAY, DEC. 26 (Evening of Boxing Day)

Under the direction of REDMOND BARRY.

THREE GREAT CONTESTS

20 Three-Minute Rounds Contest :

KID LEWIS v. MATT WELLS

(Ex-World's Welterweight Champion.)   (Ex-Lightweight Champion.)

20 Three-Minute Rounds Contest :

PAL MOORE   v.   EUGÈNE CRIQUI

(America.)   (France.)

(Criqui takes Ledoux's place, owing to the latter's serious illness.)

12 Three-Minute Rounds Contest :

JOHNNY GRIFFITHS v. FRANCIS CHARLES

(America.)   (France.)

Commence at 8 p.m. sharp. Doors open at 7 o'clock.

GEORGES CARPENTIER

(Champion of Europe)

will positively appear and spar four rounds exhibition.

Prices from £1 1s. to £9 9s.

Box Office now open at the Albert Hall and the usual Agencies.

PART THREE

The Prodigal Returns

Boxing, NOVEMBER 24, 1920.
Vol. XXII. No. 586.

BOXING

Three Pence Every Wednesday.

Vol. XXII.
No. 586.

The Only Paper in the World solely devoted to Boxing.
NOVEMBER 24, 1920.

Registered at the G.P.O. as a Newspaper and for Canadian Magazine Post.

A "BATEMAN" VIEW OF LEWIS AND BASHAM.

As will be readily recognised, Mr. Nicolle will never earn a living as a portrait-painter. This cartoon is supposed to indicate that Basham and Lewis will fight next Friday for the European middle-weight championship. To no purpose, for the title has been already sequestrated by the illogical French Federation, with the high approval of the British Board of Control. We regret having to explain the joke, but you might not see it otherwise.

19 The Lonsdale Belt Again

'We had hardly passed the Aldgate Pump when we heard a shout "There's Kid Lewis!" And before you could say Jack Britton our car was surrounded by a huge crowd.'
Charlie Rose

TK let no one see how much the loss of his title meant to him. But from Elsie he couldn't hide the truth. When he returned from training at Boan's gymnasium, she noted his tight lips and white face. He had been used to being called 'champ' and being lionized by the other boxers. Now, though he was still respected as one of the greatest fighters campaigning in the States, he was discovering the vast difference the prefix 'ex' can mean. His pride was hurt.

His father, too, was unhappy. He had blossomed in his son's fame and was always ready to pontificate on boxing, as if his son's success had invested him with a deep knowledge of the sport. Charlie Harvey reassured his fighter's father that the loss of the title didn't necessarily mean a drastic reduction in his purses, but even then Mr Mendeloff felt the defeat almost as keenly as his boy. He liked the glory of being the father of a champion.

Once again Elsie decided that her husband should get away from boxing and recover his health in the country. But they had barely settled in at their mountain hotel when TK's father joined them. Mr Mendeloff had heard of a wonderful new doctor who had more experience of sleeping sickness than anyone in the world.

And TK took little persuading. He was hankering after the ring and felt that his life was drab now he no longer wore the purple robe of champion. So he grasped at the straw and, despite Elsie's protests, returned immediately to New York with his father. But while Dr Zipser's treatment helped, it certainly did not cure him. Charlie Harvey was just as concerned as Mr Mendeloff that TK should recover fully. They had something in common. TK was their breadwinner. So the manager insisted TK should enter the Vincent Hospital for observation. Once again the doctors were optimistic, though their efforts proved abortive. But TK's will to recover had been rekindled and slowly he returned, if not to full health, at least to a better mental state.

On 4 July, Independence Day, he was introduced from the ring in Toledo, before the world heavyweight championship fight.

The new challenger for the giant Jeff Willard's title was a beetle-browed young fighter who sported a three-days' growth of beard and was unable to sit still in his corner, so anxious was he to fling himself across the ring at the champion. TK knew the feeling. He also knew Jack Dempsey.

'I had met him previously when he was just climbing the ladder to fame. He was training for Gunboat Smith at the time . . . we were staying at the same San Francisco hotel and after working out I suggested to Jack that he should come to the local theatre with me.

' "Righto," he said, highly pleased as he went away to put on his glad rags. I was wearing a big single stone diamond ring at the time and Jack, doubtless in a spirit of emulation, appeared at dinner wearing a diamond pin. I chaffingly said, "I like your pin, Jack," and quick as a flash he replied, "Don't kid me. I shall have a ring like yours some day."

' "Too sure you will, Jack. The Gunner is easy for you and when you've settled him there are not many more to beat," I replied.'

As TK sat at the ringside and watched the young Jack Dempsey thrash the Kansas giant to defeat, he envied him the frenzied yelling of the fans. He resented the cheers of the crowd for Dempsey. . . when they could so easily be for him. And he was determined to get back into action. Not in a month or two months, but next week. Charlie Harvey was equally enthusiastic, having been indulging in a gambling spree, with the inevitable result that he was once again broke and, at the same time, TK's fight purses were only just keeping up with his spending. There were now nine in his extended family as well as Alec, plus all the hangers-on and this, in itself, was a persuading element.

TK's father was equally encouraging and if Elsie bit her lips as she listened to the enthusiasm with which her husband discussed his first contest in four months, she made no comment.

Ten days after Jack Dempsey had become world champion, TK was fighting against Steve Latzo. He won well without, however, being able to call up the vicious attacks of the past. A fortnight later he climbed through the ropes with Jack Britton, the world champion, for their nineteenth contest. Another fighter with a less resilient temperament might have felt apprehensive at facing a man who had defeated him so decisively five months earlier, especially as he knew that he had not yet reached peak condition. But TK merely tightened his lips and resolved that he would make his old enemy understand that never again would he easily defeat the tough London fighter. If there had been a decision there is little doubt that it would have been awarded to the champion, but TK was satisfied with his performance because, though his own punches were lacking their full power, Britton was completely unable to repeat his former performance and had to be content with a narrow points victory.

Two days after this contest, TK was leaving the flat for his training quarters when he met Dr Muth, a well-known New York dentist and a keen fight fan. They travelled to the gymnasium together and the doctor commented that he had noticed TK was lacking his usual zest. The outcome of their talk was that he invited TK to his consulting room. Having examined his teeth, the dentist told TK that there was little doubt as to the cause of his lethargy. He could forget all about sleeping sickness. The real trouble was that his teeth were decayed and he was continually swallowing the poison. Without delay the dentist extracted four of TK's teeth, and though TK wondered briefly whether he had been wise to accept the dentist's decision, he was to be extremely grateful for his interest for, from that moment, he began to feel really fit again and celebrated his lost teeth by once again defeating Steve Latzo, this time with the utmost ease.

His determination to prove himself again was fired by the additional worry of lack of finances. Charlie Harvey, following a disastrous gambling spree, was broke; TK's family needed feeding; Alec, too, had grown used to a certain standard of living. . . Elsie's reservations were thus overruled.

Now fully confident, TK was back at his best. He accepted a match with the new middleweight champion, his old enemy, Mike O'Dowd, who had recently won the world crown by knocking out Al McCoy. TK had to give away 21 lb. to one of the toughest fighters in the world, and to a man who already held a twelve-round victory over him. Nevertheless, though he would probably have lost the verdict had one been given, he took all the Irishman's best punches without flinching or being in real trouble, and succeeded in cutting the champion's eyes in the final session.

The press, although expressing surprise at his ability to last the full distance with the man who had KO'd McCoy at the height of his power in six rounds, stated that they thought Lewis far too ambitious in taking on men so much heavier . . . what was his manager trying to prove?

Once more TK visited Dr Muth, and a further two teeth were removed. This time he celebrated their extraction by knocking out K.O. Laughlin in the first round and repeating the dose five days later, this time the patient being Jimmy McCabe. Two more weeks passed and he travelled to Atlanta to face Jack Able, whom he defeated clearly on points over ten rounds.

TK now felt that the run of victories entitled him to a return with Britton for the championship. But Britton had other ideas. He remembered how TK had kept him waiting for his chance and politely, though firmly, told TK that he would have to wait.

However, TK wasn't too downhearted. He was feeling fit again – fitter than he had been for a long time – and confident in his ability to take on the world. But he was becoming restless, he wanted and needed more work.

One day after finishing sparring, an expatriate came over to TK, saying that he had heard he was going back to England to fight Matt Wells on Boxing Day at the Albert Hall, that he looked fit and shouldn't have any trouble with Wells.

'This was the first I had heard about it, in fact I was delighted and hoped it was true. I thanked him and hurried over to Charlie Harvey's office.

'Well, Charlie, I feel fit and ready to work. Got anything lined up?' TK thought he'd play Charlie at his own game. He'd wait him out.

'Well, the situation is tough. The top welterweights prefer to go after Britton, because if they fight you and lose, their position would be hurt. And for the middleweights that can draw money with you, they feel that they are expected to beat a little guy, and would look bad if they lost to one.' For a moment TK was speechless, then regained his composure. 'I don't understand. Are you saying that it's hard to get me work? It sounds like you have been pushed out of the managers' ring!'

'Well, yes, but only for a little while. I've got something going but, in the meantime, I've fixed you up with a fight on 26 December.'

'But that's nearly a couple of months off!' TK exclaimed. Settling down again, he asked calmly, 'How much, where and who with?'

Charlie felt a little better. '$25,000 purse. $15 grand to the winner at the Royal Albert Hall against Matt Wells.'   TK grinned broadly. He had little doubt that his manager's accepting a contest without telling him had little connection with the reasons he was now giving, but for once didn't resent Harvey's lack of consideration. For some months now he had been hankering to see his old friends and to visit the scenes of his youth. The only disadvantage was in fighting Wells, who had been one of his childhood heroes, and was a good seven years older than himself. Then he shrugged. He wasn't in the fight game for sentiment. If Charlie Harvey had contracted for him to fight Wells, then Wells it would be – and, besides, it would be a good payday for Matt.

Two weeks later found TK and Alec on board the SS *Olympic* bound for Southampton. Elsie, Morton, TK's mother, father, two brothers, and one sister, were to follow as soon as he settled in. His parents were delighted at the news for though they had enjoyed New York, they were looking forward to seeing their two married daughters and grandchildren.

Although he had been extremely popular in London at the time he had sailed for Australia, TK had not realized how many friends his victories in the States had won him amongst the British fight fans.

As the ship docked, a swarm of newspaper reporters sought him out. Also on the quay to greet him was Joe Beckett, the British heavyweight champion, who was training at Southampton. Arriving at Waterloo Station, TK was amazed to find hundreds of sports fans, many of whom had been waiting for hours to catch a sight of the East End boy who'd not only won the world crown twice, but won them both in the States. TK's eyes were shining and he was close to tears as people pressed forward to slap him on the back or to shake his hand. Here and there he managed to call out to friends of the old days before being swept through the barrier. It was a reception he was never to recall without tears welling up in his eyes.

His first visit was to Gardiner's Corner, to call on the cafés where he'd hung about as a boy, and to walk the streets through which he'd led the Jewish lads to battle against the waiting goys. Everywhere there were handshakes and applause. Gershon, as he was to his friends, was King of the East End.

However, the prospect of fighting Wells did not fill him with pleasure: 'Matt and I had been staunch pals for some time in the States and he had frequently been in my corner and we were very fond of one another. However, Matt later explained he had been given a very tempting offer and he hated to refuse so large a sum of money.'

The contest was the first of a series of big fights to be held at the Royal Albert Hall, and great interest was being shown. TK thus went into hard training at the Star and Garter in Windsor. Crowds turned up every day to watch him, and he even had the assistance of several Guardsmen stationed in the town.

'It was here that I got a little of my own back on Sid Burns. . . I still retained memories of the hidings I took from him a few years back when he was in training for his welterweight title fight with Johnny Summers. Now I engaged him as my sparring partner and I repaid the debt I owed him. But Sid was a real asset, his knowledge was unlimited and he took all that came his way with a smile.'

On the day before the fight, Charlie Harvey arrived, escorting Elsie and Morton. TK had not wanted to break training, so he had sent his sister Bessie and her husband Manny Littlestone, who had never met Elsie, to Southampton with just a photograph to identify them. When they duly arrived at the Star and Garter Hotel there was, quite naturally, a reunion celebration. In fact, Charlie Harvey was never to forget it.

'Up till then he had been twenty years without touching strong drink but the occasion called for something and I made him "break the pledge". . . We broke a bottle of champagne, toasted the King and then toasted everyone else, after which I bade them goodnight.'

Next morning Harvey was missing at the breakfast table, and no one had seen a sight of him. TK went to his room and found him lying on his bed fully clothed with ten or more empty champagne bottles around him! It took almost half an hour to bring him round and then he had to be put back to bed until it was time to attend the weigh-in ceremony in London.

However, the biggest laugh TK had and which he used as a party piece for years to come concerned Elsie, not Harvey.

As Elsie boarded the Southampton boat train, she noticed a Bovril poster, and during the train journey to Victoria Station Bovril posters were to be seen everywhere as they passed from station to station. About twenty minutes out of Southampton, she turned to Bessie and said, 'Gee, this Bovril sure is a big town!'

The tournament at the Albert Hall was the first time that big boxing had come to this grotesque Victorian wedding cake of an edifice. The Barry Brothers were promoting, and they promised TK two further contests if he made a good showing. After all, he had not been seen in England for nearly six years.

This first tournament turned out to be a disappointment for the promoters because the boxing fans had evidently decided that it was more prudent to sleep off their Christmas Day after-effects than to venture out to Kensington on a night lashed by hail and rain.

The referee was that famous entrepreneur of boxing, J.T. Hulls, and TK had George Shinn and Sid Slogg in his corner with, of course, Alec Goodman.

Matt Wells was almost as embarrassed as TK when they touched gloves in the centre of the ring, for he, too, remembered TK with considerable affection. But both were professionals, and though they might not relish fighting each other, it was a job to be done and they were paid to give of their best.

TK opened at full speed, and quite bewildered his robust opponent as he darted in and out, throwing combinations of punches. All Matt could do was to grab his tormentor and try to hold him still long enough to get at least a short punch into his body. But the referee was having none of this. Immediately, he stopped the contest and warned Wells that they were there to box, not wrestle. On the bell, TK landed a left hook of such force that it threw him off balance, as well as rocking Wells back on his heels.

The second round came and TK hotted up the pace, with Wells unable to cope with TK's speed and punching power. All he could do was to try to hold and to hit, which incurred further warnings from J.T. Hulls.

By the third round, few in the ringside conceded Wells much of a chance as a vicious left hook opened a gash over his right eye and his mouth began to seep blood. But Wells was nothing if not brave, and though taking a continual beating, mauled and wrestled his way through round after round, until many in the crowd were calling for the referee to stop the contest. TK threw everything he had to try to finish the fight to save Matt going the distance. As TK had to make a good showing, he had to continue to do his best. This slaughter continued round after round. Matt could have gone down from any one of the dozens of punches he received, but he was tough and brave.

By the twelfth round TK and the ring canvas were covered with Matt's blood. The referee stepped between the boxers and said, 'Sufficient', to the relief of TK and the spectators. Even then Matt Wells had his little joke. He turned to J.T. Hulls and said, 'I've been trying to think of that word for the last nine rounds!' Matt used this story whenever given the opportunity at dinners or at the many boxing classes he supervised. After the referee held up TK's hand to signify the winner, the two friends clasped each other, and TK told him, 'It would have been different a few years ago.' Wells couldn't answer. For once in his life he was lost for words, but his expression showed his gratitude for this generosity on the part of his opponent. As well as his purse, TK was awarded a gold cup. Once more, Mr Mendeloff carefully examined the hallmark before remarking: 'This is real gold. This we shall keep.'

Elsie fell in love with London. Until now she had never been outside the States and, indeed, had travelled very little in America before marrying TK. She had been apprehensive about coming to England. The image she had was that all the English were snobs and that she would be expected to curtsy to the aristocracy, who she would no doubt meet daily. Instead she found herself warmly welcomed by all her husband's admirers; furthermore, at parties when she did encounter London society, she was delighted to find it very little different from the rest – just as eager to shake TK's hand and to hail him intimately as 'Ted', 'Kid' or 'Gershon'.

As for Solomon Mendeloff, he spent his days in Whitechapel, talking all the time about his son's success in the States and about what a magnificent house they had there, until his old cronies, who had welcomed his return, began to wish that if everything about America was so wonderful, he would return there at the earliest opportunity.

The tournament at the Royal Albert Hall had cost the promoters too much money for them to show any eagerness to take up their option on TK's services. Anyway, as far as the Albert Hall was concerned. But they were also promoting in Manchester and they matched TK, a fortnight later, against Frank Moody, a heavy-punching, square-faced middleweight of whom great deeds were expected.

But TK was anxious to prove to the British fight fans that he was ready for an immediate tilt at the home title, currently held by Johnny Basham. Immediately on the bell, he crossed the ring and hit Moody with two left hooks to his prominent jaw. Moody was thrown out of his stride with the speed of the assault and fell back. TK nailed him with an overhand right and Moody crashed to the canvas to be counted out. The bout lasted sixteen seconds, including the count.

After the contest, TK received a most welcome visitor in his dressing room: Ernest Mogford, his old backer. Mogford still took a proprietary interest in TK and told him: 'Paris is the European boxing Mecca today, Gersh. As soon as I heard you were coming over, I contacted the promoters at the Boxing Club de Paris. They want you next month against Prunier, an up and coming Froggy welterweight.'

Charlie Harvey grimaced. He was the manager, and here was an amateur having the impertinence to usurp his office. 'But do you get a square deal there? Can you trust the Frenchies?'

'As far as you can trust anyone in this game . . . even an American,' TK remarked quietly. And Charlie Harvey, no doubt with memories of certain of his past transactions at TK's expense, coloured.

Harvey tried again. 'It's just I don't want you taken for a ride, TK. You can never trust the frogs.'

Ernest Mogford was about to interpose a comment, when TK anticipated him. 'This is your first French trip, Charlie. I've fought in Paris before and have no complaints. So let's fix it, shall we?'

It was put as a question but Charlie Harvey had no doubts as to the real meaning. He contented himself with a 'Well, I hope it's OK. But the money better be right.'

The money was right and the match was made at the welterweight limit. Elsie, despite TK's encouragement, had decided to stay in England; she was still so engrossed in discovering London and setting up house that Paris held no immediate attractions for her.

Without her presence, Ted enjoyed the Paris cuisine rather more than he should have done, with the result that at the weigh-in, to Alec's and his surprise, he was a 1¼ lb. overweight. Prunier could have claimed forfeit, but instead clapped TK on the shoulder: 'I do not claim francs from so great a fighter. I am proud to meet him.'

Prunier's manager, however, insisted that TK make the limit within two hours. TK and Alec went to the local steam baths and within an hour, made the stipulated weight, at 4.30 pm. They returned to TK's hotel for a meal of raw eggs and milk and went to bed.

Prunier's style was similar to the American fighters', for he was a busy, two-fisted puncher. The French fans were standing on their chairs by the end of the first round and were kept there throughout the following eight rounds as the two men punched away without pause. By the ninth round, however, the gallant Frenchman was exhausted and a combination of straight left, left hook and following right stretched him unconscious at TK's feet.

The French fans gave them both a tremendous reception, for their man was young and would, no doubt, have learned much from this encounter with a fighter who was now one of the most experienced in the world. They also gave the referee, J.H. Douglas, generous applause for his handling of a contest which could so easily have got out of control.

At the ringside for this contest was Georges Carpentier, the Orchid Man, now the idol of the French crowd. Apart from his good looks, his skill and his savage punching, he had a fine record as a wartime pilot. When the referee had counted the final second over the inert Prunier, Carpentier was one of the first through the ropes to shake TK's hand. The French light heavyweight champion had good reason to like British boxers, for he had already accounted for Bandsman Rice, Bombardier Billy Wells – twice having knocked out the handsome British heavyweight champion – Dick Smith and Joe Beckett.

Despite this outstanding record, TK immediately issued a challenge. Carpentier grinned: 'Of course, I will fight you, Ted. But not yet.'

'Why not?'

'Because I have another fight . . . I am matched to meet Jack Dempsey. And if you should beat me. . .' The French champion spread his hands expressively, '*Pouf* goes so many, many dollars.'

Naturally TK was disappointed, but these were facts he could not contradict. He envied the Frenchman his opportunity but, remembering the Manassa Mauler's power, looked almost sympathetically at the comparatively lightly built French fighter.

Instead, TK met Jerry Shea at Mountain Ash and treated the Welsh fight fans to a sixty-second exhibition of non-stop punching by which time Shea, an extremely durable fighter, was lying against the ropes, quite unable to defend himself, and the fight was over in one minute.

Four days later found TK facing Gus Platts, the Sheffield publican, over twenty rounds, at 11 st. Platts, who only just managed to make the weight, was tough and experienced. He was determined to be there at the last bell and, though taking a trouncing in every round, had the fans of his home town yelling with excitement as it appeared that he might do what no other fighter had done since TK's return . . . require the referee to give a verdict.

But in the eighteenth, TK unleashed his most vicious attack, and, much against the wishes of their principal, the Sheffield man's seconds sent the towel fluttering over the ropes.

Seven days later TK was fighting again, this time with an added incentive, for the British middleweight title was at stake. There

Elsie's engagement picture, 1916

TK sent this picture to Elsie Schneider a few weeks after their first meeting in 1915

TK and Elsie in Milan for the Bruno Frattini fight, 1924

Elsie and TK on their ruby wedding anniversary, 1957

Morton and Elsie pose for the press while TK trained for the
1921 Basham fight

TK's favourite car, 1922

Morton, Elsie and Mingtoy on board the SS *Union Castle,* travelling to South Africa

Morton at the door to the cricket nets where he was knocked out by a ball hit by Frank Woolley, who also took this picture

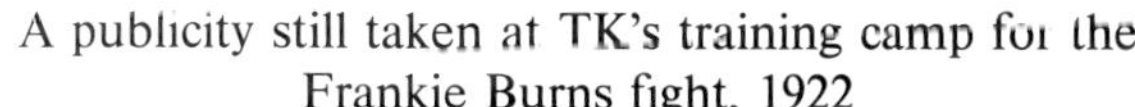

A publicity still taken at TK's training camp for the Frankie Burns fight, 1922

One of TK's greatest pleasures was to entertain at his children's outings

Second Lieutenant (Instructor) US army

Presented to TK by George VI when, as Duke of York, he was inspecting the Boxers in Uniform, 1919

Hungary, 1927. TK poses with his army boxing squad
Morton is on the right

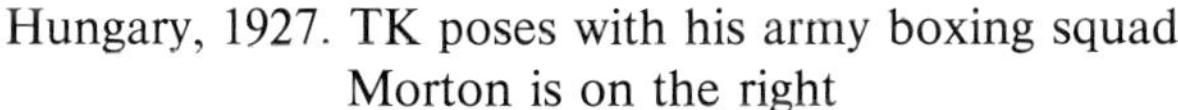

TK leading the reception cheers for Jack Dempsey's arrival at
Southampton, 1922

At the Anglo-American Sporting Club, 1967. TK with promoter Mickey
Duff, manager George Biddles, boxer Wally Swift and Jack Dempsey

Charlie Chaplin (Morton's godfather) entertaining TK at his studios in Hollywood

TK tries to match Douglas Fairbanks's agility at his home in Hollywood

TK with old opponent Maxie Rosenbloom (left) working on a film set with George Raft, also a former boxer

TK refereeing the Jack Hood/Vince Dundee bout. London, 1931

TK discussing his fight ticket with a young Reg Gutteridge
at Jack Solomons' gymnasium. 1947

had been much argument as to who had the soundest claim to the title, and the NSC had been talking of matching Jim Sullivan with Tom Gummer for the title. Charles B. Cochran, however, had other ideas, and beat the Club for the championship by matching TK with Johnny Bee of Birkenhead. Although 'CB' was offering a far larger purse than the Club, they, of course, had the Lonsdale Belt to encircle the waist of the winner of their version.

The contest lasted only four rounds, Bee being down three times in the first round, and once in the second and third. The fourth ended in a quick knockout. Tom Gummer won the NSC version of the championship, so it seemed only logical that he and TK should meet to remove any doubts as to who the real champion was. But Gummer made such extravagant claims that no promoter could have afforded the contest, and so British boxing had two middleweight champions, both of whom were confident that theirs was the only justifiable claim.

Whilst waiting for a chance to fight Johnny Basham for the welterweight crown, TK took on Kid Doyle at 11 st. 8 lb., at Liverpool Stadium. On 5 April, he stopped Doyle in eleven rounds, and three weeks later repeated the dose at the Stadium Club in five rounds.

By now, arrangements had been made for the Basham contest. In all, three titles would be at stake: the British and Empire titles, held by Basham, and the European title won by TK from Albert Badoud.

Johnny Basham was one of the most popular sportsmen in England. Not only was he a most skilful boxer, who had won a Lonsdale Belt outright, but he was good-natured and always had a warm welcome for his fans. The public interest in the match was tremendous, and the fighters were matched to meet at Olympia on 9 June 1920. The purse was £5,000 – £3,000 for the winner and £2,000 for the loser.

The story was a 'natural' and the press made the most of it. Photographers dogged TK as he ran in the early morning through the Brighton streets, where he'd taken up his training quarters. His favourite photograph showed him wheeling a motorbike with his young son, Morton, perched on the handlebars.

Unfortunately, his return to Brighton also heralded his return to gambling. He had never been able to resist betting upon the turn of a card or on dice. But since his marriage he had at least kept this mania in some sort of control. But Brighton had always been the British Mecca of gamblers, and soon he was venturing large sums.

On the night of the fight there wasn't an empty seat in the arena. Ted Kid Lewis was back, and he gave the fans what they wanted, ability and personality. He brought class and made British boxing big-time entertainment. His fight with Basham was to sweep away all his financial worries for some time to come. It was to re-establish him on the international stage and was the first of three tough fights he was to have with Basham.

'What a game fellow Johnny was that June night. I split his lip in the third round and the blood spurted unceasingly from it, bathing my chest and trunks in blood. All the time he kept up a running fire of light-hearted comment while we were fighting, though he must have known that his chances of victory were very slender with such a handicap to carry.

'What a fuss he kicked up when Danny Davies threw in the towel at the end of the ninth round. One would have thought his best girl had been stolen from him by this action, instead of it saving him eleven more rounds of punishment. . .'

And Ted Kid Lewis was the new champion.

Ted Lewis—Being Generous

20 Transatlantic Commuter

'Don't be silly Darby. Me beat Kid Lewis? The world's greatest fighter? Didn't I go the full twenty rounds with him? That's good enough for me!'

Jack Bloomfield

As the holder of three titles, TK wasn't lacking enticing offers, and not only to fight. The music-hall producers realized the attraction of his popularity and arranged a tour for him. TK's act was much more polished than it had been when he had toured six years earlier. He was altogether more confident and assured.

He would enter from the wings in his dressing gown and stand talking to the audience; describing his fights and answering their questions. Then the curtain would rise behind him to reveal a ring. He'd skip for a round and then shadow-box. After that, his sparring partners entered the act, so that apart from making him money, the tour also kept him in fair condition.

This was the heyday of silent films, and few suspected that within a few years the stars would be speaking aloud and many of the favourites of the day would pass into obscurity. A film company offered TK a small part. He accepted. The strong spotlights, the making-up and the excitement were very much to his taste. Many professional champions have toured the halls and tried their hands at films, men like Jack Johnson, Jack Dempsey, John L. Sullivan, Robert Fitzsimmons and Max Baer. But TK had far more inherent talent than most of them.

The Dempsey-Carpentier championship contest had run into difficulties, and it seemed as if it might be postponed. TK, therefore, renewed his challenge to the Frenchman.

Carpentier was impressed by TK's persistence; but there seemed to be little glory in beating a man so much lighter and Carpentier left for the States to fight Battling Levinsky for the world lightweight crown.

In the meantime, TK received a cable from New York: 'Have

possibility of title fight against Britton, how soon can you come over, regards Charlie Harvey'. With a match against Carpentier shelved for the time being, TK didn't need much persuading to try to regain his title. He went home and exclaimed to Elsie, with what was to become an ongoing catch-phrase with the Lewis family, 'Pack up, we're leaving'. Elsie was getting used to TK's impetuous decisions, and knew how badly he wanted to be champion again. So with bags packed, TK, accompanied by his mother, father, Elsie and two-year-old son, sailed for New York.

Charlie Harvey embraced TK on arrival, shouting to the newspapermen that this time he and TK would make a million. But TK was less gullible than he had been in the past. Now, when his manager talked so confidently, he suspected a hidden meaning in the words.

And he was right. 'Dumb' Dan Morgan had refused to let Britton fight TK. Instead, he was contracted to fight Mike O'Dowd.

For a moment TK was angry. He had come to fight Jack Britton and to regain his world welterweight championship. Instead, he was to fight O'Dowd, a man over 18 1b. heavier, who had already given him a hot time in three contests. There was little to gain in beating O'Dowd and much to lose. But TK could never resist a challenge and a chance to make money and once more allowed his manager to manoeuvre him into the position of accepting a contest which could not be remotely in his interest. Furthermore, he found that Charlie Harvey and his former partner, the 'Boy Bandit', had buried their past disagreements and were working together again. He had thought himself free of Jay Jay's tentacles . . . but it was not to be. The octopus of the American fight game had him tied once more to a manager of dubious repute.

Elsie, naturally, was pleased to be back with her mother who had been sad to see her daughter sail for England. Now Elsie was busy finding a new home and telling all her family and friends about London and how she had been received by Teddy's multitudinous fans.

O'Dowd was still the middleweight champion of the world, since beating Al McCoy in 1917. He was to defend his title against Johnny Wilson, so it was vital for him to maintain an unbeaten record. The result was that he and TK served up a vicious, unrelenting fight. Try as he would, TK was unable to overcome the substantial weight disadvantage. It was a no-decision contest and TK shared the newspaper verdicts.

TK still had Carpentier in his sights, however, and he managed to upstage the Frenchman by seizing the opportunity to fight Carpentier's sparring partner – Marcel Thomas – on the same bill as the Carpentier-Levinsky contest. The fans were still talking about TK's skill and speed when the immaculate Carpentier climbed through the ropes for his world title contest – a contest which ended summarily when he stopped Levinsky in the fourth round.

Once again TK threw out his challenge but still Carpentier ignored him, preferring to concentrate on trying to entice the Manassa Mauler into the ring.

TK became restless, sidetracked by Britton, with the trip so far only bringing him two meaningless contests. The fact that Harvey and Johnston were giving him excuses for lack of work made him frustrated because he was losing time that could never be recovered. He began to think his luck had run out when he received a cable from Major Arnold Wilson who had taken over promoting at the Royal Albert Hall, offering terms to defend his three welterweight titles against Johnny Basham. Elsie was disappointed; she had started to make the flat very comfortable, hoping they would be able to settle in New York. But TK explained his situation, that the offer from London was too good to turn down and, if a bout was arranged with Britton, they would return. TK cabled his acceptance and, with his entourage, 'packed up' once again and sailed for home.

On the night of the Basham fight, the Albert Hall was packed for many of Basham's supporters – especially his Welsh countrymen – were convinced that he had only been beaten the last time by the savage injury he had received to his mouth so early in the contest. Furthermore, they knew that Johnny Basham was the sort of fighter who learned from every contest. Certainly, Basham had realized that at in-fighting Lewis was his master and this time he resolved to keep the contest at long range.

Basham had trained assiduously and at the weigh-in was 10 st. 6 lb. in his vest and boxing gear. TK had been taken ill once again in training, a secret which had been kept from the press. He had suffered an internal haemorrhage for which the doctor could find no explanation. It later turned out to be bleeding piles. Thus, looking even more drawn than usual, he weighed in at 10 st. 4½ lb. and was so pale that the odds which had started at three to one shortened to seven to four!

Johnny Basham entered the ring first to a mighty roar of 'Land of My Fathers'. TK's supporters were no less noisy and this was what he needed. The crowd were with him – a big smile came over his face. He acknowledged the cheers, walked over and shook hands with Basham, and then proceeded to shake hands with numerous friends, leaning through the ropes to reach them. This was a show of real confidence; he now looked and felt like a real champion and he was back in his element (as the Pathe Newsreel of the event reveals).

TK was determined to repeat the dose of their first meeting. His plan was to work his way inside, and to cut Basham up at close quarters and, at the same time, because of his internal pains, he would have to pace himself so that he would still be strong in the twentieth round, should the contest go the distance.

The contest opened at a fast rate with Basham using his skill at feinting and side-stepping to keep the champion on the end of his left hand. In this he was most successful and try as TK would, he could not penetrate that long, classic left hand. Once more 'Land of My Fathers' rent the air as the Welsh enthusiasts saw their man regaining his titles. TK had to continue to pace and conserve his strength for a grandstand finish.

The betting was now five to two on Basham, because although his face and ear were in very bad shape, he was well ahead on points and TK would have to knock him out to win. As he prepared to leave his corner for the nineteenth, TK could hear his friends still taking the odds. This made him determined to put Basham away; he had two rounds to do the business and not let his supporters down.

TK left his stool as the bell went, intent on doing damage, and Basham, on instructions from his corner, to box and move and keep out of trouble. TK took all the left-hand shots and kept shuffling forward. He then leaped in with a one-two punch, only to receive a left hook on the chin. They reached the centre of the ring when TK measured Basham with his left, followed by a right cross. The Welshman's legs became rubber. He stumbled backwards and hit the canvas. He rose at five. When TK had a man on the hook, he never let him go. He chased Basham around the ring, landing with every punch he threw. The Welshman backed on to the ropes and TK had him. He came in with a left hand and, in desperation, Basham threw his best ever right, which landed flush on TK's chin. TK took his medicine and at the same time threw his right to Basham's chin, which left him floundering and swaying. TK followed this up with a smashing double left hook and the Welshman crashed to the boards. All but unconscious, Johnny Basham began to claw his way up the ropes. He struggled to his feet at six, but the referee decided the end had come and raised TK's hand – he was still triple champion.

Despite this clear victory, the National Sporting Club still disputed TK's claim but, as far as the boxing fans and the press were concerned, Ted Kid Lewis was now established beyond all doubt as the top welterweight in Britain, Europe and the Empire.

With reports of the contest being featured in the American papers, Johnston and Harvey were overwhelmed with offers for TK's services. At first TK ignored their urgent cables, until the offer came that he had been secretly hoping for – to fight Jack Britton for the championship in New York. But the fight was not immediate, so he took a holiday motoring round the Sussex Downs, proudly introducing his son Morton to everyone he met. Elsie was impressed again by the warmth and naturalness of all the fans she met. A walk along Brighton Parade was in the nature of a royal procession. Every few yards they would be stopped and Ted, with Morton's little hand in his, would say: 'And this is my son.' His pride in his offspring was ingenuous and endeared him to all he met.

Early in the New Year, the Lewis family sailed for the States. On board ship, TK boxed every morning with members of the crew, and so famous was he by now that they queued up for the chance to share a ring with him. A black eye at the gloves of the champion was a disfigurement of which any sailor could be proud. The passengers would flock to watch the champion every day and TK's delight was to see Elsie, sitting ringside, controlling Morton's excitement in the occasion.

This was the nearest Elsie had been to see her husband in the ring and, even though they were wearing big 16-ounce sparring gloves, she couldn't bear to see one of his sparring partners, however occasionally, land a punch on his face. Elsie saw little of TK during the voyage for when he wasn't training, he would be shooting crap or playing cards with anybody who was willing – and there were plenty of takers. As always, his enthusiasm for gambling wasn't matched by his skill as a boxer. He was a big spender and everywhere he went on board, he treated his admirers. He had earned many thousands of pounds but even now, with a championship fight just behind him, he was short of ready money by the time the ship docked at New York.

Charlie Harvey and Jimmy Johnston were at the docks to meet and escort them to their new apartment. Once installed, TK started training for his fight with Jack Britton. During a break in training, TK went to watch a team of British amateurs boxing an American team. TK and Alec started to give loud vocal encouragement to the British boys. Their English accents brought cat-calls from the American spectators. Mallin, Chandler, Brown and Watson did well and were all grateful to TK and Alec for their tremendous support.

The championship fight was staged in Madison Square Garden over fifteen rounds, but the arguments between Morgan and Johnston surfaced once again over TK's gumshield. Although TK was the first to wear a gumshield and by now the majority of American boxers wore such protection, Britton did not. Morgan would not let him fight if TK did not remove it. TK, against his manager's advice, took out the gumshield and by the time the fight got under way almost everyone except TK had lost their temper.

Throughout the contest, TK maintained his attack, but Britton boxed beautifully, outsmarting TK and keeping the contest at long range. At the last bell, there could have been little between them, but the judges decided that Britton had done enough to keep his title. The two boxers embraced each other and Britton told him, 'You're a great guy. You shall have another crack at the title, I promise you.'

TK thought he had done enough to win but had to content himself with the thought that he would get another crack at the title.

With Britton's promise in his mind, TK decided it was politic to stay in America and wait for his next chance. To keep in top condition he told Johnston to fix more fights for him. The 'Boy Bandit', delighted with the prospect of a rich harvest, agreed with enthusiasm, and four weeks after losing to Britton TK took on Jack Perry over ten rounds, no-decision, in Detroit. Three weeks later he took on middleweight Nate Siegel in Boston – and lost on points. A week later, with a 12 1b. weight advantage, Augie Ratner took a fifteen-round points decision from him in New York. It was a moment of truth.

TK was faced with the unpalatable fact that he had lost three out of his last four contests. Something was missing. He trained as enthusiastically as ever. He was sure he could punch as fast and as hard as he had ever done; but somehow his timing was at fault. At night he wasn't sleeping and Elsie found him irritable and tetchy.

Dan Morgan, meanwhile, still smarting over the insults thrown by Jay Jay during their championship fight, made it clear that there was little chance of a twenty-first meeting with Britton.

So, when TK received an invitation from the NSC to defend his middleweight title against Jack Bloomfield, he was delighted. Elsie was not surprised when TK told her, 'I've accepted a fight in London.' It was her third trip. Once more, the Lewis and Mendeloff families packed their bags and sailed for England.

For the contest with Jack Bloomfield, the NSC decided to change its usual venue and to stage the bout at the Holland Park Skating Rink – the very first time they were to award a belt outside the club. Apart from the purse, Jack Bloomfield's backer offered a sidestake of £1,000 on the result, which TK took up personally.

J.H. Douglas refereed what proved to be a somewhat dull contest for, though Jack Bloomfield was a skilled boxer, he showed great respect for TK's reputation by never opening out and leaving it to TK to do all the attacking. If TK had fought the same way, there would have been no contest at all. TK won well and his father crowed with pleasure as he assessed the value of the new Lonsdale Belt.

Once more TK toured the country for two months with his music-hall act. It was good for his income, but not for his training which, compared to his work in the theatre, was becoming a chore. He liked the life in the theatre. However, TK received a letter from Harvey saying that he was arranging with Morgan for a return bout with Britton for the title. He added that there was a lot of work in the States now available and he advised TK to return there as soon as there was money to be made in the meantime.

With a contract for a title fight with Johnny Basham in October already signed, TK considered the risk worth taking, and so the Lewis family 'packed up' and departed once more for the States. TK hurried to meet Harvey in his office on arrival, only to find that nothing concrete had been settled and the Britton fight looked unlikely to materialize.

Harvey and Johnston had done it again. They had fallen out with the managers' 'ring' and though TK spent much of his time issuing challenges to every middleweight of note, there were no takers. With two families to support and with over two months since his last fight, TK was once again running short of money.

He was offered a fight in Toronto on 20 September, however, against the Canadian welterweight champion Ernie Barrieau and he immediately cabled his acceptance. It was a way out – he could earn enough money in Toronto to get everyone back to the United Kingdom. Thus he and Alec left on 16 September, leaving Elsie and Morton in New York.

In Toronto TK spoiled the evening for the Canadian spectators by knocking out their champion in the tenth round. He was pleased with his performance, and was once more in funds.

Returning to New York the next day, TK checked with Harvey and Johnston to see if any fights were coming up. He received the same answer, 'Nothing settled yet'. TK was becoming worried, the fights were fewer and further apart, his money was now going out faster than he could get work in the States, and besides, it was almost time to return to London for the Johnny Basham fight. So, once again, the Lewis and the Mendeloff families packed up and left for England.

TK was able to do some training on the ship – more to keep himself occupied and the passengers entertained than to keep fit. They arrived in London and moved into Manor House, a new block of flats in Marylebone Road, while TK set up training camp at Wembley. With Alec now deciding to retire to take a pub down in Brighton, TK engaged Jack Goodwin to look after him, assisted by Alf Mansfield, the former flyweight champion. Three weeks' strict training did TK the world of good and he was in better condition than he had been for the past two years. He was still annoyed at being unable to secure a return bout with Britton. This seemed to add to his punching power from which his sparring partners had to suffer.

The Royal Albert Hall was packed to capacity when Johnny Basham entered the ring, and once again Pathe News covered the proceedings, as the film of their first two fights proved most successful. TK entered the ring in his usual manner, smiling as he acknowledged the applause from the packed house. Once again after shaking hands with his opponent, as the Pathe News Film shows, he walked to the ringside and shook hands with his friends through the ropes.

They did not use the first round as a feeler. Basham decided to use his boxing skill, but TK had other ideas, the mean streak. Johnny was going to suffer because of Britton. The spectators were going to see TK at his best. He would show them why the press called him 'The Smashing, Dashing, Crashing Kid'. Basham had all his work cut out in trying to keep out of trouble as round followed round. TK bombarded his opponent with every punch in the book. By the ninth round, Basham was a sorry sight, bleeding from cuts to his eye and mouth, with a left ear the size of his fist. Basham forbade his corner to throw in the towel. Near the end of the eleventh, Basham went down for a count of nine from a vicious right hand, only to be saved by the bell. Once again he argued with his seconds to allow him to continue.

The bell went for the twelfth round and TK decided to end the massacre, and immediately went into a two-handed attack. Basham instinctively tried to keep away but there was no way. He was reduced to a helpless bloodstained mess as TK landed a combination of six punches to the head, the last one splitting Basham's ear. The blood covered both men. TK backed off and looked pleadingly at the referee who went to stop the slaughter as the towel floated in.

TK was now holder of five titles and looked for other fields to conquer. He issued a challenge to fight Joe Beckett for the heavyweight title, with a side-stake of £5,000, but Beckett wasn't interested. So Major Arnold Wilson immediately proposed to TK that he fight Boy McCormick, the light-heavyweight champion of Great Britain, who had just taken on Joe Beckett for his heavyweight title. McCormick had shown good for twelve rounds until Beckett's weight and punching took its toll.

TK jumped at the chance. A victory would mean that Carpentier would have one less excuse for not wanting to meet him.

The fight took place at the Holland Park Rink, and the newsreels show that TK outclassed McCormick until the fourteenth round when the referee stopped the contest. TK was now Britain's premier boxer and in demand both in and out of the ring.

Wherever he went he was recognized, asked for his autograph, slapped on the back. One evening in London's Kit Kat club, an incident ocurred that demonstrated how much of a national celebrity he had become: '. . . a man came over and whispered in my ear. I was delighted with his question. When the band struck up, the Prince of Wales came over and asked Elsie to dance. Afterwards, he brought her back, we shook hands and he bowed to Elsie – how about that!'

Following the McCormick victory, TK put in another three weeks in the music-halls and, at the same time, took over the Premierland to promote boxing in partnership with Joe Morris as manager and co-promoter. Matt Wells and Ted Moore topped the bill on the opening night in December 1921. The gate was quite fair and TK was now in business.

By defeating McCormick, TK could have claimed the light-heavyweight championship, as they were both inside the weight limit, but as it didn't include the Lonsdale Belt, TK didn't bother.

But TK was not satisfied with his last performance. He was looking despondent, and Elsie told him so. 'You should take a rest from boxing, you look tired, you've had a fight nearly every month.'

TK tried to defend himself. 'I only had eight fights this year, and in 1917 I had twenty-eight and won the world title as well.'

Elsie eyed TK nervously. 'That was four years ago and you were younger then.'

'Younger!' TK exclaimed. 'I'm only twenty-eight and not ready for the old age home yet.'

This was the first time she had the opportunity of guiding him; she couldn't stop now. 'But you've been fighting and training for nearly fifteen years. You said yourself that there was something wrong with your stomach, whatever that means. Why not try to take a real rest?'

TK could see some logic in what Elsie said. 'Well, Jack Callaghan wants me to meet Tom Gummer at the Dome in Brighton in February. That's three months away. I can lay off boxing until then, and accept the offer of six weeks touring the music-halls. How about that?'

Elsie considered that better than nothing, and smiled.

'Besides, the money's good on the halls.' TK felt he had complied with her wishes.

Following the successful music-hall tour, TK got down to serious training at Maidenhead for the fight with Tom Gummer, made at 11 st. 6 lb.

At the weigh-in on 16 February 1922, TK was well inside the limit – he did not need to remove his overcoat in fact. . . But when Tom Gummer stepped on to the scales, the arm rocketed, hitting the metal stop with a bang! More weights were added and TK eventually burst out laughing, when 13 st. 10 lb. finally settled the scales. However, TK waived the forfeit, declaring that he would fight Gummer even if he weighed a ton; after all, the boxing show at the Dome, Brighton, was in aid of one of Sir Harry Preston's charities. In fact, Sir Harry visited TK's training camp on several occasions for publicity purposes and had become firm friends with Elsie and TK. It had been Sir Harry himself who had persuaded and cajoled Elsie to come to the Brighton fight: 'It's a charity show and you would lend a little class to the affair.' Elsie had looked questioningly at TK who had replied: 'It's a good idea: you should see me in action.' And she had agreed.

The Dome was packed, and once more Pathe News was there. Elsie sat between Georges Carpentier and Sir Harry, trying not to look nervous. Georges was doing his best to explain what was going on during the preliminaries. Then Gummer entered the ring to a good reception from his followers, to be followed by a tumultuous roar as TK climbed through the ropes. He didn't do his customary hand-shaking with the ringsiders, but nodded and smiled at Elsie and her two escorts. He was determined to put up a good show in front of Carpentier who was now the one man he wanted to fight more than anyone else. It had become an obsession with him. TK sat on his stool, waiting for the bell, and rolling his gloves on his thighs as he clenched his fists inside them.

At the bell, he wasted no time. He tore into the middle of the ring and threw a right-hand which landed on Gummer's shoulder. If it had landed, the fight would have been over then and there. TK started a two-handed body attack which had his opponent holding on as tightly as possible. They both lost their balance and fell on the bottom ropes, with Gummer on top. Sir Harry held Elsie's hand to calm her down. She couldn't bear to see Gummer lying on top of TK. The referee parted them and in the centre of the ring, TK measured his opponent with a left, followed by a smashing right cross to the chin. Down went Gummer for a count. Elsie was battling too, to contain her excitement. Gummer rose at seven and grabbed TK with both arms. Two strong right-hands to the heart made Gummer release his hold and back away. TK sprang in with a perfect double left hook which can be seen clearly on the Pathe film – and Gummer collapsed in a heap as the referee reached five. Gummer tried to rise, and a woman's voice was heard shouting, 'Kill him, Teddy, kill him, Teddy.' TK turned slightly, to see Elsie on her feet, being restrained by both Carpentier and Sir Harry. She was, in fact, still calling out 'Kill him, Teddy,' after the referee had reached ten. TK smiled over to her and blew a kiss before walking over to console Gummer, then left the ring without waiting for the official announcement. He did this out of habit, as most of his fights in the States were no-decision bouts. He was immediately recalled and as he re-entered the ring, Elsie grabbed Georges. 'Does he have to knock him out again?'

Georges laughed, put his arm around her, 'No, he was called back to be declared the winner.'

'But he won, didn't he?' she questioned.

'Yes, but it's the boxing tradition to have his hand raised by the referee.'

Having showered and dressed in almost as many minutes as the fight took, he found Carpentier and Elsie with a number of other celebrities, including the press, at a party hosted by Sir Harry. Everyone was teasing Elsie who was still too excited to grasp the situation. TK entered and was congratulated by all as he made his way over to Elsie, and kissed her. A newspaper reporter asked what he had to say. TK laughed and pointed to Elsie. 'Elsie has just seen me fight for the last time.' He then turned with a smile to face Carpentier. 'Thanks for looking after Elsie,' he said. 'But why won't you fight me?'

Carpentier looked at Elsie with his handsome smile which had become so famous. 'I'd rather fight you than Elsie,' he said, and the room filled with laughter. 'That is, if you can get anyone to stage the bout.'

'I'll stage it!' said Major Arnold Wilson, standing near by. 'And I'll put it on at Olympia – and we'll charge twenty-five guineas for ringside seats.'

TK was bubbling over. He turned to Georges and calculated out loud. 'That's . . . one hundred and thirty-one dollars a seat. Why, Georges, they only paid fifty dollars a seat to see you and Dempsey.'

Georges smiled. 'Let's hope we give them their money's-worth.'

A reporter standing near by asked TK, 'Why were you in such a hurry with Gummer?'

TK smiled as he had his little joke. 'Well . . . I didn't want Georges to learn too much. And, besides, you don't get overtime in this business!'

21 Carpentier

'You could tell if they were hurt, and if they were you had to watch out for their dying Sunday punch, their last throw of the dice . . .'

TK

Thus at the modest Dome in Brighton, TK agreed to terms for the one contest he wanted above all others – though the formality of signing did not take place until several days later when the contracts read that the bout would take place at Olympia on 11 May 1922 at 12 st. 7 lb. And the prize? The light-heavyweight Championship of the World, and, for good measure, if TK won, it would include Carpentier's light-heavyweight and heavyweight championships of Europe. What an incentive!

The only condition was that Carpentier should nominate Joe Palmer as referee, to which TK readily agreed. All he said to the promoter was, 'As long as he can count up to ten'. TK was determined to stop his opponent inside the distance. But he would live to regret accepting Palmer as referee.

In every paper, the contest was headlines. Many sporting columnists pointed out that if TK could beat Carpentier when so much lighter, he would undoubtedly bear comparison with the ring giants of history. Others ventured words of warning and the old adage: 'A good big 'un will always lick a good little' 'un,' was frequently quoted.

TK trained for this most important contest at Harrow-on-the-Hill. He had always loved children and was creating a tradition by sending East End children for a seaside holiday twice a year. Now, once again, he thought of the children – or rather youths – for he applied to the headmaster for permission for the pupils of Harrow, the famous school, to be allowed to attend his training sessions.

As Alec Goodman was no longer in the fight game, he cabled Charlie Harvey to come and look after his interests. Harvey demanded $5,000 for his services and a first-class return fare to

New York, quite apart from training which could cost TK over £750. But TK knew the value of Harvey as a top-rate man in his corner and he agreed to Harvey's demands. Besides, at the same time, TK would now have the opportunity of proving that he too was a businessman.

Jack Dempsey made a special trip to see the fight, accompanied by his manager, Jack Kearns, and Joe Benjamin, his sparring partner. TK went to meet Jack and Joe at Southampton. Arnold Wilson gave a cocktail party in Jack's honour, and both TK and Carpentier were present.

Dempsey visited both training camps several times during his stay, to the delight of the reporters. During one of the visits, Jack made a cryptic remark to TK. 'If you can beat the Frenchman, we'll have a talk.'

Jack Kearns smiled and chimed in with, 'Yeah, it should draw a big gate.'

Whether this was just small talk or not, TK replied, 'Well, I'll do my best. I can't let an opportunity like that go by without trying.' TK meant it. He would fight anybody for money. He'd fought big men before – he knew no fear. After all, if he did beat Carpentier, he would be a big man in drawing power, if not in size.

Jack brought Joe Benjamin, his lightweight sparring partner, to the training camp to spar with TK. The spectators and press were given three rounds of fireworks which showed TK at his speediest. Sir Harry Lauder visited the Harrow-on-the-Hill training camp and had a rousing reception when he proceeded to make a speech. TK took the opportunity to raise some funds for the vicar of 'The Little Church Around the Corner', and went around the gym with a collecting box. Nobody refused, and when he reached Sir Harry, the press photographers asked for pictures, with Sir Harry putting in a half-crown. Immediately the pictures were taken, Sir Harry caused a roar of laughter as he put the half-crown back in his pocket. It was a joke on the part of the great comedian, who later put a pound note in the box.

TK's training camp became a rendezvous for many stars of the theatre such as Sophie Tucker, Josie Collins, Edith Day, Pat Somerset, Lord Oliver-Kerr, Harry Green, Stanley Lupino, the Marx Brothers, Syd Walker, Con Conrad, etc. And one day, just as TK finished, that great sportsman and financier, Woolf Joel, presented TK with a most magnificent gold-braided dressing gown, which bore the handiwork of practically every well-known cartoonist of the country.

'This is for you Ted . . . may it always bring you luck!' said Woolf. 'I have had the sleeves made double the size.' As he held it for TK to put on, 'So you don't have to struggle to get it on when you're wearing gloves.' TK was delighted and continued to wear it for many years.

Elsie and Morton made an occasional visit to Harrow when TK would jog around the packed gym all smiles with his son Morton on his shoulders for everyone to see. While TK would skip, punch the bag and spar, he would watch and see the famous personages shake his father's hand. He was too young yet to appreciate why the great ring giants, like his father, were focal points for the famous and the infamous.

The weigh-in took place at the Ring, Blackfriars. The arena was packed to the rafters and the crowd outside was so dense that extra police were called to control them. Carpentier tipped the scales at exactly 12 st. 7 lb., while TK, fully clothed, weighed in at 10 st. 10 lb. François Descamps, the Frenchman's voluble manager, looked slightly embarrassed when he saw how light TK was. His Georges could gain little glory in beating this little fellow. But Carpentier did not share this confidence. He had seen TK fight.

TK left for home where he had a light meal, followed by a walk through Regent's Park, and returned and went to bed for his customary sleep. The flat in Manor House, Marylebone, was packed with friends and family, all talking quietly so as not to disturb TK. A messenger brought a big cut-out black cat to be put near TK's corner. The note said, 'To our Champion. Break a leg.' It was the way theatrical people wished one another luck. It came from Stanley Lupino and Seymour Hicks.

At six o'clock, TK was awakened by Charlie Harvey and his trainer, Harry Stokes, who gave TK a thorough massage. During the hustle and bustle of excitement of leaving for the Olympia, Harvey forgot to take the lucky black cat. It was discovered in the car that it was missing, but it was too late to return.

The doctor who examined the boxers before they entered the ring declared later that while TK showed no evidence of nerves, Carpentier's heart was racing alarmingly.

The ring lights were extra bright – for Pathe News was there to record what was hoped to be the British fight of the century.

A tremendous reception greeted TK as he climbed through the ropes, sporting his new dressing gown. The whole East End seemed to have made a pilgrimage up town to cheer their idol.

Carpentier followed as world champion, receiving, for once, a mixed reception. Descamps declared that one of TK's supporters had actually kicked his ankle as he led his fighter down the gangway. Maybe this was true for he was so angry that he followed 'Dumb' Dan Morgan's example by declaring that TK would have to remove his gumshield before the fight could take place. This time, however, the promoter stood firm. The ringsiders booed, and the much criticized gumshield remained in place.

The Carpentier-Lewis fight will be talked about as long as boxing is allowed. Argument will never die and certainly – as a basis for disagreement – it ranks with the 'long count' between Dempsey and Gene Tunney.

TK had watched Georges Carpentier box and was determined to set the pattern for the contest and to be the 'guvnor' from the first bell. He met Carpentier in the centre of the ring, and as soon as he could draw a light left lead, stepped in with a hard right, which landed clean to the Frenchman's jaw. A look of apprehension flickered in the champion's eyes. Immediately, TK stepped in and drove both hands into the body. The referee tore them apart and the crowd, with an intake of breath, noticed the two tell-tale, raw patches on the Frenchman's body. TK shook himself and once again punched to the body. The champion grabbed TK's arms and held as the referee, Joe Palmer, again pulled them apart. Then, as TK stepped back, the Orchid Man threw a long left which landed low.

TK ignored the punch, and once again made the body his target. Now in-fighting, both fighters used their heads dangerously. They looked more like Roman gladiators fighting to the death than modern-day pugilists. The fight experts whispered to their companions that they were seeing as vicious and as uncompromising a fight as they'd ever seen . . . or were likely to see.

The referee had noticed the bitterness creeping in and took every opportunity to try to part the boxers, speaking to them all the time. 'Stop holding, both of you. Watch your heads.' The ringsiders could not understand why the referee was interfering with the action. But, even if Carpentier held or used his head, TK had no intention of changing his tactics. Immediately he set up a body attack which had the Frenchman hanging on. Once again Carpentier's counter-punch went low, and the boxers' heads crashed together with sickening impact.

Joe Palmer, the referee, prised them apart, this time issuing a warning to TK. 'Don't hold, Lewis.' TK stepped back. He wasn't holding. He was fighting the fight of his life. He looked with surprise at Palmer. Carpentier, seeing the opening as TK was still looking at the referee, threw his whole weight into a straight right cross, smashing on TK's jaw. The same punch nearly dropped Dempsey. TK slumped to the canvas. There he lay with staring eyes as the hall erupted in protest as the referee began his count. TK rose instinctively just after ten was called, still dazed. The rule requiring a boxer to stand in a neutral corner had not yet come into effect. Carpentier, who was standing very close to his fallen opponent, immediately jumped forward as TK rose to help him to his corner. He was trying to regain his image of a gentleman with the crowd. TK, realizing now what had happened, elbowed Carpentier away, who in turn instinctively ducked out of range, fearing that TK wanted to continue fighting.

TK believed to his dying day that Carpentier transgressed, if not the rules of boxing, then certainly the spirit of sportsmanship with a 'win at any cost punch'. Others remember the rules: 'A boxer shall defend himself at all times', but whatever were the rights or wrongs, as far as the record book is concerned, Ted Kid Lewis had been knocked out by Georges Carpentier in the first round.

TK had suffered from adverse decisions before, but no injustice had affected him as had this one. He said he was in better shape mentally and physically for this fight than he had been for years. He believed that he had not only let himself down, but also all his supporters. His pride was hurt. The anti-Carpentier critics were ably supported in their argument whenever the Pathe News film of the fight was shown.

As to the result of the contest which he had sought so avidly, TK's disappointment was mollified by an open letter to the press from Lord Lonsdale.

'Lewis scored more points than Carpentier, who was the original cause of the holding. The referee should have separated the men and made them stand back. When he put his hands on the men to separate them he should either have walked between them or sent them right back. This I imagine was his intention. From what I saw, it appeared that he had hardly taken his hand off Lewis before Carpentier delivered the blow. Carpentier committed an 'accidental' foul if he had not understood the referee. It was the referee's fault the accident occurred. Lewis scored more points and did more execution. He hit harder and marked Carpentier on his body and mouth. Carpentier butted no less than four times and should have been disqualified.'

The following day TK met Carpentier at a lunch given for them by Jack Dempsey, the world champion, whose comments to the press as to the impossibility of a man as light as Lewis giving away weight to Carpentier merely added to TK's fury. After all, Dempsey did not complain when he fought the lighter Carpentier. But Georges was, if anything, a master of diplomacy. Raising his voice so all could hear, he asked TK: 'I hope you have no ill feelings towards me? The fight was fair. This time I win . . . next time . . .' he shrugged his shoulders expressively.

TK, with difficulty, accepted his comments. 'OK. That is if you will . . . give me another chance.' The Frenchman nodded his agreement. But his manager, who was not known for philanthropy, made sure no other contest ever took place.

The next day, Jack Dempsey, who had been a close friend of TK's for the previous five years, published an apology for the words attributed to him, as having been misinterpreted.

As the years passed, TK was to meet Georges Carpentier many times at training camps, boxing matches or social functions. In Paris, inevitably the cameramen would pose them together. They became firm friends and the record shows that both of them suffered as 'the good little 'un' – Carpentier against Dempsey and TK against Georges.

THE MAJOR INTRODUCING HIS LATEST AND GREATEST.
"And now, ladies and gentlemen, Lewis will endeavour to add still further to the collection of championships he balances so miraculously on his nose."

22 Britain's Premier Fighter

'Ted and Elsie took me and some of the entertainers from
my show – Lupino Lane, Stanley Lupino and Olson and
Johnson – to the East End, where they gave a party for
400 Jewish Free School boys! I'll never forget it!'
Sophie Tucker

TK was desperately disappointed, especially as several sporting
writers commented that now he was well past his best. Indeed,
some of them, with the best of intentions, suggested that the
time had come for him to hang up his gloves while he was still
on top. TK was somewhat nettled by their words, although in
his heart he knew they were right. How could he retire? He
was only twenty-nine and still felt strong. And he could still
earn money in the only game he knew. He had signed a contract
with Peggy Bettinson prior to the Carpentier contest, regardless
of the result, to defend his Empire middleweight championship
on 19 June, against the young, hard-hitting Australian, Frankie
Burns.

Holland Park Skating Rink, the venue for the fight, was packed
tight with spectators. TK's corner men were Harry Stokes and his
school chum, Curley Carr, who through the years was TK's number
one fan and best friend until the day Curley died. Burns was good,
young and strong. But he came up against a dedicated man who was
out to prove something. TK flattened Burns with a left hook and
he would have been counted out but the bell came to his rescue at
the count of eight. Burns at twenty-two years of age made a good
recovery and a most exciting fight ensued. In the fourteenth round,
Curley got so excited that he lit a cigarette in the corner as TK landed
a left hook and right uppercut flush on Burns's chin, which lifted
him bodily from the floor over to the far ropes where he fell flat
on his back, rolled over and was counted out. The crowds roared
their approval and Curley, who was dancing around the ring, could
not have been more excited if he had administered the final blow
himself.

The excitement enveloped Pathe cameraman Billy Williams Snr, too, to such an extent that the knock-out was missed. Billy's story was, 'I ran out of film and didn't have time to reload.'

TK, however, said, 'I was told he got so excited, that he forgot to crank the handle.'

Whichever story is correct, the film company did not get the knock-out and had to move fast as they did not have an ending. They arranged for the ring and lights to be left standing, and for another boxer to double for Burns with his back to the camera. TK was persuaded to get back in the ring and knock him out all over again. The successful re-shoot took place two days later. TK did it in three takes, but word leaked out that it had been faked and all the theatre bookings were cancelled.

This bout now left TK with six titles and his Lonsdale Belt. He felt he had made his point with the pressmen.

The week following his latest victory, TK relaxed in his own way by taking over five hundred East End kids on an outing. Horley Woods rang with their happy laughter. Elsie, TK and his brothers and sisters made it a red-letter day for the children. They were served sandwiches for lunch and later in the afternoon tea and cakes. They had the free run of the local fairground which was the arrangement TK had previously made. The day finished with TK personally handing each child a shilling to take home. TK was in his element. He loved children and his enjoyment was to see them happy.

TK did a six-week tour of the music-halls after which he received a call from his partner, Joe Morris, to say he needed a top-liner for the Premierland on 4 September, and to ask if TK would meet Marcel Thomas. TK was delighted. He had not boxed there since he had beaten Paul Til for the European featherweight championship – and that was eight years earlier. He readily agreed. It would give him the opportunity of appearing before his people and at the same time ensure a packed house as he was, after all, the co-promoter.

The Premierland was packed from floor to ceiling. Hundreds were unable to get in and had to be content to follow the proceedings via a running commentary from the lucky ones inside.

A number of French supporters, whose judgements were coloured by the French press reports of the Carpentier fight on TK's ability, had raised £1,500 to back Thomas. TK obliged and covered the bet. It was bad luck for Thomas that TK was still allergic to Frenchmen. He still could not get Carpentier's action out of his mind and was burning to get a return. Unfortunately for Thomas, he had to bear the brunt and received the treatment from TK that he had no opportunity to administer to Carpentier. And Thomas was knocked out in the fourth round after being down for two counts of six earlier in the contest.

TK played the music-halls again for a month until he was contacted by Peggy Bettinson with an offer to defend his middle-weight titles against Roland Todd for the National Sporting Club at the Holland Park Skating Rink. He contacted the theatre owners, asking to be let off the following week, with a promise to do a return date after the Todd fight, and assuring them that the extra publicity would ensure good takings at the box office. TK got their agreement and returned immediately to London as he had only six days left in which to get in shape.

Once again TK drew a capacity crowd to the Holland Park Skating Rink. TK was to discover that Todd was a clever spoiler and a subtle boxer who carried a big punch. But Todd refused to be drawn into outright battle, and TK won the twenty-round bout on points. Although TK was awarded the verdict, he appreciated that there were signs that he was slowing up. So once again he plumped for the bright lights and good life of the music-halls and cabaret performances. It brought in the money, but it was not conducive for a boxer nearing thirty to keep fit.

TK's music-hall activities captured considerable attention. Wherever he appeared, the theatre was sold out. The act would start with a film, showing the last rounds of each of the Johnny Basham fights and his first and only round knocking out Tom Gummer. The public loved it. They made it quite plain that though TK had been defeated by Carpentier, he had lost no whit of their respect.

Near the end of 1922 TK decided that music-hall, cabaret and film work, plus the training he would soon have to start for his forthcoming defence of his middleweight title against Roland Todd in February, would not allow him any time to concentrate on a public house he had taken, which was now becoming a drain on his finances – although the takings had trebled since TK took over the ownership.

It was normal procedure for anyone of TK's family – his father, mother, sister and both young brothers – who were living above the premises, to help themselves to the silver that was stacked near the cash register which always seemed to be open. There were three barmen and very little control. The money was never right but the suppliers had trebled their deliveries. And so another business venture evaporated for lack of a business brain.

It was February 1923 when TK climbed into the ring, three months since his last contest. He was facing Roland Todd again, defending his middleweight title. The Lonsdale Belt was not at stake as the fight was not under the auspices of the NSC The contest was largely a repeat of their first meeting, with the heavier man taking care never to be drawn into an out-and-out fight. And certainly Todd did better this time. The harder TK tried, the more Todd defended. Nevertheless, TK's supporters were amazed to see the referee raise Todd's hand at the end of twenty rounds. This opinion was echoed by most of the sporting press. TK and some of his supporters took the opportunity of seeing the film the following week and it seemed that Todd had received the verdict for his defensive work.

This contest cost TK three of his titles and, despite the arrangements, his Lonsdale Belt. TK immediately issued a challenge for a rubber match and proposed that the Belt should be awarded to the winner. But the National Sporting Club were not interested in contests promoted by other organizations and without informing TK they collected the Belt from his home while he was out. The NSC representatives simply told Elsie that they required it at the club, in order to have it repolished for the new champion. After all, TK had just lost the title. Elsie did not know they were misrepresenting the situation and so she handed them the Lonsdale Belt. TK was infuriated at this devious way of obtaining it. Indeed, it was possible, in view of the contracts for the Roland Todd contest, that he could have charged them with larceny. Elsie was most upset and TK consoled her. 'It's OK, darling. You couldn't have known. Not to worry. I'll just have to win it back!'

Then, following the Todd fight, TK had to appear in court as he was being sued for non-appearance at the Rotherhithe Hippodrome, London, on 26 June 1922, the week after he had defeated Frankie Burns. Once again, TK couldn't understand the position. Prior to the Burns fight, he had agreed verbally to postpone the appearance until a future date. But he did not have the agreement in writing, and the claim was for the loss of £341.

TK told his story to the judge, and his lawyer asked for an adjournment until the following day. In the meantime TK, as usual, paid up. The court was informed that the case had been satisfactorily settled out of court. The judge, Lord Acton, said, 'The offer to pay was a very satisfactory termination of the proceedings and one entirely to the credit of Lewis. So far as Lewis was concerned, there could not be any imputation against his conduct in the matter.'

Feeling a little fed up after the Todd fight and the theatre episode, TK decided to take an extended rest. Elsie was delighted when she heard the news that he had fixed up a number of music-hall dates in South Africa and also one fight with the up-and-coming young heavyweight Johnny Squires. She was even more elated when TK said, 'This will be our holiday. Just you, Morton and me. No family, no trainer, nobody, just us.' He did not tell her that he had left his family one thousand pounds to see them through until his return.

Elsie, TK and Morton boarded the SS *Union Castle* with their pekinese dog, Ming Toy. They had a first-class suite and an adjoining cabin for Morton. TK felt great. He had paid for three first-class returns, left money for his family, and had £2,800 in his pocket. To add to his pleasure, the MCC touring cricket team were also on board. The side was captained by F.T. Mann, and included in the party were such great names as Percy Fender and Frank Woolley.

TK arranged with the purser to train every other day with any of the crew who were willing to spar. A number of the cricketers promised to join in. TK would take the collection box around for the Seamen's Charity. The passengers were delighted to think that they were going to be entertained by the boxing champion and the MCC team during the next three weeks.

On the first day out TK and Morton visited the boat's shop which catered for most of the needs of the passengers, and which was run by the ship's photographer. Morton was looking at a Brownie box camera and as he touched it, TK asked him, 'Would you like it?'

Morton shyly nodded his head. TK picked up the camera and handed it to Morton. The photographer asked him, 'How many films would you like?'

TK looked at Morton. 'How many films do you want?'

Morton held up three fingers.

TK turned to the photographer. 'Give him three films every day and put the cost on my bill.' And so Ted Kid Lewis unknowingly made his best ever investment. He did not realize that he had started his four and a half year-old son on his career.

Morton photographed everybody and everything in sight. He took his 36 picture allowance every day, keeping the photographer busy in his dark room. One day Morton took four rolls of film from the shop. TK heard about it and Morton received his first and only scolding from his father. During the trip the MCC team had set up nets on one of the decks for batting practice. Morton as usual wandered all over the ship. He opened a door, not knowing it opened on to the batting practice deck and, as he stood watching in the doorway, Frank Woolley hit a hard drive that landed in the pit of Morton's midriff. He collapsed then and there. He was quickly gathered up and taken to the sick bay, with all the team worried that they had just knocked out Ted Kid Lewis's son. Who was going to tell him? Mann, the captain, decided to risk it, saying, 'I'm the captain. I'll tell him – besides as I haven't volunteered to spar with Ted it may be all right.'

TK and Elsie hurried to the sick bay, by which time Morton had recovered and was feeling none the worse for the blow – especially as he had become the team's mascot during the trip. Frank Woolley insisted on taking a picture of Morton standing in the doorway where it happened – with Morton's camera.

When the ship docked in Cape Town, TK handed out old white ten-pound notes along a line of white-jacketed members of the crew. There was no question about it, TK did things in style.

TK and the theatre company worked out a format for his show and arranged a schedule which would cover theatres in Cape Town, Durban and Johannesburg, but when TK contacted the promoter to confirm the date for the Johnny Squires bout, the promoter informed him that Squires had changed his mind and did not consider himself ready to meet TK. A proposal to get Don McCorkindale, though agreeable to TK, was refused by the South African Boxing Commission – McCorkindale was some four stone heavier than TK!

TK thus toured the music-halls and gambled large sums at the races, winning and losing comparative fortunes . . . but when he received a cable from Major Wilson, offering him terms to meet Augie Ratner at the Albert Hall on 31 July, he was eager to accept. TK asked Elsie how she would feel about returning to London in a couple of weeks. Elsie was delighted. They had put Morton into a kindergarten boarding school, the first of the thirty-two schools he attended, and felt he should soon be starting a proper school either back in England or in the States, wherever they were going to settle.

TK cabled Wilson accepting the offer, and saying that he would return the following week after he had completed his music-hall date in Durban.

The closing night of the show was one TK would remember for a long time. He had become friends with a former boxer, Fireman George Anderson, who became TK's trainer and on several occasions he acted as sparring partner during the tour. As usual, one of the other acts came to the front of the stage and asked for volunteers to box three rounds with the welterweight champion. Quite a number rose to come forward but they were pushed back by a hefty young Boer, well-built and weighing about fifteen stone. He mounted the stage and removed his jacket and shirt. TK's usual routine was to take all the punches for two rounds, but to take them on his gloves and act groggy. Then, in the third round, to stage a grandstand finish with speed and a lot of left hands, without hurting his opponent for the night, and at the conclusion the whole company would come forward to take the curtain calls.

They were both gloved up and the bell rang. The young Boer sprang in, throwing punches like a windmill. TK had to use all his skill and guile to avoid being hit, hoping his man would run out of steam. At the end of the first round TK told Anderson to tell this chap that he was being paid to box an exhibition and not to have a real fight. Anderson relayed the message and brought back the reply. 'He said he was here to fight. He was going to show his friends in the audience how good he was.'

TK replied, 'Well, George, I'll have to show them, won't I?'

The bell went for the second round. TK went to the centre of the ring and extended his right glove to shake hands. The Boer refused to take it. 'There's another round after this.'

TK took his hand back. 'No, there isn't. This is the last round.' Then TK stepped back, feinted, threw a left hook followed by a right to the stomach and as his head came forward, he brought up a left uppercut to the jaw and the young Boer crashed to the canvas with no further interest in the proceedings. The management, fearing the worst, dropped the curtain. There were no final bows for the troupe that night.

TK dressed and went to the stage door, where he saw a mob waiting. He recognized several who had been sitting in the front row. He was prepared for the worst when one of them stepped forward, smiling, with his hand extended. As TK shook his hand, the remainder of the group were cheering and laughing. It appeared that TK had deflated the local bully who had ruled the roost and was feared throughout the town. Everyone was delighted.

A few days later the Lewis family and Ming Toy embarked for England. TK managed to get some light training and sparred with some of the crew. After seven days, he began to feel slightly feverish. Elsie noticed the change and insisted he visit the ship's doctor who immediately diagnosed a touch of malaria and ordered TK to the sick bay. Two days before the end of the voyage, TK felt much better and spent the time walking around the decks for exercise. No sooner had the boat docked when the family experienced a shock. They discovered that Ming Toy would have to go into quarantine for six months. Another shock followed soon after they had settled into their new home in Gordon Square. It was a summons for non-payment of a £250 guarantee which TK had signed for a friend to purchase a taxicab back in October 1922. TK had not realized what he had signed. His friend said it had been 'only a formality'.

'I can't understand why it hasn't been paid. He's working,' TK told the court. However, he paid the sum, then and there, including costs.

The funny side was when the claimant's lawyer, Mr Croom Johnson, told the court, 'The defendant was known as Kid Lewis.'

In spite of the fact that TK's name was continually splashed across the newspapers, Mr Justice Horridge replied, 'That name seems familiar.'

Mr Johnson added, 'The name is well known in certain circles.'

TK laughed. 'He means rings, my Lord.'

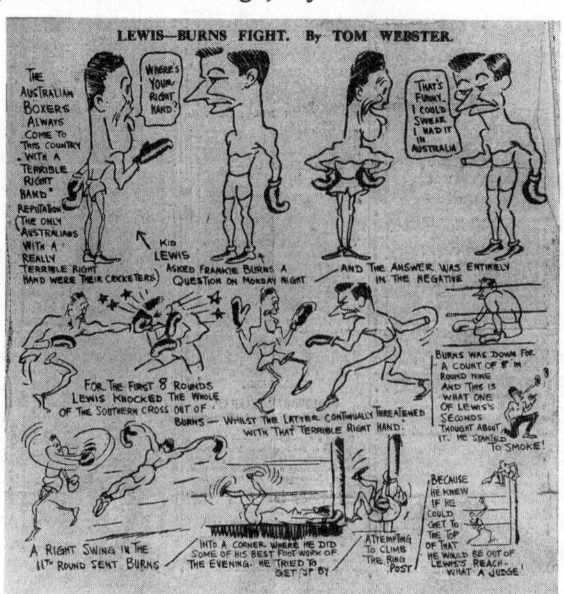

23 The Continental Tour

'I knew if I was fit I could out-smart, out-gun most of them. Sometimes I would come unstuck – but that's the fight game. After all, what else did I know?'

TK

TK's immediate concern was to get fit for the Augie Ratner fight and chose to train at Shoeburyness. With Alec Goodman unavailable, TK was delighted when Jack Goodwin offered his services. Terms were agreed but, after waiting two days for his trainer to show up, TK was informed by his schooldays chum, Curley Carr, that Ratner's London manager, Harry 'The Horse' Levene, had offered Goodwin more money to look after his man. TK was irritated by this lack of loyalty. He had been good to Jack in the past. Also, he was not in the best of health. He was still suffering from his touch of malaria and was not in a pleasant frame of mind. Curley sized up the situation. 'Don't worry. You can do without fair weather friends like that. Gus Wilson, Carpentier's trainer, is in town and I took the liberty of arranging for him to train you. Did I do wrong?'

TK was delighted. He put his arms around Curley and hugged and kissed him. This was TK's way, when his emotions overcame him. It helped to hide his wet eyes.

He returned Curley's favour, however, in a more substantial way. Some months later Curley opened a billiard hall in Cable Street, in London's East End. Curley's son Sydney recalled: 'Ted came for the opening with a bag full of silver, "to start his old mate off". The place was packed as he walked around the snooker tables stuffing money in all the twelve pockets for the crowd of locals to help themselves. They sat there astonished, I'll never forget their faces. Ted was mobbed, word got around he was in the club, the street was jammed calling for Ted, it was great!'

Gus Wilson duly arrived, bringing Paul Frisch, Billy Palmer and his famous father, Pedlar Palmer, as sparring partners. Pedlar was always the court jester, as well as being the hardest man to hit. He could stand on a handkerchief and defy anyone to hit him in the face. After two days of training, the trainer, the sparring partners and Curley ganged up together and told TK that he was not well enough to face the strong Ratner. TK wouldn't hear of calling off the contest. 'I'll be all right. We'll just have to work a little harder – and Gus will have to pull some magic out of his little black bag. Besides, I'm getting well paid and I can't let Major Wilson down. He needs the fight more than I do.'

The Albert Hall was packed once again with TK's drawing power. TK followed Ratner into the ring to the roar of the crowds. He shook hands with Ratner, determined to try to get his own back from Augie for the defeat of two years earlier. The introductions were made and the bout was ready to start when Harry Levene raised the old objection to TK's gumshield.

TK allowed this gamesmanship to rattle him and at first refused to allow referee Jack Smith to examine the shield. After all, since TK had first started to wear a gumshield back in 1911, most boxers in England and, for that matter, in the States, were using them. It had become part of their gear.

TK, however, took it out, showed it to Smith who found it quite in order. The contest finally started. It proved to be a 'fight' in every sense of the word. The bout was extremely close and TK genuinely believed that he had won. Jack Smith, however, thought otherwise and raised Ratner's hand at the end of twenty rounds.

The Premierland was meeting with little success from a financial point of view and eventually TK's partner, Joe Morris, decided to withdraw, leaving TK to run it alone. TK was not ready for the rat-race of promoting fights. He told his brother-in-law, Manny Littlestone, who had been working in the Premierland box office for some time, 'If you could find someone to join you to run the place, I'll assign the lease over to you.'

Manny found Victor Berliner, a local sportsman, to partner him, and suggested that, to help them to get started, TK sign for two fights later in the year. They would pay TK 55 per cent of the gate. TK agreed, providing it was not before October as he had been booked for a six-week music-hall tour.

Berliner and Littlestone propositioned TK to top the Premierland bill in a return with Frankie Burns on 4 October, and guaranteed him a packed house. TK agreed and managed to get a week's training. Burns did better in this contest and lasted the full twenty rounds, though losing by a wide margin on points. The takings were so

successful that TK agreed to a further two fights to round off
the year. The first was in five weeks' time against Fred Archer,
which gave TK time for another three weeks on tour and a week
to train. Once again the arena was packed. TK was never troubled
and, like the crowd, was surprised that the referee, the former light-
heavyweight champion Dick Smith, allowed the one-sided fight to
go the full twenty rounds.

There then followed four more weeks of touring and one week's
training, to get fit to meet Fred Davies on 26 December. This was
the second time that TK had fought on Boxing Day. But this time
the hall was packed to see TK give Davies a boxing lesson over twenty
rounds.

Nineteen twenty-four opened with Ramsay MacDonald winning
the election, and leading the first Socialist party to power. TK
celebrated the new government by touring with his music-hall
company. Though he was no longer middleweight champion, he
still held his welterweight titles. These could surely be marketed,
and he could still make 10 st. 7 lb. fully dressed. This he proved when
meeting Yorkshireman Sid Pape on 22 January. After knocking out
Pape in two rounds, TK dressed and drove back to London through
the night in his AC sports car, with his friend Albert Levy.

Whilst in the Midlands prior to the fight, TK had purchased the
first miniature two-wheel bicycle for his six and a half year-old son,
Morton. TK and Albert took turns driving while the other held the
bike on the running board.

Albert Levy was a great fan of TK's who followed him about all
over the country. One of his hobbies was photography and Morton
spent hours with Albert's son and daughter in their Clapham
Common home, watching Albert developing and printing his
pictures. All this helped cement Morton's interest in photography.
Albert's other hobby was stealing cars, repainting them in his garage
workshop and re-selling them. The AC sports car which TK was
driving at the time was a present from Albert. However, TK was
not to know about Albert's affairs until twelve years later, when he
was finally caught.

TK now felt that he was in good physical condition and should profit
from it. With this in mind, he turned his attention to the continent. A
tour by a champion was always rewarding. Arrangements were made
to fight in Milan, Paris, Hamburg and Berlin.

TK arranged for Phil Richards, a fairly capable middleweight from
London, to accompany him on the tour. Phil was the older brother of

Benny Caplin, who, in the 1930s, fought a fifteen-round draw for the featherweight championship of the world against Freddie Miller.

Phil, besides being sparring partner, chief cook and bottle-washer, was also nursemaid to Morton. In Paris, TK contacted Gus Wilson, who was waiting to travel to the States with Carpentier, and arranged for Gus to act as trainer as long as he could. TK's first opponent was Bruno Frattini, the middleweight champion of Italy. The contest was billed as for the middleweight championship of Europe.

TK and Elsie received a warm welcome in Milan. Accommodation and training quarters were arranged by the promoters. Everybody was most helpful and TK and Elsie made a host of friends, each one vying for the privilege of wining and dining them. TK did not realize that they were trying to kill him with kindness. All of them were Frattini fans, and their aim was to soften TK up. Of course they did not know that TK was a non-smoker and practically a non-drinker, but Elsie, Phil and Gus enjoyed the hospitality.

TK entered the ring to the usual applause afforded a visiting foreign boxer, and waved to some of the ringsiders, who had for the past week been TK's admirers. The scene changed when Frattini climbed through the ropes. The house rose to him, and the cheering was deafening. TK noticed that his ringside friends stood up to be counted. They had now declared their loyalties. TK had Gus Wilson, Phil Richards and Darby Sabini, that colourful London character, who was in Milan at the time and who had volunteered to work in the corner.

Although Frattini proved no match for TK, TK was content to outbox Frattini. The apparent ease with which TK handled his opponent irritated the fans rather than rousing their admiration. Gus whispered, 'I just heard that you won't get the verdict if the fight goes the distance. You've got to knock him out to win.' Gus was anything but alarmist. TK nodded. He knew what was required.

The bell went for the seventeenth round. TK changed his tactics and shuffled forward after a few measuring left leads. He landed a left swing to the solar plexus and, as Frattini bent forward, finished him with a right uppercut to the chin. Frattini fell as if poleaxed – out to the world.

The scene that followed was one TK remembered for a long time. All hell broke loose. Bottles, paper, banana skins and an assortment of missiles were thrown. The crowd were making their way to the ring with bottles and chairs in their hands. As they approached the corner steps, TK shouted,

'Phil, you and Darby take that corner. Gus and I will take the other.'

To this Darby shouted back, 'You're not in England now. You're in my country and you're on your own!' And with that, he jumped through the ropes and out of the ring. TK and Phil were knocking the men off the ring as fast as they could, with Gus doing his best with a chair which he managed to grab from a spectator. Two shots were fired. These shots must have come from the police in their efforts to gain control. About fifty police mounted the ring with drawn batons. TK, Phil and Gus were hurriedly escorted from the ring to the dressing room by a posse of policemen, while bottles rained down above their heads.

All three were covered with bruises from the kicks and TK's head had a slight cut from a bottle. The police locked them in the dressing room and kept them there for two hours – hoping things would quieten down. Eventually the Chief of Police arrived and ordered ten policemen to escort the party back to the hotel, with instructions that they were to take the next train out of Milan.

News of the riot had reached the hotel and Elsie was frantic with worry. When TK arrived at the door with a police escort, she thought the worst – that he had killed Frattini. TK was told that the next train out was to Paris and that he and his party were to be on it. They packed hurriedly, dressed Morton (who was delighted by all the excitement), and travelled separately from Phil and Gus to the station, escorted by the police who waited until the train had pulled out.

On arrival in Paris, the train was met by Joey Madden, an American friend who had settled there after the war, and had established himself in the nightclub business. He asked TK to join him and together they would run a club called the 'Ringside'. With TK greeting the customers, they would make a 'killing'. TK convinced Elsie that here was a good chance to start a new life, but Elsie was not sure. However, Morton was sent to the English-French boarding school near Maison Lafitte and three nights later TK started on a new career – nightclub owner.

The first week was quite a success. Maurice Chevalier headed a big list of well-known artists who visited the club, while Georges Carpentier and his manager were frequent visitors too.

Elsie and TK took French lessons and they began to settle down. Gus Wilson had arranged for TK to train at La Guerche, a training camp owned by Descamps and Carpentier as TK was due to box

Francis Charles, the French middleweight champion, in two weeks' time. Although they found the new life interesting and rewarding, it was hard on their sleeping habits. They would rarely get to bed before eight o'clock in the morning. TK managed to get ten days' training and, during this period, he managed to get to bed before eleven o'clock. Carpentier, who was training there at the same time, would accompany TK on his road work and was helpful in every possible way. Georges offered to go in TK's corner but TK declined. 'Thanks, but that wouldn't increase your popularity, with me fighting a Frenchman.' However, Georges sat near to TK's corner throughout the contest.

Both TK and Charles, the French champion, put up a good show. TK made several all-out attempts to end the contest, but Charles was a good defensive boxer and was determined to go the distance. At the end of fifteen rounds, with the French crowd loving every minute of it even though it was a one-sided bout, TK won the verdict.

It was quite a night at the Ringside after the fight. The club was packed, with everyone helping TK to celebrate his victory.

The nightclub business was going quite well until TK had to get down to the business of training again for his fight with Chic Nelson, which was to take place in Hamburg. TK was beginning to find training a strain. He was having to take more punishment to achieve the same results and of course he had the added problem of advancing age. He was thirty-one and the grind of training was taking its toll. But his confidence in his ability and experience gave him the will to continue. When he entered the ring in Hamburg, he found it difficult to get going against Nelson. Although both TK and his supporters thought he had done enough to win, the local referee declared the contest a draw.

Seven days after the Chic Nelson fight, TK entered the Berlin Sports Palatz to face Eric Milenz, the middleweight champion of Germany. The German boxing fans were to witness their champion take severe punishment, with Milenz hitting the canvas nine times before he was counted out in the seventh round.

TK returned home to Paris to another big celebration at the Ringside. That night he was offered another contest, to meet Piet Hobin, the Belgian welterweight champion, eighteen days later at the Paris Velodrome. The European title was not at stake as the match was at 10 st. 11 lb., over fifteen rounds. TK was now well caught up with the nightclub life and when the time came to start training, he found it difficult to getting down to the required weight.

'House Full' signs were up at the open-air Velodrome arena when TK climbed into the ring. He received a warm welcome. Paris had taken to him. Both men took things a little easy, expecting the contest to be stopped until the rain subsided. But the referee had other ideas. As the rounds rolled by, TK found it difficult to get going and, at the end of twenty rounds, the referee declared the contest a draw. The crowd who had braved the weather were struck dumb. Following the action of raising both men's arms to signify a draw, the referee jumped from the ring to take shelter underneath it.

Once again the takings at the Ringside were up as those present celebrated. Elsie and TK were finding it difficult to think of ways of evading drinking. Both were privately non-drinkers and eventually Joey had the idea of keeping a special bottle for drinks for TK and Elsie. The drink was cold tea, coloured to look like whisky. Both TK and Elsie felt that this ruse was cheating, but Joey convinced them that it was better to cheat a little than to upset the customers by refusing to drink with them. After all, it was a drinking club. TK and Elsie were always in fear of being caught out with their cold tea drink. They either drank it down in one gulp or made sure that it never left their hands until the glass was empty.

However, TK and Elsie were increasingly having second thoughts about the nightclub. They did not think the business was their scene, and the late hours did not give them much of a family life or time to see Morton.

Two weeks after the Hobin fight Major Arnold Wilson called TK and asked if he wished to defend his welterweight title against Johnny Brown of Hamilton, Scotland. The fight was to take place at the Albert Hall. TK said he would think about it and call him back. TK turned to Elsie. 'It was the Major. He wants me to defend my title against Johnny Brown, 3 July in London. This might give us the chance to break away from the club business.' They had the dilemma of how to break it to Joey. TK took the easy way out. He agreed to Elsie's suggestion that she would talk to Joey and he would go to London in the normal way to start training. TK called the Major and accepted the fight, said his goodbyes to Joey and Morton, and left for England.

TK arrived in London and allowed himself two weeks to get fighting fit. He secured the services of Alec Lambert whom he had defeated for the British featherweight championship back in 1913.

Alec had now become a first-class trainer. During the final week's preparation, Alec Goodman visited TK, and the smell of sweat and rubbing embrocation was too much for him. He offered his services for the one fight. TK and Alec Lambert were delighted with the idea and felt that Alec's experience in the corner would be most valuable. Alec was the first to recognize the fact that it was taking TK much longer to get into shape and, having seen Johnny Brown in action, suggested to TK that he change his usual tearaway style.

'You can outbox Brown, and slow him up with counter-punches.' TK agreed. He knew, and Alec knew, that he couldn't keep up his usual aggression for twenty rounds. The final week found TK boxing rings around his sparring partners, deliberately trying not to drop them, so that they could continue to go forward throwing punches.

The sporting press were sceptical as to whether TK could comfortably make the weight. However, TK came in at 10 st. 7 lb. while Brown scaled 1 lb. more. Once again TK packed the Albert Hall. The fight turned out to be exactly as Alec had planned. Brown did all the attacking and TK all the boxing, scoring points with his counter-punching. By the fourteenth round, it was obvious to the crowd that TK was the stronger of the two, and at the sixteenth round Brown was showing signs of tiring, and also showing the marks of the punishment he was taking.

At the final bell, the referee immediately raised TK's hand in victory. He was still the welterweight champion. TK was pleased to read in one of the papers the following morning: 'Lewis fought what was probably the brainiest battle of his career.' He wished Alec would change his mind and come back.

The following day TK had a call offering him dates for a three-month tour to take a show on the road, starting 28 July. He was delighted with the offer and told them to pencil it in and he would confirm it one way or the other as soon as he returned to Paris. Elsie, Morton and a crowd of friends met TK at the station in Paris. TK's first question to Elsie when they were alone was, 'What did Joey say?'

Elsie was all smiles. 'Joey understood and his only concern was that we should be happy and whatever we wanted to do would be OK with him.'

TK hugged Elsie. 'Maybe you should be our business manager.' It was unfortunate that in years to come he did not take his own advice. 'We've got dates for a three-month tour starting 28 July if we can get away in time.' There was no way out, TK now had to face Joey, and if anybody could ever have called Ted Kid Lewis a coward, it would have been then.

Joey was sorry to lose them. 'You're not to worry, kids. Everything's OK,' putting his arms around Elsie and TK. 'I understand. Besides, you've helped me build the place up. I've no complaints.' Joey laughed. 'Besides, I'll now be my own boss,' as he side-stepped a playful right swing from TK. 'When do you want to leave?'

TK and Elsie looked embarrassed as they gazed at each other. TK plucked up courage. 'We've gotta be there in a couple of weeks' time.'

'Well, that's no problem. Make arrangements to leave at the end of the week. That will leave you plenty of time and give me a few days to check the books and see what's owing.' He patted them both on the back and departed.

TK and Elsie were delighted by his reaction. But then, 'What did he mean, check the books and see what's owing?' Elsie inquired. 'What do you think it will cost us?'

TK was lost for words. He didn't expect it to cost him anything.

Joey and TK did not mention the books during the remaining five days before their departure. There was a farewell party given by Joey at the Ringside, the night before they left. The party was packed with celebrities. Joey made a speech, saying how sorry he was to lose such a partner and that TK and Elsie would always be welcome to return. He presented Elsie with a beautiful dressing case and to TK gave a gold tiepin and an envelope. TK opened the envelope which contained a note and a cheque and, with his emotions getting the better of him, read the note to Elsie:

'Dear Ted, What can I say? It won't be the same without you two wonderful people. You can always come back and take up where you left off. But in case you don't, I have checked through the books and I figured your third share was worth £1,850 and I have pleasure in giving you this cheque.

Take care of each other. I love you both. Joey.'

TK and Elsie were missing for the next thirty minutes, Elsie putting on new make-up and TK washing his face in cold water.

The next morning, Joey and five carloads of friends escorted them to the train. TK, Elsie and Morton waved goodbye from their carriage window until they were out of sight.

They were never to see Joey Madden again. Six months later, he was killed by a hit-and-run driver. It was a sad blow for Elsie and TK when they heard the news.

24 Hollywood Calling

'I liked what money could buy – independence, recognition – the courtesy, the pleasure of seeing what money brings – that's what I enjoyed the most.'

TK

The Lewis family arrived in London and checked into the Strand Palace Hotel. Their immediate tasks were to hire Teddy Finch, a comedian, who was resting at the time, to stage-manage and organize the show. Then to enrol Morton at Macauley House, a boarding school in Cuckfield, Haywards Heath, East Sussex, while Elsie went to Harrod's to get Morton's school outfits. The boarding school was necessary because TK and Elsie would be living in theatrical boarding-houses and hotels until the show ended the tour.

Rehearsals started and the following week the show was on the road. This was quite an enjoyable time for TK and Elsie; it was the first time they had had the opportunity to be alone. They had all day together, except for two matinées and six evening shows a week. They met old friends and made new ones in every town they played. There was no early morning road-work to contend with and no gymnasiums to worry about. TK kept fairly fit (for an actor) by boxing in the show and riding a couple of mornings a week. It was the first time that the grind and worry of the fight game was not hanging over them. Elsie was hoping that the longer the show ran, the longer TK would be out of boxing and thus that little bit older.

The bookings ended on Saturday, 25 October – a date easily remembered: Morton's birthday. They moved into a furnished flat in Clanricarde Gardens, Bayswater, and TK, for the first time, found himself with nothing to do and no immediate prospects. Several business offers were made, but they all required TK to put up money, and money was not too plentiful, in spite of the three-month tour. He found that their expenses, his entertaining bills and the Mendeloff family's constant drain on his funds had left him very little in the kitty. TK was becoming restless. Elsie could see the signs and was fast coming to understand where all their money was going. She could never get TK into a position to complain that it was time the Lewis family came first, and that his responsibility for the whole Mendeloff family must end. Every time the mention of money came up, his reply was, 'Don't worry, there's a fight next week', or, 'There's this deal I'm involved in, so don't worry, we'll be all right'.

TK started to make the rounds, seeing boxing promoters and regularly visiting boxing shows, where he would always receive a big welcome. Offers began to come in. One was from Charlie Harvey, to fight the new welterweight champion of the world, Mickey Walker, who had beaten Jack Britton for the title. Another came from Liverpool to fight Billy Mach, the new local idol, and the third from Edinburgh promoter Nat Dresner who proposed a title fight with Tommy Milligan.

TK considered the offers. The Walker fight was the most attractive, but it was too soon. It meant departing for the States immediately and leaving no time at all for training. This would not have bothered TK in the past. He would have willingly taken a fight without a day's preparation, but the good life had set in, and he was getting older. He could drop out of condition in a couple of days and it would take much longer to return to fighting shape. He went for the Milligan fight in Edinburgh as it worked out best financially and he wouldn't have too far to travel. TK gave the usual story to Elsie: 'I'm sitting around wasting time, and time is all I've got to sell, so while I'm still able and a drawing card, I am defending my welterweight title against Tommy Milligan, and besides, it's very good money.' Elsie understood his reasoning, but was not happy. He had not trained for nearly four months and had turned thirty-one. He was now fighting solely for money, not prestige – he already had that, and had earned it.

There were over 20,000 packed into the Industrial Hall for the bout, and practically all of them were rooting for Milligan. This did not worry TK. In fact, it urged him on. Milligan turned out to be better than TK had envisaged. In the fourth round, TK went for the kill. He threw his best left hook to Milligan's chin, but it landed a little too high, and he felt an agonizing pain shoot up his arm. His left hand was useless. TK knew that there was no man living who could be a match for Milligan with one hand and, for the next sixteen rounds, he had to fight to stay the distance. TK would try one of his right-hand haymakers, but to no avail. Milligan was too clever to be caught by a one-handed fighter. As Milligan increased his pace, TK began to slow down. When the final bell rang, TK didn't have to look to the referee to see who had won. He knew.

And so did Elsie. She waited for TK to return home and was at the front door as he arrived. He knew immediately by her anxious expression what she was looking for, he smiled and turned his head from side to side, 'See, no damage.' She was relieved and could see he was unhappy, but he shrugged it off when she asked him if he was all right. 'I'm all right, darling. I'll win it back as soon as I get another chance.'

The damaged hand caused TK to take an extended lay-off and, as he was approaching the end of his boxing career, every day that he didn't train meant an even harder effort if he were to maintain fighting fitness.

By the end of 1924, TK's hand had healed and he started to do some road-work in the afternoon, with Morton when on holiday accompanying him on his bicycle.

Just after Christmas, Harry Jacobs called TK. 'I'd like you to top the bill against Francis Charles, at the Albert Hall on 22 January, at 11 st. 6 lb. I'll give you three and a half thousand, can you make the date?' TK didn't need much persuading. The money was good and he had beaten Charles in Paris the previous year, and in front of his own crowd. It would be a cinch. 'OK, Harry. I'll take it.' Charles weighed-in 5 lb. overweight, TK scaled 11 st. fully dressed and waived the forfeit.

The fight went the full twenty rounds and although TK won well on points, he had slowed up considerably. Still, the spectators were well satisfied with his performance, as were the press. Harry Jacobs was delighted with the box office results and offered TK a return with Tommy Milligan on his 19 March show.

'I can arrange the fight at catch-weights. It would suit Tommy as he, like you, is finding it irksome to get down to 10 st. 7 lb.'

'I'll take it. Same money? It should pack them in,' TK replied.

'You're on, but don't tell anybody what you're getting,' Jacobs replied.

TK wasn't worried about that. He was more concerned about telling Elsie. Luckily at the same time he was offered two weeks' music-hall work, which would leave him just under two weeks to train for the Milligan fight. He accepted. This gave him the courage he needed to tell Elsie. TK led with his left. 'It seems the publicity for beating Charles was good, because we've got two weeks' music-hall work.'

Elsie was delighted. Maybe this would eventually lead to more theatre work and possibly film work.

Then TK threw his right. 'You see, I'm still a good drawing card.' He let that sink in. He was getting good at making excuses to Elsie. 'So Jacobs offered me three and a half thousand to fight Milligan again.'

Elsie's joy was short-lived. She had no defence against TK's attack with, 'The money's good and we need it'. So they completed the music-hall dates, and TK gathered up his retinue of trainers, sparring partners and the usual hangers-on and set up camp at the Star and Garter, Windsor.

The Albert Hall again showed 'House Full' signs as the bell went for the first of the twenty rounds. TK had decided that though their first contest had been hard, it had been fought mostly at long range. This time, however, TK elected to make it a test of in-fighting. Inevitably such a style of boxing leads to clinches and the referee had to prise them apart again and again. Eventually, realizing that neither was going to give way, the referee issued a general warning – and appealed to both men to box at long range. TK knew he could win only at close quarters and nothing would divert him from his pre-fight plan. However, the referee was just as determined and in the fifth round, he disqualified TK for holding.

TK was dreadfully disappointed, for though he knew he was at fault, he thought Milligan at least shared the blame.

Disappointed or not, TK was giving an after-fight party at Harry Adams's nightclub and, much to Harry's surprise, he arrived, putting on his usual happy smile. A good time was had by all. After the party TK went to Harry. 'How much do I owe you, Harry?'

'You were good enough to show up after losing and not spoil the party. It's on me.'

They had been friends for years and were to remain so for the rest of their days.

TK spent a few days making the rounds, visiting his family and, as usual, left a good part of his purse money as well. Elsie never knew what money TK had, nor realized how much he gave to cover the demands of his family, until many years later. Then TK had a call from Sam Brown, representing Warner Bros of Hollywood. They would like him to go to Hollywood and be featured in a boxing film starring Bert Lytell! TK was flattered when Brown said his name on the bills would make the film a success over there. He became interested.

'How long would it take?'

'The filming would take five weeks, allow three to four weeks' travelling, say nine weeks.'

'What are they paying?' TK asked.

'£1,000 and two first-class returns,' was the reply.

'I'll think about it and let you know in a couple of days.' TK was getting more than interested, so he immediately called Elsie. 'How would you like to visit the States? I've been offered a part in a film.' Elsie was delighted, as she would be able to see her family and friends again.

'When?' she inquired.

'I'll know in a couple of days.' TK then visited Wardour Street, the film centre, to see his producer friends, Albert and Moss Goodman. They listened to his story, thought it was a good idea, as film punches don't hurt. However, Albert agreed to accompany TK to meet Brown to discuss a better financial deal.

The meeting took place the next day, when Albert and TK met Sam Brown in the lounge of the Strand Palace Hotel. Albert got right down to business. 'It's a good idea to have Ted Kid Lewis featured on your posters, it will play to packed houses, but nine weeks is a long time in a busy boxer's life, and you know the kind of money he's getting.'

Sam was cornered. His instructions were to get Lewis at the best price he could and he knew the time factor was against him, so he inquired as to what TK was worth.

'Worth!!' exclaimed Albert. At that point, TK squirmed, went red in the face, got up and excused himself. He needed the Gents. Albert felt he had the upper hand. 'You couldn't pay what he's worth.'

TK was hiding behind one of the columns in the lounge, too embarrassed to look. It was the type of business approach he had never understood. 'But as he would like to do it, I think he'll take five thousand and three first-class returns.'

'Dollars or pounds?' Sam inquired. Albert told Sam he was in England, therefore it was pounds, or 25,000 in dollars. Sam swallowed, shook hands, stood up, looked, but couldn't see TK. 'Tell Ted to come to the office tomorrow and sign the contract,' and departed.

Albert kept TK in suspense as he walked over inquiring what had happened. 'Sit down, Ted. Yes, you're going. I got three first-class tickets, so you can take Morton. Who knows how long you may stay there.' TK smiled; Albert was enjoying himself. 'And . . . twenty . . . five . . . thousand . . . dollars!'

TK couldn't believe it and in his usual way of showing affection to his friends, kissed Albert on the cheek. 'You're a wonder, Albert. You must take your cut.' But Albert wouldn't hear of it.

Sam met TK next day. They signed the contract for twenty-five thousand dollars and three return tickets, with TK reporting to Warner Brothers studio by the third week in April. The usual instructions prevailed. TK told Elsie to 'get packed' while he drove down to Cuckfield, once again to take Morton out of school. Then TK left the Mendeloffs very well provided for, and the family and a crowd of friends travelled to Southampton to see them board the SS *Mauritania*. TK, Elsie and Morton stood on the top deck waving goodbye until they were nearly out of sight.

The Statue of Liberty looked good to Elsie. It had been three years since she sailed past it on her way to Europe. The family reception committee ensured a happy reunion. They stayed in New York for four days before departing for Hollywood. During their stay, TK made the rounds, taking Morton along. They stopped at Grupp's gymnasium where TK used to train and watched Johnny Dundee, Benny Leonard and other great names work out. Morton was introduced to them all by his proud father. He was wide-eyed with excitement at meeting all these great names. TK stopped off to say hello and to tell Charlie Harvey of his plans. Charlie let Morton look through all his fight photographs while he tried to talk TK into having a few fights while he was in New York. TK, however, had made up his mind. He was going to try his luck in the film business. Jimmy Johnston was the next call, and there TK introduced Morton to the 'Boy Bandit', who wasn't much taller than Morton. 'Your Pop was a great fighter. I wish he was in his prime now. Why, he could lick any light, welter or middleweight in the country.' Jimmy looked at TK. 'Wanna take a couple of jobs while you're here?' TK smiled and shook his head. 'Nope, I'm going to Hollywood.'

Elsie had a wonderful time seeing all her family and friends. Jack Dempsey and his wife gave a farewell dinner for Elsie and TK and the following morning they took the train to Hollywood.

It was a hot day when the train pulled into Los Angeles station. They were greeted by a Warner Brothers publicity man who directed his photographer on the type of stills he wanted. Dave Marks, who had met TK on his previous visit, acted as the reception committee of one. A house was rented for TK and his next-door neighbour was Victor McLaglen, another British boxer who had switched to film-making.

TK reported to the studio, and was introduced to Bert Lytell, the star, by Dave Marks, who was to be the assistant director on the new film, *Sporting Life*. TK was told that he would be on call from the following Monday and was instructed to get fitted out in Wardrobe.

TK and Elsie were recommended to send Morton to the Hollywood Military Academy where most of the stars sent their boys. Morton was duly enrolled and kitted out, and once again he started in yet another new school. Until they wanted him to box. Elsie heard about it, and promptly enrolled him in another school.

The film took just over four weeks to shoot. As TK was required on the set every day, he took Elsie to visit his friends. Their first call was to see Douglas Fairbanks Snr., and there they had lunch with Douglas and his wife, Mary Pickford. TK was pleased to tell Douglas that he was there to appear in two films and that he hoped to be able to stay and find other work in Hollywood. Douglas said that he was sure TK would make it and offered him a small part in his next film which would be starting in about six weeks' time.

Sydney Chaplin, the star of the original *Charley's Aunt* film, dropped in to see TK and Elsie and arranged for them to visit his brother, Charlie, and to bring Morton along to meet his godfather.

TK was playing the part of the champion in *Sporting Life* and one of the early sequences to be shot had Bert Lytell, playing the part of the big-hearted playboy who could box, boxing the champion. Their see-saw fight Lytell won by a knockout. Elsie and Morton visited the studio on the day the fight was to be shot and the knockout scene was taken fifteen times before it was judged to be right. Each take required Bert to land a right cross on TK's chin, knocking him through the ropes and on to the ringsiders, who were supposed to be gangsters. Morton couldn't understand why his father should be knocked out in the first place, much less why he should be knocked out so many times, of course the reason became clear to him in future years.

The day spent with Charlie Chaplin, first at his studio and then at his home, seemed to Elsie and Morton like being in wonderland. TK visited Charlie a number of times during his stay in Hollywood. Both TK and Elsie were invited to numerous parties and they became firm friends with Richard Bennett who, besides being the father of Barbara, Constance and Joan, was a star in his own right. John

Barrymore, drinking too much even in those days, was a great host and he and Wallace Beery were regular visitors with TK to the Friday night fights at Hollywood Legion, where TK was always called upon to take a bow when the Master of Ceremonies called out the names of the famous boxers in the hall.

TK's part in *Sporting Life* finished ahead of schedule. In his second contracted film, he had a small part in a Billy Sullivan leather-pushing film, *The Champ Strikes Back*. At every opportunity TK worked out in the Hollywood Athletic Club, where he would be joined by Douglas Fairbanks, Charlie Chaplin, Bert Lytell, Bill Sullivan and Victor McLaglen, sparring with them, wearing 16-ounce gloves, and making sure he did not hurt their faces. He also trained with two of his old opponents, Jack Perry and Phil Bloom, who had been the first boxer TK had faced in the States, back in 1914.

The life and work in Hollywood suited TK. He was looking good and feeling fit when his friends suggested that they would like to see him in action. TK was flattered. He was in fair condition and was talked into having one fight at the Hollywood Legion.

He was matched against Bob Sage, a twenty-two year-old tough and heavy puncher who was beginning to make a name for himself on the West Coast. TK trained in downtown Los Angeles, and called upon his old friend, Gus Wilson, who was now managing West Coast fighters, to train him and work in the corner.

Friday night, 10 July 1925, found the Hollywood Legion totally packed. Every big name in Hollywood, with the numbers of female stars nearly equalling the male, were in the ringside seats. It was the first time an outsider held his own in the cheering stakes against the local man. The fighters were introduced. 'Ted Kid Lewis at 152 lb. in the red corner and Bob Sage at 178 lb. in the white corner.' The bell sounded and the six-foot Sage came rushing forward wanting to make a name at TK's expense. TK hit him with every punch in the boxing manual, he rocked and swayed but he would not go down. TK realized the grim truth – his punching had lost its snap. He received the verdict at the end of ten rounds, and the tumultuous cheering for TK did not do much to restore the feeling that he had had his last big fight.

Douglas Fairbanks gave a party that night for TK. It was held at his house, 'Pickfair', where TK was congratulated for his brilliant display, and for his generosity in letting the local boy go the distance, by doing only enough to hold him in check. Several promoters were at the party, wanting to arrange more contests, but TK excused himself by saying that he had hurt his right hand and it now needed a couple of months' rest. It was an old injury.

For the first five of the six months during which TK lived in Hollywood, he was in a number of films. But then it seemed that the bottom fell out of the boxing films market and TK was out of work. This inactivity seemed to affect him and once again he began to have stomach pains, which lasted a few weeks. Then TK cabled Joe Morris, inquiring whether he could fix up a couple of fights. Four days later TK received an offer for three fights, the first against Marcel Thuru on 8 October, the second with Simon Rossman on 8 November, and the third on 27 November with Len Johnson. The money was good. He still had three return fares, and here he was twiddling his thumbs – no film work, no business interests, and he had been gambling again over the past two months with disastrous results. TK talked it over with Elsie.

'I'm doing nothing here. Gambling, while waiting for work, and this offer is pretty good. Besides, I can always work the music-halls. We've got more chances in England.'

Elsie understood his predicament. She had become aware of how he handled money. He had not worried in the past: there was always another fight in a few weeks. But now the fights were few and far between. Perhaps TK was right in thinking that their future was in England.

TK cabled his reply to Joe Morris and, once again, the Lewis family packed up and left for England.

Back in England, TK and Elsie set up home in Finchley Road, Golders Green, and enrolled Morton in yet another school. TK started training at Windsor for the Marcel Thuru fight and found little enjoyment in his efforts to get fighting fit.

TK weighed in at 11 st., with Thuru touching 11 st. 12 lb. Once again the Albert Hall had a 'House Full' sign, as TK and his opponent climbed through the ropes. At the bell, Thuru rushed at TK with a two-handed barrage, which drove TK on to the ropes. TK covered up, weaved out of trouble and, with a look of 'If this is what you want, let's go', TK leaped forward and started to hand out a combination of punches to the head, finishing with a left and right to the body which sent Thuru to the canvas. The referee started to count. At five Thuru started to get up when one of the seconds shouted, 'Stay down, stay down' in French, while the other screamed 'foul' to the referee. TK looked on flabbergasted, as the referee waved his arms, signalling that Thuru had indeed won on a foul! TK had been disqualified! Pandemonium broke out and the referee had to be escorted out of the ring and required police protection when he left the Albert Hall two hours later.

TK returned home and was comforted by Elsie. 'I hit him clean and square to the body. He went down. His seconds pulled a fast one – win at any cost. I think my luck has changed.'

Elsie kissed his cheek. 'Why don't you call it a day? We'll find something else to do.'

TK shook his head. 'I can't yet. I'm signed for two more fights. If I don't do well, I'll quit. That's a promise.'

Elsie accepted this, hoping against hope that he would not change his mind when the time came.

Training for his next fight found TK moody – not his usual self – no gags, no fun, and he sparred without his usual flair and showmanship. He decided that in his fight with Simon Rossman, a heavy-set middleweight fighter, he would make an effort to redeem himself. Then, after eight rounds of tough in-fighting by both men, each in turn doing his share of holding, it happened again. TK was disqualified. The referee had had a tough job separating the men and must have run out of patience, and adjudged TK to be the greater offender.

TK was having a bad run. His engine was cracking up and his luck was running out. Elsie was upset to see him in this mood but inwardly thought, 'Two down and one fight to go'. She wondered if she would be wrong in half hoping that he wouldn't beat Len Johnson. It would mean the end of this tough business. TK had been fighting now for the best part of eighteen years against most of the top boxers. He should have retired two years ago. How long could a human body take this grind? She shuddered to think of it.

TK was now a shadow of the old fighter. He began to accept the inevitable, but his confidence was not completely impaired when he entered the ring to fight the black middleweight from Manchester, Len Johnson. It was a tough fight. TK did well for the first three rounds until Johnson discovered that he was not facing the original smashing, crashing, bashing Ted Kid Lewis, and for the next four rounds, they stood toe to toe, exchanging blows. Johnson was becoming stronger and too fast for the ageing TK who had suffered a severe laceration of the mouth. The referee looked at the cut after the seventh round and TK waved him away. Half-way through the eighth, TK's mouth became worse, and the referee stopped the fight.

Elsie waited up all night for TK to return. He was driving back from Manchester with Albert Levy and Curley Carr. TK arrived to fall into Elsie's arms, breaking down in tears. 'What a way to finish. I really tried.'

Elsie was more concerned about TK's cut and swollen lips. She fingered them gently.

'Don't worry, they'll heal up soon,' said TK as he put on a big smile for her.

TK kept his word – 'That was my last fight' – and started to think about the future. They took things easy for the rest of the year, with TK again having slight touches of malaria. Elsie was delighted to have TK home and spending more time playing with Morton.

Nineteen twenty-six started with TK being offered six weeks touring the music-halls. Having recovered and feeling fit, he was delighted to accept and, as usual, knew he could use the money. Whenever TK did have money, he would spend it. He might have originated the saying: 'Spending money as if it were going out of fashion.'

Show business to TK was really an extension of what he had been doing all his life – showing his boxing prowess to an audience – and now he was doing the same without taking the punches. And, he was generally enjoying the life.

TK's brother-in-law, Manny Littlestone, and his partner, Victor Berliner, called backstage to see TK. Victor pleaded with TK. 'We're having a lot of trouble. Can't get anybody who can half fill the Premierland. If you could do two shows for us, it would start the public coming back again.' Victor was persuasive. 'We'll give you 55 per cent of the gate – and two easy opponents.'

TK replied, 'There's no such thing as an easy opponent. They've got two hands like anybody else.'

Manny chimed in, 'You wouldn't have to work any harder than you do in this show.'

They finally wore TK down and he agreed to box Billy Prichard on 7 March, a week after the show closed, and Billy Mattick two weeks later.

TK, having committed himself to Victor and Manny, had to face Elsie. He would rather have had to face Carpentier again, but he was sure she would understand. 'It's not really a comeback, darling,' TK proclaimed, 'it's just two fights. Manny's in trouble and besides, the money will come in handy. It's really easy money.'

Elsie had heard about 'easy money'. 'Easy money! How can you say it's easy money when you're being punched?' But Elsie knew too that she was fighting a losing battle. It was the 'the money will come in handy' that really worried her. Where had all the money gone? 'Well, if you think it will be all right . . . I suppose. . .'

TK kissed her. 'I knew you would understand.'

TK had a week's training for the fight and entered the ring weighing 10 st. 11 lb., giving away just over 16 lb.! He started cautiously, keeping Prichard at bay. Prichard was more aware of TK's reputation than of his age. As the rounds went by, TK boxed himself into condition and in the tenth round changed his tactics. With a sudden change of pace he leapt in with a right cross and a left hook to the chin. That finished the bout. Everyone was delighted with the result and with the way TK had performed.

TK's first thought was to prove to Elsie that he was right. 'See, darling,' as he turned his head from side to side, 'not a mark. He didn't lay a glove on me.'

Elsie was relieved and now only had to wait another two weeks before she could relax again. TK had no trouble with Billy Mattick and by the fourth round had his opponent hanging on whenever possible. The referee warned him to stop holding and make a fight of it, but in the fifth round, the referee had had enough and disqualified Mattick for holding.

Elsie had heard the result from a friend and was waiting with open arms as TK came home, smiling and showing both sides of his face. 'OK, darling, like you said, it was easy, and I've now retired for the second and last time.' They embraced as Elsie cried with joy.

The two fights created further interest with the music-hall proprietors and TK toured for a further five weeks. Then TK received an offer from a most unexpected source. Would he be interested in a boxing instructor's job, working for the Hungarian government on a six months' contract for £3,000 and fares? Would he? His reply was just as it might have been to Jay Jay in the old days: 'Let's grab it!'

PREMIERLAND.
COMMERCIAL ROAD, E.
The Largest and most Up-to-date Boxing Arena in England.
Under the Personal Direction of HARRY MORRIS.
SATURDAY NEXT, MARCH 14th.
IMPORTANT 15-ROUNDS CONTEST.
KID LEWIS
(Feather-wt. Champion of England)
v.
HARRY BERRY
(Of Ireland).
EXTRA SPECIAL 10-ROUNDS CONTEST,
JACK MORRIS
v.
BILLY WILLIAMS.
Special 10-Rounds Contest.
DIXIE BROWN v. TOMMY LEWIS.
Also several Six-Round Contests.
Prices—
Gallery, 1s.; Ring Seats, 2s.; Stage Seats, 3s. and 5s.
ROYAL ALBERT HALL
FRIDAY, DEC. 26 (Evening of Boxing Day)
Under the direction of REDMOND BARRY.
THREE GREAT CONTESTS
20 Three-Minute Rounds Contest:
KID LEWIS v. MATT WELLS
(Ex-World's Welterweight Champion.) (Ex-Lightweight Champion.)
20 Three-Minute Rounds Contest:
PAL MOORE v. CHARLES LEDOUX
(America.) (Bantamweight Champion of Europe.)
12 Three-Minute Rounds Contest:
JOHNNY GRIFFITHS v. FRANCIS CHARLES
(America.) (France.)
Commence at 8 p.m. sharp. Doors open at 7 o'clock.
GEORGES CARPENTIER
(Champion of Europe)
will positively appear and spar four rounds exhibition.
Prices from £1 1s. to £9 9s.
Box Office now open at the Albert Hall and the usual Agencies.
Free Trade Hall,
MANCHESTER,
13th January, 1920, at 7.45 p.m.
THREE GREAT INTERNATIONAL BOXING CONTESTS
H. BARRY presents in a 15 3-minute Rounds Contest,
TED ("KID") LEWIS v. FRANKIE MOODY
Ex Welter-weight Champion of the World Wales' Leading Welter Weight
Conqueror of Matt Wells.
10 3-MINUTE ROUNDS.
TED LESTER v. MARCEL DENIS
Champion Light Weight of Scotland. French Light Weight.
10 3-MINUTE ROUNDS.
TED BREWER v. BLAZY
Welsh Light Weight. Promising French Boy.
Prices: 5/-, 10/6, £1 1s., and a few Ringside Seats at £2 2s. Tax extra.

PART FOUR

I Knew Him Before You Were Born

HOLLAND PARK HALL, HOLLAND PARK AVENUE, W.
MONDAY, JUNE 27th;
20 ROUND CONTEST FOR THE MIDDLEWEIGHT
CHAMPIONSHIP OF GREAT BRITAIN
and the LONSDALE CHAMPIONSHIP CHALLENGE BELT.
KID LEWIS v
JACK BLOOMFIELD.
15 ROUND CONTEST AT 7st 10lb for £250.
JOHNNY BROKER v BILLY MORRIS.
Tickets on sale at the National Sporting Club, Covent Garden,
Holland Park Hall, and all Agencies.
PRICES—RESERVED SEATS £5, £3, £2, £1 & 10s. (Including Tax).

ROYAL ALBERT HALL
FRIDAY, OCT. 14, at 8
Under the Direction of J. ARNOLD WILSON.
Middle-Weight Championship of Great Britain & Europe.
JOHNNY BASHAM (Wrexham)
v
TED (KID) LEWIS (Aldgate)
THEIR FIRST CONTEST AS MIDDLE-WEIGHTS.
TICKETS NOW ON SALE.
BOX OFFICE: Wisden's, 23, Cranbourn Street, W.C.2. Ger. 2120; Albert Hall; and
usual Agencies.
PRICES (inc. tax), 12/-, £1 4s., £2 7s., £3 10s., £5 16s.

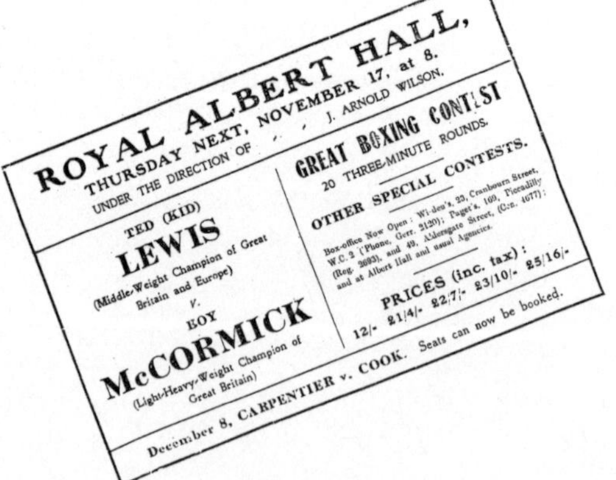

ROYAL ALBERT HALL,
THURSDAY NEXT, NOVEMBER 17, at 8.
UNDER THE DIRECTION OF J. ARNOLD WILSON.
TED (KID)
LEWIS
(Middle-Weight Champion of Great
Britain and Europe)
v.
ROY
McCORMICK
(Light-Heavy-Weight Champion of
Great Britain)
GREAT BOXING CONTEST
20 THREE-MINUTE ROUNDS.
OTHER SPECIAL CONTESTS.
Box-office Now Open: Wisden's, 23, Cranbourn Street,
W.C.2 ('Phone, Gerr. 2120); Paget's, 169, Piccadilly
(Reg. 2693), and 49, Aldersgate Street, (Cen. 4677);
and at Albert Hall and usual Agencies.
PRICES (inc. tax):
12/- £1/4/- £2/7/- £3/10/- £5/16/-
December 8, CARPENTIER v. COOK. Seats can now be booked.

25 Further Continental Adventures

'Yes, it gets harder every year, every month, every day.
But you keep going. Where else is there to go?'

TK

TK's story now becomes my story too – or rather the story as seen directly through my eyes. The trip to Europe in 1925 marks the point at which my memories become so vivid that it almost seems like yesterday. And more than that, Europe in 1925 marked the beginning of the almost indivisible threesome: Elsie, TK and me. No entourage, no Mendeloff family, just the three of us and a set of suitcases.

The Hungarian offer had come out of the blue, giving credibility to TK and Elsie's philosophy, 'all will be alright tomorrow'. They were over the moon; this was the opportunity they had been waiting for – a chance for TK to establish a new career as a boxing coach.

As a ten year-old boy, I was too young to understand all this, when watching my father box in Hungary and later in Berlin, sparring with men from the military and police, I thought it was authentic when he knocked out all three! It was the same later on that year when he entered the ring once again in London, in order to secure enough funds to get us out of hock. I did not realize his opponents were no longer top-liners but were simply awed at being in the same ring as a boxing legend. For that is what TK had become by the time I was old enough to watch him fight – a living legend.

With the loss of his welterweight titles to Tommy Milligan in March 1925, TK's boxing career as a top-liner had come to an end. It then took him more than two years to appreciate fully that boxing could offer him little more than a way, the only way, of making money in an emergency. He was never under the illusion that he could regain his former glories, nor had he become the punch-drunk ex-hero yearning for the golden days to return. He was to make many genuine and determined attempts to establish a new life for himself outside the ring. But, unfortunately, he would always be thwarted by the financial demands constantly being made upon him by his business partners and his 'extended' family. Then boxing would be the final trump card he could deal when all else failed.

The time had also come for TK to consider the position of his parents, his two brothers and unmarried sister Dolly. At a family gathering, his father decided they liked the life in New York and could live near their married daughters. Both Lew and Lionel thought that settling there was a good idea and felt they too would have a better future out there. TK was delighted with their unanimous decision and agreed to pay their fares and give them enough money to settle down and get started in whatever they decided to do. In the meantime, Dolly had become a saleslady and earned a good living, so things looked bright all round.

The trip to Hungary was to prove a happy interlude for the family and a great way to start a new career. Elsie became more relaxed; TK would be at least six months older by the time this assignment finished and that much further away from any comeback plans. Budapest was a beautiful city, they were very satisfied with the hotel, TK was in funds and his wages would more than cover their outgoings. I was sent to a small private school (just 24 pupils) for the children of English residents in a large house in Pest.

TK's job was to instruct a number of men from the army and police in the finer arts of boxing, which he found most rewarding. He was allowed to enter five men at various weights in an open competition in Berlin. TK was delighted with the warm welcome he received when it was announced that he would be working in the team's corner. He was even more delighted when all five won their contests. Before leaving the arena, he was asked if he would be interested in working in Berlin after his completed contract in Hungary. He agreed to think about it. On his return to Budapest, TK was received by Count Addenskolski and the Prime Minister and was rewarded with a number of medals. He was also invited to give them both a series of training sessions to keep fit.

The streets were full of beggars, three or four on every street corner. I remember each time we went into a restaurant, TK's first order was for a couple of dozen sandwiches. We would then walk around, handing them to the poor people. When the sandwiches ran out, TK would give them money – until that ran out. There were very strong anti-Semitic sections in the capital, yet somehow it went unnoticed by my parents. That is, until TK and Elsie became very friendly with a Dr and Mrs Kagan who insisted on having the Lewis family as house guests, so that they might enjoy good Jewish home cooking and at the same time be told the facts of life.

When TK discovered the truth about the anti-Semitism, he wanted to say something to the top brass. TK was always one for saying what was in his heart. But the doctor advised him against it. If he wanted to help, and of course he did, then the only way at that time was with money. TK didn't need much persuasion to give money; he had been doing that all his life!

During the following week, TK became feverish and complained about stomach pains. The doctor examined him and during the examination, checked his teeth. He was certain that TK's problem was his front teeth and he arranged to have them extracted within the next two weeks. Following this TK recovered and during his training classes felt his strength returning. He felt a new man. The training was easier and he was now enjoying the work.

TK continued his association with the Count and the Prime Minister and told them both that he was Jewish. He received the usual answer whenever such an occasion arose. 'Yes, we know, but you're different.'

When the six months were up, TK was presented with a beautiful silver cigarette case from the Count. The case bore the Count's coat of arms and was inscribed 'To Ted Kid Lewis. A most remarkable man.' This inscription was raised and in the Count's handwriting.

In later years TK had several well-known figures add their names to the case, but when Major Arnold Wilson took it to have his signature added, TK never saw it again. Excuses and promises were accepted and as time went by it was forgotten.

After the 1928 Olympic Games, TK received a letter from the Count to say that one of TK's former pupils had won the flyweight championship, and he enclosed a cheque for £100 as a token of gratitude.

When TK told Elsie about the offer to coach in Berlin, she readily agreed; it was, after all, what they wanted. It was to be a refresher course of six weeks for twelve boxing instructors and if he made good it could develop into a longer contract. So, once again, the Lewis family left, this time for Berlin. We moved into the Adlon Hotel where we had previously stayed and I was enrolled with a private tutor with ten other pupils. TK then reported to the official in charge and arranged to start work the following week.

An American/Hungarian by the name of Tony Kranz made

himself known to TK. He had done a little boxing in the past and was looking for a job in Berlin. TK, always ready to help, got the officials to take Tony on as an assistant trainer, someone who would, if needed, be able to stay on after he left. The officials agreed. With Tony in tow, the Adlon became too expensive even for TK, and we moved into a smaller hotel in Unter den Linden. I shared a room with Tony, who taught me to speak a little German and Hungarian.

Towards the end of the contract, TK was to box three men, all heavyweights and all over six feet tall. Tony heard a rumour that they were going to try to beat TK up. The first two would tire him out and the third, the best of the three, would knock him out. Elsie wasn't pleased with Tony's story. I remember TK laughing and saying, 'Well, we'll wait and see. After all, it's only an exhibition and if I give them a good show, they might extend the contract.' TK then insisted that Elsie should come and bring me along to watch.

TK entered the ring wearing 16-ounce gloves, only to discover the first man was wearing 8-ounce gloves. TK went over to the official in charge, and demanded they both wear 16-ounce gloves, or give him 8-ounce ones instead. The official was embarrassed. He had a quick consultation with the boxers and suggested they all wear 8-ounce gloves, if that was all right with TK. 'That suits me. I'm not sure it will suit them,' was TK's reply.

The officials sent for a smaller pair of gloves. While they were being fitted, the smile on TK's face slowly disappeared. They were taking him for a mug. Determination had set in. There was to be no mercy. The bell went. They shook hands. TK stepped back, feinted to the left and threw an overhand right to the jaw. The man dropped like a log. It was fifteen minutes before it was possible to escort the man from the ring. I couldn't understand what all the commotion was about; it was just what I had expected – so why hadn't they?

The second man did not fare much better. He was able to make three wild rushes which TK easily avoided. At the fourth attempt, TK ducked under his opponent's right cross, and landed a straight right to his mid-section. The man stopped in his tracks and dropped to his knees, supporting himself with both arms, and gasping for breath. There was no need to count. TK looked at the officials, beckoning with his right hand. 'OK, bring on the last one.'

I became over-excited, and Elsie had her hands full trying to restrain me, while smiling to the people around us. I said, 'I knew he could do it!' I even think I started to shape up, that is until I felt my ear being twisted, which seemed to do the trick.

The public began to clap and make cat-calls, while the officials were dragging the second boxer to his corner. The officials didn't like what was happening to their men. They went to TK's corner. They felt they shouldn't let the next man appear, that it would not be appreciated by the public. TK agreed to let him go the three rounds, providing he did not try to be clever.

The bell went for the first round. TK played with him, dancing around with left-hand leads, then going in close and tying him up. His opponent did not make one wrong move during the three rounds and was still on his feet after the final bell. The crowd changed its attitude. However, I couldn't understand and asked Elsie, 'Why didn't Daddy knock him out?'

Elsie smiled. 'He's a friend of Daddy's, that's why. You don't hurt your friends.'

The following day TK was informed that they would not be requiring his services, or those of his assistant, after the six weeks were up.

In the meantime, TK discovered what he considered to be a natural heavyweight, Hans Segal. Hans was twenty-four years old, six foot two inches, blond and weighing 14 st. 10 lb. He had no experience but shaped up well. TK arranged to pay Hans living expenses, £5 a week pocket money and to give his father £10 a week until his first fight. Tony became his trainer and our chief cook and bottle-washer.

At the end of four weeks of constant schooling in the art of boxing, Hans was looking great. In the meantime TK had run out of money (with Tony and Hans eating as if there was no tomorrow). The hotel manager was friendly and a fight fan and prepared to wait for his bill. TK contacted a Hamburg promoter, who agreed to give Hans a bout, provided he could see him spar first. The trial came and Hans looked good, that is, until the fourth-rate heavy they had dug up threw a left to the stomach and a right to the chin!

The following day Hans left for home and a change of occupation. I never liked Hans, I thought he was a big show-off and stupid. It was rather ironic, because two weeks earlier I had reason to call him a *Dom Kop* (my German was improving!). He got annoyed and threatened to leave, but Elsie and TK made me apologize as he could have been the ticket back into big-time boxing.

Things were now getting serious. I would be sent to the local restaurant where we all used to go, to eat by myself and to tell the manager to put it on my father's bill. I never realized how bad things were, only that when there was a problem, TK would come up smiling. But it seemed there was nowhere for TK to turn.

He told Elsie, 'Look, I'm feeling well . . . and fit, and the only way we're going to get out of here is for me to fight. There's nobody here who could beat me.' They were in a foreign country and TK knew no other way. Elsie accepted the situation. TK tried all the promoters he knew but could not get a fight. The usual promises were forthcoming but nothing materialized. TK didn't want anyone in England to know of his plight, so, grasping at straws, he decided to cable Charlie Harvey. Charlie owed him $8,000 which he could account for. The cable read 'Stranded in Berlin with family stop please cable a thousand dollars urgent stop address Hotel Linden Berlin stop will repay upon arriving London regards Ted Lewis'.

TK and Elsie waited for two terrible, nerve-racking days until the answer arrived. TK couldn't open it fast enough. His face changed. He went white and slumped into the armchair. He looked as though he had seen a ghost. He handed the cable to Elsie. 'What do you think of this?'

She read it out aloud. 'Received your wire stop kidding. I don't like these jokes regards Charlie Harvey.'

Elsie handed the cable to Tony. 'This is ridiculous,' she said and with that, she went to the wardrobe and took out her mink coat. 'This will have to go.' TK objected but she wouldn't hear of it. She handed it to Tony.

'Pawn this and let's get the hell out of here.'

Tony knew where to go. What TK didn't know, however, was that Tony had pawned two of Elsie's rings during the past four weeks. He thought the money she kept coming up with was some she had put away.

Tony came back with the money, only to find that it wasn't enough to pay the hotel bill and four fares back to London.

'Pack my bags,' TK told Elsie. 'I'm going to London. You and Morton stay here. Tony will take care of you.'

Elsie was already packing his bag, as Tony went to fix the travel arrangements. TK left that night. Two days later, a cable arrived with enough money to pay the hotel bill, cover three fares back to London and to reclaim the coat and the rings from the pawnshop. Elsie was relieved. She told Tony, 'Pack up. We're leaving. Teddy's done it again.'

26 The Comeback Treadmill

'You could Kid Doyle, Kid Berg, even Kid Lewis – but
you couldn't kid Mummy!'

TK to Morton

The first thing TK did on his return to London was to see his old
school chum, Issy Farrar, a furrier, who was also backing boxing
shows, including the Premierland. He lent TK enough money to
bring us back from Berlin and to set us up in an apartment. TK
met us at the station, grinning from ear to ear, very excited. 'My
old pal, Issy Farrar, has great ideas for me, he's going to show me
how to make money.'

TK had rented an apartment with four bedrooms, in Maida Vale,
so there would be room for sister Dolly and Tony until he got settled.
Farrar splashed TK's name all over the boxing posters; he became a
great drawing card and the crowds came to see him referee, and he
received £50 per show. Farrar then approached Joe Morris, a boxing
manager, asking whether, if TK made a comeback, he would draw
the crowds. Morris was quite sure he would, as long as he was kept
away from the top-flight men. They put the idea to TK, suggesting
a number of opponents whom TK had seen box and, in fact, in a
couple of cases, had refereed. He would have to ask Elsie.

Once again, TK prepared for his hardest fight. He told Elsie it was
against six men he could easily beat. Elsie bit her lip. She had heard
it all before, but TK hurried on: 'It will put us on our feet and settle
our debts, and it's only six fights in three months.'

Elsie protested; she would find a job and go to work. TK wouldn't
hear of it; it would be over his dead body. That was the cue for Elsie's
punch-line: 'That's what I'm afraid of, it'll kill you!' But TK won the
battle. He had promised Issy and he couldn't go back on his word –
Elsie had no chance.

TK set up training camp at Southend for his second comeback, with
the help of Joe Morris, Curley Carr and Tony Kranz acting as one of

his sparring partners. I visited the camp on weekends when I could get away from the new school. I enjoyed watching TK train. He was in good spirits and didn't seem to mind the gruelling routine. In fact, if truth be known, he had missed it. TK even arranged for Tony to take me to see the first fight, that was if Elsie did not object. At first she did, but my 'Daddy promised me' won the day.

The press were not over-enthusiastic, but TK was still a good draw and the Ilford Skating Rink was sold out. TK weighed in at 11 st. 1 lb., and his opponent, Joe Green, at 11 st. 12 lb. The crowd roared as TK climbed into the ring, shaking hands with a number of ringsiders through the ropes. He waved and blew a kiss to the press table where I was seated.

Then the bell went and I thought my heart had stopped beating. But all was well. TK looked good to me, and Green seemed to be either grabbing TK around the shoulders or running backwards. TK was having trouble with his cup, which in those days was only attached to a jock-strap. He backed into a corner, fending and feinting Green off while he shook off the cup and, as it slid down his leg, he kicked it away. In my excitement, I tore up a bundle of handbills for the next show, as TK finally caught up with Green, and in the sixth round Green retired.

Everybody seemed more than satisfied with TK's performance; the excitement in the dressing room was overwhelming. Everybody was trying to get close to shake TK's hand or, failing that, were patting my head and saying how good my father was. I didn't need to be told; I was there to see for myself.

Back home, Elsie was relieved when TK showed both sides of his face – she could see he was unmarked. TK picked me up and put his arm around Elsie. 'Morton brought me luck, I'm going to take him to all my fights as a good luck charm.' Elsie had no answer to that! Over the next eleven weeks, I saw TK have five more fights, all at the Premierland. His opponents could not be termed worthy of his steel, but TK could still fill most of the halls in London. Following the Green fight, TK knocked out Jim Carr in three, Noel Steenhorst in nine, Ted Coveney in six, and the imported Belgian, Ansemes, in one. The prices were increased for the last bout, because his opponent was of a higher grade. Joe Rolfe had a 12 lb. advantage. Nevertheless, TK gave him a good working over, before knocking him out in the eleventh round.

Once again, the Lewis family were back to normal, and following a two weeks' rest, TK took his show on tour and was once again in funds, with a goodly share being sent out to the Mendeloff family. News of TK's successes reached South Africa and the boxing fans wanted to see TK in action, as he had not fought during the 1923 visit. He was offered two fights and, as a sweetener, a music-hall tour. The money was good and he accepted. And he had his story already prepared for Elsie. 'How would you like a trip to New York?'

Elsie couldn't believe her ears. 'Would I? When do we go?'

'Next week if you want to, that is, you and Morton. I'll meet you there later.'

Elsie was puzzled and couldn't understand. TK then started his spiel, that he had been offered music-hall dates in South Africa, that she and Morton could go with him, but if she went straight to New York, it would save a lot of money and, besides, it would give her more time to spend with her family.

Elsie didn't need the sales talk. She had been to South Africa, and perhaps this would be an opportunity to settle in the States. TK's subterfuge worked and once again the Lewis family 'packed up and left', this time Elsie and I left for New York, and TK for South Africa, with enough money for his trip after giving half his bankroll to Elsie and the other half to the Mendeloffs.

Elsie and I arrived in New York and with the help of her family and friend Ada, found and furnished an apartment in Eastern Parkway, Brooklyn, and located another school for me. In the meantime, TK was still on board ship travelling to South Africa. He managed to do some light training during the trip, to the delight of the passengers, and declared, 'The trip did me the world of good. I felt great.' The press and his old friend Fireman Anderson were there to welcome him. TK stayed with the Anderson family, prior to the three-week music-hall tour.

In New York, weekly cables kept on arriving from TK, usually containing a banker's draft, with a message stating: 'Feeling great. Show doing well. More news and money next week. Love to all, Teddy.' For the first time Elsie began to relax and enjoyed getting the apartment ready for when TK arrived. In the meantime the South African music-hall tour ended, and though the press had been kind, they were really looking forward to his first contest in Johannesburg. His opponent was to be South Africa's light heavyweight champion, Alex Storbeck.

TK trained hard for the contest. The match was to be at catch-weights. He weighed in at 11 st., with Storbeck tipping the scales at 12 st. 12 lb. This did not worry TK, as it was his usual fate. The fight caused a sensation and surprised most of the fans, as well as the press, most of whom now regarded TK as an old man in the boxing sense, as he was, after all, in his thirty-sixth year.

One sportswriter wrote: 'The Storbeck versus Lewis fight sensation: Kid Carter, former boxer and referee, gave the usual instructions, and the boxers touched gloves. Both were in the centre of the ring as the bell went, Lewis feinted, threw a left hook which put Storbeck down for a count of eight. Another left hook dropped him again for a nine count. This occurred five times, five left hooks, five counts. Then the old Kid measured his opponent with a left and crossed him with a right and the fight was over.'

This display caused considerable interest in the press and a match was made with Johnny Squires, the heavyweight champion of South Africa, for the following month.

Elsie and Ada had finished the apartment when TK's first letter arrived, which was sent prior to the forthcoming Storbeck fight which, of course, was not mentioned. The letter was full of good news, that the show was doing well, that they all loved him and would she consider living there, as it wouldn't be difficult to earn a living in South Africa.

However, the day after the fight, Elsie's brother Harry was so delighted when he read in the sporting press that TK had stopped Storbeck in one round, that he rushed to show Elsie, who couldn't believe what she saw. She cabled TK: 'What's going on? Worried. Seen newspaper report of fight. I thought you were retired. Cable situation. Love Elsie.'

I couldn't understand why Elsie was worried. I was delighted and told her so. 'Mummy, Daddy couldn't have done any better, it only went one round.'

She smiled. 'You wouldn't understand, we all know he's good. But Daddy's retired, he's too old to fight.' But I still didn't understand. After all, wasn't he the best?

TK's reply to Elsie's cable soon came: 'Still touring. Easy fight offered with good money. Took it between show bookings. Letter follows explaining everything. Love Teddy.' Elsie had no alternative but to accept the position, knowing he would do what he thought was best for the family.

TK did three more weeks touring the music-halls, leaving the last ten days to train for the Squires fight. He found the climate hard going but kept in fairly good condition. Weight was no problem. In fact, he scaled 10 st. 12 lb. to Squires's 14 st. 8 lb. The press, on the day of the fight, described the boxers as Mutt and Jeff because of the difference in weight and height.

The fight went the fifteen rounds and the referee declared it a draw. TK thought he had done enough to win, but accepted the fact that it was Squires's home town. Many years later, TK told me the story of the fight.

'He was at least six foot three tall and almost four stone heavier. I tried to do him in the first couple of rounds, but he didn't want to come forward. He saw what had happened to Storbeck and didn't want to take any chances. I caught him with a right cross and double left hook in the ninth round and he fell forward and grabbed me. I couldn't try to finish him – he was too big and they were my best shots, and there were six more rounds to go. I was satisfied to get into the clinch and grab some rest. I kept leading with my left in his face, feinting, moving and trying to outbox him. Every time he got me in a corner, I swayed from left to right, and said, "Don't hit the old man" and kidded him into another clinch. I think the bell for the end of the fight sounded as good to him as it did to me. He came into the dressing room after the fight, shook hands and thanked me for not finishing him in the ninth and letting him go the distance.'

TK then grinned from ear to ear. 'Little did he know, I would have if I could, but I couldn't.' He always enjoyed telling that story.

The promoters immediately offered TK a return bout, but he said he needed a rest and would let them know. TK toured the halls for another three weeks when he began to feel under the weather. He decided to return to London; the promoters were certainly disappointed. But he consoled them by saying he would return in about three months and fight Squires again. He cabled Elsie that he was coming to New York, but would stop off in London for a couple of weeks. He then boarded ship at Cape Town for the journey home.

On the second day out, TK had difficulty in getting out of bed. The ship's doctor was unable to diagnose the complaint and TK was immediately removed to the sick bay, where he was to receive treatment for the remainder of the trip. On arrival at Southampton, with his condition gradually worsening, the ship's doctor arranged for a stretcher. This TK declined. He was met by Joe Morris, Curley Carr and Manny Littlestone. They were shocked by TK's condition. He was taken to see a doctor in London who immediately told TK that he had typhoid fever and ordered him into hospital where he remained for seven weeks. It was touch and go – a veritable life and death struggle. Twice a rabbi was called in to say prayers. TK's main worry was Elsie. He had his sister Dolly write once a week on his behalf, saying he was unable to write as his right hand was bandaged.

To the astonishment of the doctor and all concerned, TK made a remarkable recovery and was beginning to feel himself, when he received a cable from South Africa asking, 'When are you returning to South Africa?' TK overestimated his recovery and considered the trip. He cabled Elsie. 'Have offer for another tour of South Africa. Will be leaving in a couple of weeks.' TK thought the voyage would do the trick for his complete return to health. However, Elsie replied, 'Never mind South Africa. Come to New York. I know what's been going on.' Elsie had had a visit the day before the cable arrived from a friend who had just arrived from London and who had told Elsie the good news of TK's recovery.

27 Desperate Days

Within seven days TK was on his way to the States. The voyage
did him the world of good. The Lewises and the Mendeloffs were
amazed to see how well TK looked as he came down the companion
way. There followed a happy and relieved family reunion with
TK attempting to explain his subterfuge to Elsie, which was not
necessary as having him home and well was enough for her. They
decided to take the Mendeloffs' suggestion to go to Atlantic City for
a couple of weeks, as it would do them both good and they would
look after me.

TK's mother and father were now settled in New York amongst
Flo, Rose and their husbands and, much to the delight of TK and
Elsie, they were becoming financially independent. It was just as
well, as TK's bankroll would not last for ever. It was now April
1928 and he had to think about making some money and plans for
the future. When TK visited Charlie Harvey he took me along as a
precaution in case he lost his temper. Charlie looked pleased to see
him and patted me on the head (I took a lot of such punishment over
the years until I grew tall enough to be out of reach!).

TK wasted no time in telling Charlie what he thought. It was
the first and only time that TK ever swore in front of me. 'It's no
thanks to you, you son-of-a-bitch. The first time I ever asked you
for a favour, and you joked about it.'

Charlie acted hurt. 'I didn't know that telegram was for real, I
thought it was one of your gags.'

TK composed himself. He had said his piece and could see no
profit in continuing. 'Yeah. Some gag. Had you going – but you
didn't *know* it was a gag, did you?' They both smiled and shook
hands. Charlie had heard that TK had done well in South Africa,
and wanted to know if he was in shape and interested in work.

TK said he was thinking about turning it in, but would bear it in mind.

Our next stop was the great Madison Square Garden to visit Jimmy Johnston. I got the usual pat on the head, but his hand had to reach up higher than usual – we were the same height! TK asked Jimmy if there was any work he could do in the game, other than fight. Jimmy did not think so, but said he would see. TK did his best to get something going, but New York wasn't London. He fell for a number of get-rich money-making deals, which all proved abortive and, in all fairness, were so well promoted that most people, let alone TK, would have been taken in.

In the meantime, he had completely recovered his health and, for the first time in his life, there was nothing medically wrong with him. He began to get that urge again.

TK had a long talk with Elsie about their future which he did not think was in New York. He felt his roots were in England. 'I know everybody there. I've lots of friends. Maybe we could take another pub – or open a club – something. There's nothing like that over here for me. My folks are settled in, Flo and Rose are now able to look after them, and Lew and Lionel are working. So there's nothing here to hold us.' Elsie knew he was right.

'What do you want to do?' she asked, knowing very well what the 'something' would be.

'I'll work something out, I'll try and get a bankroll together and then make plans.'

TK knew there was only one way to get money quickly. It was his cure-all, his panacea. He'd been doing it all his life. He called Charlie Harvey to tell him he wanted a few more fights, after which he was going back to England.

Charlie was delighted and asked when he could be ready. 'I need about two or three weeks' training,' TK replied.

'I'll call you,' Charlie said, and hung up. Two days later Charlie called. 'Jimmy says he can use you on his next bill . . . in ten days' time. Good money . . . twelve grand. What do you say?'

'Who with?' TK asked.

'Maxie Rosenbloom,' was the reply.

TK knew Maxie well. He had courted TK's sister Dolly when he had been in London earlier in the year. 'Ten days isn't very long to get into shape and Rosenbloom's no mug. He's in line for a title shot.' (In fact Rosenbloom won the light-heavyweight title in 1930 and held it until 1934.)

'That's why I got you twelve grand. Do you want it or not? Jimmy's waiting to hear,' Charlie explained. He didn't explain that nobody wanted the fight, but TK could not afford to lose the chance. It was nearly twice as much as an ordinary fight.

'O.K. I'll take it.' He considered Maxie couldn't hurt him twice as much as anybody else, so it was good value. (Rosenbloom was known as 'Slapsie Maxie' because he used to extend his left hand and slap his opponent's face, using the inside and outside of his glove, which was later deemed a foul blow.)

TK now had to tell Elsie what he had done. He thought up all kinds of stories in the taxi on the way home but, when they came face to face, he couldn't remember his story and just blurted out, 'I've just taken a fight in ten days' time. It's good money. Twelve thousand dollars.' He was searching Elsie's eyes for a reaction. 'Then I'll have another fight after that and we'll have enough to go home and get started.' He waited for Elsie to reply. But Elsie didn't react. She wasn't surprised. She had been expecting it for the past three weeks.

'Well, you know best. I just hope you don't get hurt.' She leaned over and embraced him.

TK received a warm welcome considering the fight fans hadn't seen him for seven years, when he had lost to Augie Ratner. The fight started without any fireworks and ended without any fireworks, Maxie dancing around, slapping TK's face, while TK tried to get in close, the pattern for the first two rounds. The crowd could see that at thirty-five, TK's reflexes were slowing, and not only from age but from the enormous demands he had made on his health over the years. Nevertheless he tried to give them value. He kept going forward and punched away at close quarters when he could.

In the interval before the third round, TK said to Charlie, 'I thought slapping was illegal.'

Charlie replied, 'Well, it's not law yet. It's up to the referee.'

As TK got set for the bell, he said, 'Well, we'll see about that.'

For the next two rounds the crowd were amused to see TK outslapping 'Slapsie Maxie' with Maxie's speed keeping him out of danger from TK's body punches.

The fifth and sixth rounds found TK and Rosenbloom standing toe to toe, punching and holding, with the referee having trouble in parting them and, in the last minute of the sixth round, TK landed a left hook on Maxie's chin after the referee called 'break clean' – and TK was disqualified!

One reporter wrote: 'Ted Kid Lewis, the old welterweight champion, was last night the victim of the "clean break" rule, when he was disqualified in the sixth round against Maxie Rosenbloom. It was an interesting bout up to that point with Rosenbloom slightly ahead on points.'

TK wasn't unhappy about his showing but considered that the referee was wrong in stopping the fight. Charlie Harvey was satisfied with TK's performance and could see some more mileage, as well as income, in TK. Jimmy Johnston, on the other hand, was delighted. The crowd were satisfied. Rosenbloom's manager was happy and TK declared he was available to fill in whenever needed.

TK told Charlie and Jimmy, 'Get me another fight and I'll call it a day.'

Elsie was relieved to see TK in a happy mood when he arrived home after the fight. Her brother Harry assured her that TK hadn't been hurt and that the referee must have been crazy. He had spoiled the fight.

'One more fight, darling, and we'll make for home.'

After expenses and Harvey's share, TK now had $7,000 towards his bankroll. He rested for a couple of weeks.

Harvey called. 'Jimmy can put you in against KO Phil Kaplin. . . in three weeks, which gives you a little more time. What d'you say?'

TK realized that KO Phil Kaplin was in form and no doubt he hadn't got the KO in front of his name for nothing. But they couldn't get anyone else. Kaplin was good but not quite championship quality, and was being avoided. 'How much?' TK asked.

'Six grand,' came the reply.

TK hummed a little. 'Get me nine and I'll take it and finish.'

'I'll call you back,' Charlie replied. Charlie called back with a final offer of eight grand. 'Take it or leave it.'

TK took it and had two weeks' training up in the mountains. Elsie consoled herself that, come what might, this was to be his last fight. During the final week of training, Jimmy Johnston, who was matchmaker at the Garden, arranged for the press to visit the training camp to do a story on Leo Lomski. Johnston had Lomski booked to meet Maxie Rosenbloom in an eliminator for the light-heavyweight title the week after TK's fight with Kaplin. TK agreed to spar with Lomski for the press when Johnston explained, 'It will be good publicity for both of you.'

TK's brother Lew, who was helping him train, brought me up for the weekend to watch the workout. It was to be a big day in the camp.

The gym was packed with the press and newsreel cameras. I watched while both TK and Lomski shadow-boxed and punched the bag as they warmed up. They both wore 16-ounce gloves and head guards. It was very exciting when they entered the ring. I was seated next to TK's corner. Johnston signalled to the newsreel men and struck the bell, and Lomski came tearing out, swinging lefts and rights from all angles, with TK having no trouble blocking them with his arms. He seemed quite content to carry on as, after all, it was only a show for the press. But near the end of the round, one or two swings got through and TK didn't like it.

Back in the corner, TK beckoned Johnston over. 'What the hell's going on, Jimmy? He's trying for real and I'm not getting paid for this.'

Jimmy replied, 'The press are here to see how good he is.'

I'll never forget his reply. 'Well, he ain't that good.'

While Manny Seaman, TK's trainer, who in later years was to train Muhammad Ali, was wiping TK's face and putting in his gumshield, Johnston looked back, must have thought he was on a safe bet, and said, 'Well, if you think you can do better, why don't you try? They're here to see you as well.'

TK took out the gumshield and looked at Manny. 'Is he kidding?'

Manny replied, 'No, I think he means it, why don't you show him?'

TK smiled, looked at me, winked, and put his gumshield back. Lomski was waiting in the centre of the ring. They rang the bell again in case TK hadn't heard it. TK nodded towards Jimmy, rolled his gloves down his thighs and mumbled, 'Right, then,' and turned towards the centre of the ring.

Lomski came forward, throwing punches. TK blocked them, standing his ground. Leo then started dancing around, trying to pick off punches. When TK sprang forward with the first real punch he had thrown so far, a perfect left hook to the chin, Leo Lomski dropped like a sack of potatoes – out to the world.

Pandemonium broke loose! Managers, promoters, trainers, seconds, all jumped into the ring, with the press fighting to get pictures, and Jimmy Johnston trying to get in the way to stop them. It was great fun, I was jumping for joy as TK, having climbed out of the ring, grabbed me as Lew threw his dressing gown over him and made for the dressing room door. TK and Lew both burst out laughing, and I already had tears running down my cheeks from excitement. 'You should have seen Morton when Leo went down, he was jumping for joy, "That's my dad! That's my dad!" he was shouting. I managed to huddle up in front of him to keep him quiet and hide my own face.'

It took the helpers over five minutes to bring Lomski round, with Johnston making all kinds of excuses for what had happened to Lomski and, at the same time, telling the press that Lewis would do the same thing to KO Kaplin next week. In the meantime, TK got dressed and we slipped out the back door of the gym and went for a walk in the country. TK said he was annoyed at what had happened, that Jimmy was taking a liberty and that he hadn't like showing up Leo. But he agreed with Lew that Leo was trying to put him away, so perhaps they had both got their just deserts.

We got back to the camp a couple of hours later, to find most of the press still there with Johnston trying to build a story to suit both men. TK made excuses and said it was a lucky punch. 'What, with 16-ounce gloves?' one scribe commented. I burst out laughing, but stopped suddenly when both TK and Johnston turned to me and held their fingers to their lips.

The press were not to be fooled. Those who were the promoters' men kept the story in low profile, but one paper said: 'Old-time welterweight champion, training to meet KO Kaplin next week, still looks good at thirty-five. Yesterday in an exhibition bout for the press, he pole-axed Leo Lomski in two, with a great left hook. The same Lomski that's training to fight Maxie Rosenbloom in a title eliminator.'

That night after dinner, in front of everybody, TK apologized; his apology was gracefully accepted by Lomski, who went on to box a fifteen-round draw with Rosenbloom. Lomski had quite a record between 1927 and 1930. He beat world champions Tiger Flowers, Pete Latzo, Mike McTigue and James J. Braddock, lost on points to Micky Walker and Tommy Loughran, and also lost three and drew three times with Maxie Rosenbloom.

The publicity TK received from the Lomski affair cheered him up no end. But the training grind was beginning to tell. He was becoming moody for the first time in his life and he declined to join in the usual card games in the evening after training.

TK weighed in for the Kaplin fight and came home for his usual sleep before a fight. Everybody spoke in hushed tones, until Charlie Harvey came to collect him. We all wished him well as he left with Charlie, Lew and Harry by taxi to the Garden. It was to be an exciting evening as the fight was being broadcast, but when the time came to tune in, the door opened and in walked Lew and Harry followed by TK, with both hands bandaged up!

Their taxi had been involved in a smash and, in an effort to protect himself, TK had damaged both hands. But nobody else had been hurt.

Elsie went white. 'Thank God, it could have been worse, it must be an omen,' she cried. The fight was called off and there was nothing TK could do. No fight, no money, and, to add insult to injury, the training expenses had to be paid for.

TK and Morton, 1935

28 The USA Bids Farewell

'I was a fighter, fighting for my life, my pride, the pleasure
of winning, proving I could still do it.'

TK

It took eight weeks for TK's hands to mend. He did a little road-work
to keep up some semblance of fitness, but the lay-off did not help his
frame of mind. He became very moody around the house, except
when we played cards, which he seemed to enjoy, maybe because
I was about the only one he could beat. Elsie was content to watch
and say to anybody listening, 'Look at my two boys playing, bless
them.' The waiting was taking its toll and during a visit to Lindy's
restaurant, where the famous, not so famous and the infamous
gathered, TK was once again conned into another sure-fire winner
and bang went the best part of his bankroll.

Expenses were mounting and nothing was coming in. TK was
becoming worried and finding it hard to hide anything from Elsie.
One evening he plucked up courage and told her, 'We may have to
give up the flat, and for the time being I'll ask my folks to put us
up.' Elsie was prepared for this. 'There's no need to worry your
folks. I've already spoken to my sister Anna. She would love to
have us and, besides, Morton would be near his cousins, and I'll
have company as well.'

TK knew Elsie was right. She didn't tell him that arrangements
had already been made and that she had given notice to vacate the
flat. So once again, the Lewis family 'packed up and left', this time
just across town. It meant changing schools again, but I was used to
moving and changing schools. In fact, I didn't know anything else.

We were made very comfortable and TK continued to make
the rounds of people he knew, but without success. He felt very
embarrassed, living in somebody else's house, and he hated being
thought of as a failure.

It was near the end of November, the temperature was freezing,
and his bankroll had gone. So TK decided the time had come to

go home, where he knew his friends would help him get something started. However, he still needed another bankroll. He told Elsie, 'I'm going to try to get some of the money Charlie and Jimmy owe me, then I'll go back to London. You and Morton stay here and as soon as I get something started, I'll send for you.'

Elsie knew it was the only way out. TK went to see Charlie and Jimmy, explaining his situation. 'Give me three grand each and we'll call it square. That way I can get back and get something going.' Charlie and Jimmy went into another room to discuss the idea and TK waited on pins and needles. They came back.

Jimmy said, 'We want to help, if only for old times' sake, but we can't do six grand.' TK was choked. Charlie waited for it to sink in. 'But we figured we could make it four grand and call it quits.'

TK recovered his composure and proceeded, in his usual way, to hug and kiss them both to show his appreciation.

TK and Elsie began to make plans. She had arranged for me to stay with TK's sister Flo in Staten Island, where I could go to school with Flo's son, Jack. Elsie would take a modelling job in a fashion house where she had worked before her marriage. TK didn't like the idea but Elsie insisted. 'It will keep me busy and help pay the expenses.'

TK booked his passage, then he and Elsie took me to Aunty Flo's in Staten Island, where I would stay until TK got settled in London. Four days prior to TK's departure, Charlie Harvey called. 'How do you feel?'

'OK, thanks. Why?' TK asked.

'Well, there's a job going in Montreal on the seventeenth. They need an opponent for Charlie Belanger, the Canadian light-heavyweight champion. I thought you could use the money – four grand. What do you think?'

'My passage is booked for the twelfth,' TK replied.

'So? Postpone it. Go the following week. Don't be a fool. Grab the dough. Look how hard you worked for the Kaplin fight and got nothing – and banged up to boot. Also . . . I spoke to Jimmy and we agreed that we won't take our cut. The four grand's yours!'

TK liked the idea. 'But I told Elsie I was through. I don't want to upset her. What can I say?'

Charlie considered the problem. 'Tell you what to do. First, cancel your ticket. Then tell Elsie I've arranged a passage for you from Halifax. Tell her I get the ticket free. It's a friend of mine – and the boat departs on the thirteenth. You say goodbye to her and leave for Montreal on the eleventh, saying that you're going to

Halifax. There won't be any publicity in New York before the fight. How does that sound?'

TK hesitated. 'Yeah, it could work. I'll take it. Thanks, Charlie. Thank Jimmy for me.'

'You can thank him yourself. He'll go up for the fight. It will only cost you his expenses.'

TK was delighted to think that Jimmy was coming up to look after him.

Elsie was disappointed with the rearrangements. It meant TK leaving a day earlier.

TK trained in the local gym for four days but found it hard to work up a sweat. It was fifteen degrees below in Toronto. Jimmy arrived well in time for the weigh-in. TK scaled 11 st. 1 1b., and Belanger 13 st. 5 1b. After the weigh-in TK noticed Jimmy in a heated argument with the promoter. He walked over. 'What's up, Jay?'

Jimmy turned on TK. 'Stay out of this, Ted,' and pointing said, 'Wait over there for me,' and he turned to continue his battle of words, while TK walked back to join the other boxers and managers.

TK watched Jimmy disappear with the promoter into an office and emerge thirty minutes later, smiling. He grabbed TK's arm. 'Come on, let's go,' and escorted him out on to the streets.

TK asked, 'What the hell's going on?'

Jimmy put his hand on TK's shoulder. 'Nothing to worry about. He was trying to cut down on the money, and I wouldn't stand for it. That's all.'

Jimmy put TK to bed, put in a call for 6.30 pm and dozed off in the armchair.

Jimmy woke TK and gave him a massage on the bed, at the same time imparting some words of wisdom. 'This guy. He's an ex-lumberjack . . . a slow thinker. Needs four or five rounds to warm up. He hits hard when he lands . . . but telegraphs his punches. He'll be green in the clinches.'

TK was relaxing, enjoying the massage.

Jimmy went on. 'They say he's a sucker for over-the-top punches. Don't waste any time. Go all out from the bell. Throw a few punches and then tie him up.'

TK turned over. 'Well, that's the way I figured it. Make it quick.'

The house was full. The crowd had come to support Belanger, the local boy, and they were curious to see what was left of the old champion. TK received some cheers from the few hundred scattered

Englishmen in the audience. Belanger's supporters raised the roof as he climbed through the ropes. The introductions were made and the bell went.

Belanger rose slowly to his six foot three inches and by the time he had taken three steps, TK was across the ring, had leaped into action, and with all his strength had thrown an overhand right, followed by a left hook, both landing on his opponent's chin. Charlie fell forward on to TK. Had TK not been there, Belanger would have gone down. TK pushed him off and landed another right to the chin. Charlie fell backwards. This time the ropes saved him. TK went in for the kill, started a two-handed barrage, when the referee stepped in and pulled him off. TK stepped back and looked at the referee, wondering what he was going to do. Charlie was still on his feet, but lying on the ropes for support, not knowing where he was. TK couldn't understand what was going on. The referee wasn't counting, nor did he make an attempt to stop the fight. TK's supporters were screaming for him to go in and finish it. TK started forward as the referee came between him and Belanger. For a few seconds, it became a wrestling match between TK trying to push the referee out of the way, while the referee was trying to hold TK back. Finally, exasperated, TK said, 'Get out of the way,' still trying to go forward, and with Charlie still helpless on the ropes. The referee threw up both hands, then pointed to TK. 'I'm the referee. Don't tell me what to do. I tell you. You're disqualified.'

TK was flabbergasted. The referee again pointed to the dressing rooms. 'Out.' He turned to Belanger and raised his hand in victory. The crowd was stunned into silence by the drama that was going on in the ring. TK, realizing what had happened, decided to accept his fate, turned, grabbed Jimmy by the arm, and left the ring as the crowd roared their disapproval.

Back in the dressing room, TK was livid as Jimmy cut off his bandages. 'He was out on his feet. I had him stone cold. I've heard of home town referees, but that was ridiculous.'

Jimmy looked up. 'You know, the whole thing was over in forty seconds. I said do it quick, but it was too quick for the referee. It's a shame he was so close . . . before you had a chance to drop him.'

TK was freeing his hands of the bandages. 'I suppose the commission will stop my money?'

Jimmy was looking in the mirror, tying his tie. 'Under the normal circumstances, yes.'

TK looked up from drying himself. 'What do you mean – normal circumstances?'

Jimmy was trying to tease TK when the dressing room door opened and two reporters came in. TK got dressed while Jimmy talked to them. TK was more concerned about his money. Jimmy used the old cliché, 'We was robbed . . . the guy was out on his feet. One push – never mind a punch – and he would have dropped.'

'What happened? Why did you argue with the referee, TK?' one reporter asked.

'Listen, I was in there to fight and I decided to try to get it over quickly. That's what I was getting paid for, I hope.'

After a few more questions and answers, the reporters left. TK turned to Jimmy. 'Well, what's the score?'

Jimmy put his hand in his hip pocket. 'Can you count?'

TK was getting upset. 'Sure I can count. It was the referee who couldn't count.'

With that, Jimmy was holding a bundle of notes. 'Hold out your hands and start counting.'

TK was completely confused. He held out his hands and his drawn appearance slowly faded and he began to smile as Jimmy counted out fifty $20 dollar bills, forty fifties and ten hundreds. 'Thirty-eight hundred, thirty-nine hundred,' and holding up the last hundred dollar bill, 'Four thousand. This one's for my expenses.'

TK gripped the bills in his hand, grinning from ear to ear. 'How did you do it?'

'You remember the argument I was having with the promoter when I sent you away?' he asked. TK nodded. 'Well, I know him from of old. He likes to make deductions after the fight and hold the money up as long as he can, and, as we wanted to get the hell out of here, I demanded money up front, or no fight. It's the old saying, Ted. Don't promote a promoter. I know the answers. I wrote the script.'

TK burst out laughing, put his arms around Jimmy and kissed him on both cheeks. Jimmy screamed in pain. TK was standing on his foot while he embraced him.

After recovering, Jimmy got down to business. 'There's a sailing out of New York the day after tomorrow. I've booked you a berth. We can travel up tomorrow. You can either check into a hotel in Manhattan and catch the boat the following morning – or go to see Elsie and make your peace.'

TK arrived home. Elsie couldn't believe her eyes. TK was all smiles. He dropped his bags and seized her in a bear-hug embrace. He did not stand on her feet as her footwork had improved over the years.

'What happened? I thought you would be well on your way by now.'

'Well, it's a long story. I couldn't tell you before. I didn't want to upset you. But I had to take the fight. You do understand, don't you?'

Elsie understood. She knew what made her Teddy tick. She could read him like an open book. 'Yes, I understand, but you can't keep doing it.'

They discussed his trip to London and decided that TK would postpone his departure until after Christmas. Needless to say, I was overjoyed and surprised to see TK when he came to pick me up to spend Christmas back in New York. TK was a different man; once again he had fought to get us out of trouble. Elsie, for the first time, looked at ease. She said, 'There's no question this time, it's over, he's fought his last fight.'

There were farewell parties at Anna's apartment and at the Mendeloffs'. TK was not to know that it would be the last time he saw his parents alive. The dockside was crowded with family and friends to see him off, including Charlie Harvey and Jimmy Johnston who had come to say their farewells, knowing that they would never see TK fight again.

Both said it had been great – they had enjoyed every moment and only wished that TK was twenty years younger. 'Why, we'd make a fortune.'

TK smiled. 'You mean *another* fortune, don't you?'

TK had tears in his eyes as the boat pulled out. He was overcome with emotion. The glamour of the ring, the crowds, the headlines, would now be things of the past. TK would be at sea as 1928 died away. He had time to contemplate. What did the future hold for him? A future in which he could not use his fists.

29 Mosley Kids the Kid

'Teddy, he's a Blackshirt, break away from him before
it's too late, he'll hurt you.'
Curley Carr to TK

TK arrived in London full of hope. He was now in his thirty-sixth
year, an old man as far as boxing was concerned, but he still had
the feeling that he could do anything. He soon realized that it was
a different world he was entering. No longer could he overcome his
problems by fighting as he had done in the past. He contacted all his
old friends, some good, some bad. He had no way of knowing which
ones fell into the good category and which ones into the bad – that
is, until someone had taken advantage of him.

Tommy Callaghan, the boxing promoter-cum-impresario, arranged for TK to tour with his show *Hello Sweetie* for six weeks.
Business was fairly good, which gave TK the opportunity to set up
a flat in Maida Vale, ready for when we came over. Elsie received
regular weekly mail from TK, each letter containing money and
news of promises and big deals he had been offered. Finally a call
came from the steamship company that they had a booking for Elsie
and Morton Lewis on the SS *Mauritania* to sail the following week.
This was followed by a cable 'Money and tickets on way. Be ready
to leave next week, love Teddy.' So once again Elsie and Morton
packed up and sailed for England.

It was a happy reunion. I was pleased to be home (I called anywhere
'home' when I was with TK and Elsie) and, as usual, started at
another school. The show was booked for a further two weeks and
once again TK was on the lookout. He also became interested in the
latest fad – dog racing – when Ziggy, an old East End friend of his,
became a bookmaker at the dogs.

I remember when Ziggy came home and propositioned TK to join
him. 'You can't win as a punter, but as a bookmaker, the owners and
trainers will confide in you and, besides, your name on the board
will bring in customers. We will print tickets with your name and

picture on them, and the punters will come and bet, if only to keep the ticket as a souvenir.'

TK smiled; he was interested. 'But I can't make a book. The only thing I know about bookmakers is that they always take my money.'

Ziggy held up his hand. 'That's where I come in. I stand up and make the book under your name. You come down every so often just to show your face and shake a few hands.' Then Ziggy said, 'The deal is, you put up the money and I get a third of the profits.'

TK looked at Elsie and both nodded their assent. 'Well, it looks like we're in the bookmaking business. Maybe this time we'll take the other mugs' money.'

All this raised Elsie's hopes. Perhaps this was the start of the new life they were striving for. But it was not to be. Ziggy would come back to the flat three times a week, when he and TK would go through a large book, and it was a rare occasion when they won. 'If this one had got beat, we'd have cleared the lot,' Ziggy would explain. Nevertheless, they lost between £50 and £75 a week. These losses, plus living expenses, went on until TK was unable to put any more money up and the bookmaking partnership with Ziggy finished. Ziggy managed to continue bookmaking, but this time under a different name.

While TK became desperate, I remember things were very bad and Elsie took two of TK's suits to the pawnshop in Edgware Road, so that the grocery bills could be paid and TK would have some money to get around town. The same thing happened the following week, and TK had a good wardrobe. Then Tommy Callaghan arranged another tour for TK and advanced him enough money to settle his debts. We moved to a smaller flat in Westbourne Grove and I moved to another school.

Tommy had brought in TK's old opponent, Johnny Basham, as sparring partner, and with both names on the bill, the show was doing fairly well. TK was earning enough for a reasonable standard of living. But Johnny was getting fat and slow; age and beer were taking their toll. The bookings were slowing up, and it was two or three weeks working, then two or three weeks resting.

Near the end of the year, they were playing at the old Collins Music Hall when, on a packed Saturday night, Johnny didn't show up. The crowd were more than a little disappointed and the publicity was bad. Tommy Callaghan told TK, 'I've got a good idea which will bring in a lot of publicity, and help us over the Basham affair.'

TK was ready for anything. 'What's that?'

'I run a fight at Hoxton Baths next month. We'll call it a "needle match" between you and Johnny because he let you down in front of a crowded theatre.'

TK didn't think it was a good idea. 'Besides, I haven't trained for months, and what about Johnny?'

'You won't have to train, it will be the same as the act you do twice a night in the show and three times on Saturdays. It will be like an exhibition, and Johnny's agreed. He said he could use the money.'

TK conceded, 'You'll have to ask Elsie; I promised her.' However, Tommy sweet-talked Elsie.

'It will only be what he has been doing every night, and the publicity will help the show get more bookings.'

Elsie knew it had reached the point of no return. 'As long as it's not a real fight.' Tommy convinced her. 'Treat it as an exhibition, in fact bring Morton, I'm sure you'll enjoy it.'

Thus, TK entered the ring in his thirty-seventh year for his fourth comeback. Johnny Basham followed him in, and though both men received a good reception, it was more nostalgia than enthusiasm. TK disrobed and looked quite fit – that is, fit for an actor, but as a boxer he looked overweight. Johnny just looked old, much older than I realized.

I remember the fight well, as I sat ringside in TK's corner, with my fingers crossed, not because of the fight, but the date – it was Friday 13 December 1928! I need not have worried. TK had no trouble in the first round. They both made all the usual moves, but rather slowly. TK landed the only blows, with Johnny ducking and weaving from experience but unable to throw an attacking punch. In the second round, TK kept shuffling forward with Johnny on the defensive. The crowd felt TK was pulling his punches and sympathized with him, but even the light punches were taking their toll. The bell saved Johnny as his seconds wiped the blood from his mouth as he fell on to his stool.

Tommy came over to the corner and whispered to TK, 'Ted, if you can finish it, do it now.' TK looked at Tommy and nodded. The bell rang. TK went slowly forward and measured Johnny with a left and threw a slow motion right cross flush on Johnny's chin. Johnny fell back on the ropes defenceless, only his courage keeping him on his feet. TK went forward to finish the one-sided bout, but stopped as he saw Johnny couldn't defend himself. He turned to the referee. 'I can't hit him any more. Stop it.' The referee responded immediately and stopped the fight.

I knew he could do it, and what's more he had done it to order.

TK and Johnny embraced; they were old friends and, after all, it was business – show business. TK had fought his last fight, however farcical, and the record books will show that he won his last contest on a TKO in the third round. The British fight fans would never again see a British fighter to equal him.

Elsie, sitting a few rows back with friends, was at last content. She knew that, come what might, TK would never enter the ring as a boxer again. TK was still a big name and had offers to go into business in various parts of the country. The Lewis family, during 1930, moved to Manchester, then back to London, then up to Sheffield, only to find that once again TK was being used. We finally returned to London, when I was enrolled at my sixth school since returning to England in 1929.

TK refereed around the small halls, and began to get a number of bit parts in films. Nearly all the directors, producers and stars were his friends and they all saw to it that TK was kept busy. While working on a Leslie Fuller–Max Nesbett comedy film at British International Pictures Studios, Elstree, TK took me along. My main interest was to watch the camera crew at work. During the lunch break, I was introduced to Claud Freeze-Green (who was the son of Walter who had invented the modern camera), also to Ronnie Neame, Ernie Steward, Brian Langley and numerous others, who were the top men in their field.

TK could see my interest, and asked me, 'How would you like to work here in the camera department?' I thought he was kidding, I was so excited, and what with my stammer, I was unable to answer other than nod.

He later spoke to John Maxwell, the boss of British International Pictures, who said he would arrange for me to start as a clapperboy when I left school, which to me seemed like having to wait a lifetime!

TK was still receiving a fair amount of publicity from refereeing, film work and personal appearances. He was good copy and, if used correctly, would attract attention to whatever he was involved in. But he was still an easy 'touch' for every confidence man he met and, in London's West End, he met most of them. He invested money in ventures that didn't have the remotest chance of success. After a meeting he would return home, his eyes sparkling with enthusiasm, as he described his newest sure-fire venture. Elsie would listen, with never a word of reproach, nor would she remind him of the many similar ideas which had gone astray.

It is necessary to appreciate TK's overwhelming simplicity in order to begin to understand and to sympathize with what was to happen within two years of his quitting the ring. For he was to make a mistake which would cost him many friends and would be used as a smear against him for many years to come. It started when Tommy Callaghan took TK to a cocktail party to meet Sir Oswald and Lady Mosley. TK was entranced by Mosley's personal magnetism and flattered when Mosley asked about his fighting career, and his opinion of present-day boxers. It must be remembered that several leading politicians – mature and certainly not naïve in the ways of the world – had prophesied that this talented, if unstable, man would one day be British Prime Minister.

TK knew little or nothing about politics, and even less about the aims of Fascism. Mussolini to him was merely a name and a rather absurd figure who was a blessing to cartoonists.

Mosley questioned TK about his childhood days and soon TK was talking to him freely about the slums of Whitechapel, the effects of malnutrition and what it was like to run the streets without shoes.

When Mosley explained that one of his main intentions was to give the youth of the country the chance of fulfilment never enjoyed in the past, TK's eyes sparkled with excitement.

'Youth must be healthy,' Mosley explained. 'They must be encouraged to learn manly sports – such as boxing.'

At the end of the party, Mosley invited TK to become the physical youth training instructor to the 'New Party'.

'Will it be a full-time job?' TK asked.

'It's yours for as long as you want it, Ted. You can start at £60 a week, plus expenses, and we'll give you a car as there will be a lot of travelling and after a while, who knows . . .? Are you interested?'

TK looked to Tommy who nodded for TK to accept. 'That's fine. When do I start?'

Mosley held out his hand, grabbed TK's and shook it. 'You've started.'

TK was never more enthused than when describing the meeting to Elsie. 'This is it. This is what we've been waiting for. Why, who knows what it will lead to?'

TK's first duty was to take over the instructor's job in a hall on the Kings's Road, Chelsea. TK organized the training and for two months all went smoothly. Then he received a call from Mosley who by now was insisting that TK should call him Oswald.

'I'm going on a tour of the country campaigning for the next election. I would like you to accompany me in case I get into any difficulties.'

TK went to a few such meetings and found the going rough. Returning to London from one of these meetings, TK asked Mosley, 'Oswald, I enjoy the way you talk, and admire your guts, but this isn't my job. I'm not a bodyguard. Even if I was, I couldn't handle the crowds you attract.'

Mosley felt a little embarrassed. 'Well, yes, I didn't think things would be that rough. What do you suggest I do?'

TK was flattered. Sir Oswald Mosley, a possible future Prime Minister, asking for his opinion. 'Well, depending on where your meetings are, you should have quite a number of bodyguards.'

Mosley interrupted. 'Can you get them for me?'

TK knew he could get any amount of tough men from the East End. 'I'm sure I could get you as many as you want. What will you pay them?'

Mosley was pleased. 'I'll give them £10 a meeting and their expenses.' TK was delighted. 'But I shall want you by my side. It will make good publicity,' added Mosley.

TK recruited between ten and fifty men from the East End, depending on how many Mosley required. He was happy to find work for his fellow East Enders. But the meetings got out of hand and once again TK found that he was acting as Mosley's bodyguard. TK told Mosley of his feelings. 'I'm here to teach boxing and to help the youth of the country. I don't like what I'm doing.'

Mosley agreed. During a press conference for Mosley's New Party, as it was called, TK was standing next to Mosley when a reporter jokingly said, 'How true is it, Ted? I hear you may run for Parliament.'

This took TK by surprise and he glanced at Mosley for moral support. 'Well, we have been thinking about it. What do you think?'

'Well,' said the reporter, 'it should make copy. After all, he's done more for the country than most of the MPs in Parliament today. Why not? Can I quote you that he is running?' he inquired.

'Not yet. We're still discussing it. I'll let you know if he does.'

When the press left, Mosley turned to TK. 'How would you like to run as a Member of Parliament?'

TK looked amazed. 'You're kidding.'

'No, I think you would do well. You could run for the Borough of Stepney – your own stamping ground.'

TK was bewitched by Mosley's personality. Mosley convinced him that he would be taught what to say, and would always have a good speaker supporting him.

A dinner was given at the Café Royal for TK, with Mosley as the guest speaker, and at the dinner TK was to explain his reasons for joining Mosley's New Party. TK had no idea that Mosley had engineered the whole idea. Mosley's aim was to use TK's name to obtain as much publicity as possible for his New Party.

TK's friends were trying to tell him that he was out of line, that what he was doing was wrong. Mosley was a Fascist and TK should withdraw from the party immediately. TK discussed the idea with Elsie who had listened to the hints dropped by friends. She warned TK that all might not be as it seemed.

'But I tell you, darling,' said TK, 'he's a great man. He wants to clean up the East End streets. You don't know what that means, but I do. He wants a new life for the poor. No more poverty. No more hunger.'

TK might have thought of himself as a trainer of Mosley's young men, but the public saw that Mosley was using him for the publicity and for protection.

When his Blackshirts were attacked at meetings, Mosley declared: 'We shall rely on good old English fists; we shall not use knives, sticks or bombs.' To TK, they were the words of a great man.

Years later, in *The Fascists in Britain*, Colin Gross wrote: 'First into action, summer 1931, known as the "Biff Boys", trained by the Jewish boxing champion, Ted Kid Lewis, a man of lively social conscience and simple outlook. . .'

The author's assessment is fair. Sir Oswald had only to speak of clearing the slums and helping the East End boys, and TK would be listening with gleaming eyes. After all, had he not suffered in his youth in the very dingy streets his leader was talking about? Had he not known what it was to go without meals; to have no soles to his shoes?

Elsie was far less gullible, and her intimate friends had talked to her of Mosley's anti-Semitic beliefs. She voiced her fears to TK. He brushed her objections aside.

'No, he's not anti-Jewish . . . I'd know if he was, wouldn't I? It's just a dirty smear from those who want no change.'

'But Sarah told me. . .'

'You know what an old chatterbox she is. . .' Then, seeing the worry in her eyes, 'OK I'll tackle him; I'll see him again tomorrow.'

And TK went to see Mosley and challenged him on the Jewish question. Mosley shrugged his shoulders and denied that anti-Semitism had ever been part of his creed. . . after all, wasn't his own wife a Jewess?

TK was completely convinced and when in October 1931, Mosley put forward 24 candidates for the election, TK stood as a member of the New Party for Stepney and Whitechapel. But though TK might be misled as to the New Party's aims, the East End wasn't. TK recited speeches on the very street corners where he'd played as a child, and found the insults thrown at him by his former friends almost incomprehensible. Why could they not see that all Mosley wanted to do was improve their lot and to erase injustice? Why could they not appreciate Mosley's crusading spirit? What they did appreciate was that all twenty-four candidates lost their deposits and TK was counted out with 154 votes.

I went with TK when he called on Mosley at his headquarters. By coincidence, Mosley had at last decided to make his real beliefs known, because, when we arrived, there were two big men, clad not in the black shirts of Mosley's New Party, but in the brown shirts of the Nazi Party. TK momentarily froze. Then he grabbed my hand and we mounted the stairs to Mosley's office, and without knocking, opened the door.

There was Mosley seated at his desk, with two of his henchmen in brown shirts standing at his elbows. It was like a scene out of a newsreel from Germany. The two men gave TK the traditional raised arm salute. TK left me standing and walked right up to Mosley. 'Is it true you're anti-Semitic? And I want the truth this time. Are you anti-Jewish?'

Mosley almost smiled at TK's naïvety. 'Yes.' Then he rose from his chair and told TK in measured tones that the time for subterfuge was over. Now he could speak the truth and reveal his full plans and began to explain their aims.

TK's face was dead white. Boxing fans who had seen him fight would have interpreted the danger signs. But Mosley or his henchmen had not seen TK in a fighting mood. One could imagine what he was thinking. Elsie was right, his friends were right, he alone had been fooled and made to appear a donkey, an ass that brayed on street corners at Mosley's command. Mosley kept on talking, and then eyed TK as if to gauge the effect of his words on TK.

Until then TK had not moved. Then, like lightning, he struck with an open hand across Mosley's face, sending him and his chair crashing against the wall. The two brown-shirted men came round the desk and grappled with TK. I remember instinctively jumping on the back of one, wrapping my arms around his head and hanging on for dear life. I wasn't being brave; I knew TK was there. And he didn't let me down. He ducked under the other man's arms and shot a short right hook to his jaw, sending him crashing to the floor, out to the world.

In the meantime – about three seconds later but a lifetime to me – TK turned and shouted, 'Morty, let him go,' which I did as fast as possible. At the same time, TK hit *him* with a left hook and he dropped to the floor like a sack of potatoes. I think we both hit the floor at the same time! I got up and stood there in ecstasy. He'd done it again! TK stood there and inspected the room. The two men were out cold and Mosley just sat on the floor not wanting to take any further part. TK took my hand and we walked down the stairs past the two guards at the front door. About twenty yards up the street, TK told me to wait a minute. I watched him as he walked back to the entrance, mounted the steps and positioned himself between the two guards. He eyed them for two or three seconds, and then, like lightning, swung a left hook at one, spun round with a right hook to the other, and calmly stepped over both men. He walked down the steps and joined me, grinning from ear to ear.

So ended TK's association with Mosley. But, though he was guilty more of simplicity than of viciousness, and though he was to regret deeply his association with Mosley, the episode was never forgotten. Always, when TK was discussed by those who had never seen him fight – or who did not know what he had done for charity – someone would say: 'But wasn't he a Fascist?. . . Wasn't he a Mosley boy?' The grapevine passed the word around – that TK had settled with Mosley in the only way he knew how – with his hands. Gradually he was to able to live it down with the help of his friends, because they understood that this lovable man had been duped.

30 Clubland

'That jury's verdict gave me back my life.'
TK to Morton

TK was once again unemployed. He obtained a boxing manager's licence and began searching for boxers whom he considered had potential. He had a little success, but in the early days boxers needed all the money they could get and TK found it hard to take his twenty-five per cent; sometimes he did, but mostly he didn't. He also managed to obtain a few small parts in films, but the going was tough.

By chance, he met an old acquaintance by the name of Ira Lethorr who owned a club in Bournemouth. The man who had been running it for Ira had walked out, together with the takings, and Ira asked TK if he would be interested. They would share profits fifty-fifty, and all the bills would be paid from London.

TK, Elsie and I were driven down to Bournemouth. The club premises and the accommodation were good and, liking what they saw, TK and Elsie decided there and then to take it. It was 'pack up and leave' again and the Lewis family moved lock, stock and barrel to the new home, and it was yet another school for me.

TK was good 'copy' for the local press who gave the opening good coverage and the club flourished. TK regularly sent the takings to London, less £25 per week, against his 50 per cent of the profits. After the first three months, however, various suppliers complained that their bills were unpaid. TK apologized and the suppliers agreed to wait.

TK then called London and was told Ira was out of town. So he decided to hold the takings until he heard from Ira. Four weeks went by and finally Ira called to ask why the takings had not been sent.

'Why haven't the bills been paid?' he demanded.

'They are all screaming for their money,' countered TK.

'Let them scream. I'm running this company.'

'Then you'd better come down and run the club as well. I quit and I'll pay the people out of what I hold,' said TK, and hung up.

TK and Elsie were shocked; this was something new to them. Although they had had their share of unpaid bills before because of lack of funds, this was different, because they had sent the money to pay the bills. Elsie had grown up and matured since TK had retired. She had developed a personality that endeared her to everybody she came into contact with. Elsie said there was only one thing to do and told TK, 'Call all the suppliers and tell them the truth.'

The suppliers assembled, Elsie passed drinks all round and cracked a few jokes until the atmosphere was right. 'Teddy will explain the situation,' she said with a smile. (Some years later Elsie told me she had had such tummy pains that she had felt as if she had lost a twenty-round fight to a body-puncher!) For the first time in his life, TK, without realizing it, had become a businessman by doing the right thing.

'Gentlemen, I've quit the job and, as you know, the company's not mine, but I've withheld four weeks' money since you all complained. I shall deduct £100 which I would draw anyway and the balance, gentlemen, can be shared between yourselves.' The suppliers were satisfied; they each received 80 per cent of their money and would look to the company for the balance. Elsie passed more drinks around, everybody drank their health and all declared they would be delighted to extend TK and Elsie credit if they opened another club in Bournemouth.

Within two weeks and with the help of one supplier, they found and opened a new club in a better position nearer the town centre. Elsie refurbished and decorated it and made the living accommodation comfortable. The club was called 'The Punch Bowl' and it became quite well known. The artists from the touring music-hall shows which played Bournemouth and Boscombe found their way to the club and enjoyed the pleasant atmosphere created by Elsie and TK. The club also became the 'local' for the RAF officers stationed in Salisbury. TK would visit them at the station and he became the squadron's lucky charm. In years to come, TK encountered all his friends again when he joined the RAF during the Second World War, and found that most of them had reached high rank in the RAF.

TK, ever on the lookout for a heavyweight prospect, was introduced to one from Southampton by the former heavyweight champion of Great Britain, Joe Beckett.

TK signed up this new heavyweight find of Joe's. He paid his father £5 a week to cover the loss of his wage-earning son. I can only remember his first name – Charles. He moved in with us and TK turned one of the upstairs rooms into a gymnasium. For three months he trained and slept there and ate like there was no tomorrow. All our friends and visitors to the club thought he looked good in the gym. It reminded me of the 'Hans' affair two years earlier in Berlin. Then came the time to be tested. TK's first-ever opponent, Johnny Sharpe, arranged a four-round fight at an open air show in Edmonton. Charles came out looking good, he danced, moved well, ducked and then led with his left – which missed. His opponent, who might have been termed tenth-rate by a kindly critic, swung a roundhouse right, more as a defensive action, and it landed in Charles's stomach. He doubled up and ran to the ropes, leaned over and vomited, and he was a big eater. TK's face was a picture of dejection. He shook his head and threw in the towel, which helped the referee who was at a loss as to what to do. I think Charles went back to Southampton and joined the police force. So much for Joe Beckett's Great White Hope! The old heavyweight champion was a great character, however, and TK told me a story about him when he introduced us that remains one of my favourite anecdotes.

In 1919, James White asked TK to introduce the leading boxers still in uniform to the Duke of York, later to become King George VI. TK: 'The Duke, like his brother the Prince of Wales, was a great fight fan and knew a lot about my record in the States. Well, the day came, the boxers were lined up, there were Bandsman Rice and Jack Blake, Sergeant Braddock, Bombardier Billy Wells, Joe Beckett and many others. The Duke chatted to each one as I introduced them, and when we reached Joe, I said, "Your Highness, this is Joe Beckett, our heavyweight champion." He said, "I know." Joe then gave a smart salute and the Duke said, "Very pleased to meet you . . . is there anything I can do for you?"

'Joe's hands went to his chest, grabbed hold of his uniform, and said, "Yeah, get me 'aht of this!" I quickly stepped in to introduce the next man. Everybody, including the Duke, was trying to control their laughter.'

TK loved telling that story and was very proud of the photograph he received a few days later, signed 'Albert'.

Later that year, when TK was filming at Elstree, he asked John Maxwell if he had forgotten the promise he made to me, as I had now left school. Maxwell was surprised that I hadn't already started.

He immediately called Stapleton, the studio manager, to inquire. Maxwell looked to TK, as he held his hand over the mouthpiece. 'When can he start?'

TK beamed. 'As soon as possible.'

Maxwell told Stapleton, 'Start him next week and give his father particulars.'

Stapleton told TK he shouldn't have gone over his head. 'However, your boy can start next week as clapperboy, at twenty-five shillings a week.' TK mentioned this to Claude Freeze-Green, the cameraman, who said, 'The bastard, all the new boys start at between thirty and thirty-five shillings a week, depending on how far they travel.' I never forgot Mr Stapleton, but TK couldn't have cared less. He had got his son the job he had dreamt of, a job in the film business and in the camera department. TK arranged for my digs with a studio prop man, at twenty-five shillings a week. There was excitement in the Lewis home that night when TK gave us the news. I was over the moon, and Elsie was overjoyed and relieved, as she had had a secret fear that she might have another fighter in the family.

The following week found TK on one stage in a film starring Bernard Nedell, and I starting as clapperboy next door on *For The Love of Mike*, starring Bobby Howes, Claude Hulbert and Arthur Risco, directed by Monty Banks and photographed by Claude Freeze-Green, all friends of TK's.

TK remained busy, trying to build a stable of boxers, travelling to Elstree for film work and to help Elsie run the club. The travelling was hard, but his main problem was to throw his friends out after hours, especially the RAF boys who wanted to stay all night if they could. TK was warned about the hours and was raided by friendly plainclothes policemen, so the fine was small, but TK and Elsie decided to return to London.

They moved into a flat in Marylebone, where I joined them, and for the first time in my 'moving career' I was not enrolled into a new school. TK then became matchmaker for a number of small shows, managed a few boxers, and continued with the occasional film work.

His next big venture was to open a nightclub in New Compton Street called the Moulin Rouge. Because of the licensing laws of the day, it was run as a 'bottle-party' club, with a fair amount of success. All the top actors and actresses frequented the club, and TK built up quite a following. But, like all good things, it had a problem.

A number of London tearaways would visit the club. One by one TK would try to keep them out. One night six men tried to gain admission and the doorman, a former flyweight boxer, Nat Simmonds, tried to stop them. The struggle got out of hand and Simmonds pressed the alarm bell. TK went to the front door which by now was smashed to pieces and between them, Nat and TK managed to hold on until the police arrived. By this time the six thugs had fled. Unfortunately, the situation didn't end there.

The following week, Nat was visiting the 'Q' club for a game of billiards. The club was well known and Jack Isso ran a luncheon counter on the premises. While Nat was playing billiards, he was attacked by four of the thugs, using the thick end of billiard cues. His head was split open from ear to ear. The police were called and the four men were arrested. Nat was taken to hospital where he spent the next two weeks, and the four thugs were eventually sent for trial.

In the meantime, Mr and Mrs Wooden, parents of Jimmy, one of the thugs, were sitting in the Mapleton Café, waiting for TK who was a regular tea-time visitor there. Mrs Wooden beckoned to TK. He walked over and was asked to sit down.

'Mr Lewis, would you do me a favour and speak to Simmonds on behalf of my son?'

TK rose. 'I'm sorry. There's nothing I can do,' and joined another table.

The following day, the Woodens were again there when TK arrived. They waited until he was leaving and then Mrs Wooden called to TK and asked him to sit down. TK felt sorry for her. Whatever her son had done, it wasn't her fault. Therefore, he felt the least he could do was be polite, so he sat down, when Mr Wooden leaned over to him. 'Would you do me a favour. Give this message to Simmonds,' and he pushed an envelope into TK's hand.

For a moment TK felt sympathetic. Then, looking at the envelope, he became suspicious. 'What's in this?' he asked.

Mr Wooden, raising his voice, replied, 'Count it.'

With that, TK threw the envelope back to Mr Wooden, saying, 'I don't want it.'

Two plainclothes policemen were waiting outside the café, waiting for Wooden to call out 'count it'. This was their signal to come in. They picked up the envelope and asked TK to accompany them to the police station.

On 11 February 1937, at Bow Street, TK was charged with attempting to obstruct and prevent the due course of the law and justice. He pleaded not guilty.

TK decided to close the Moulin Rouge there and then. He felt he could not face customers night after night with the charge hanging over his head. He was filled with shame and longed to go and hide his head. He wanted to go around shouting the Jimmy Johnston theme: 'I was framed', but would people believe him? And, most of all, would the jury believe him?

It was only Elsie's strength and support that kept TK from breaking down during the two months of waiting for the case to be heard. He would come home in a daze, spending most of the time worrying, and the rest of the time with his lawyers and counsel.

It was 12 April when TK finally went to court; his weight was down to 10 st. 2 lb. And it wasn't only weight he lost during the case; the legal fees practically wiped him out. It was TK's biggest fight, the fight he wanted to win most of all. His friends rallied round offering their moral support. The trial lasted three days and was good copy for the newspapers.

The jury were only out for twenty minutes and it seemed like a lifetime to me. They slowly came back; TK was gripping the rail in front of him, and I could see he was rocking. Elsie grabbed my hand and was shaking. I think I was the strong one at the time, only because I didn't appreciate the severity of the situation. Then, after another lifetime of waiting, it was announced – they found him not guilty! TK had got the biggest verdict of his life.

Elsie threw her arms around my neck and broke down, and there were cheers from the spectators, but TK didn't acknowledge them by clasping his hands over his head in victory as he had done so many times in the past. His hands were covering his face; he had finally broken down and was crying like a child.

The judge, Sir Holman Gregory, KC, in discharging the jury, said, 'You are quite right.' Elsie and I rushed over and TK embraced us as if he had been released from prison. He kept his head down as if he was in a clinch and whispered, 'They've just given me my life back again.'

TK did not become cynical, as one might have expected, even though he had seen the toughest time he had ever had, in or out of the ring. He became more philosophical and less flamboyant. In fact, he had slowed up; the case had taken its toll. But, fortunately, he had not lost faith in his fellow human beings. TK felt he was starting life again, and needed an income quickly.

He was still popular and decided to open another nightclub. He found new premises in Dean Street, Soho, and with another loan, from an old friend (Justice McNaughten, chairman of the British American Tobacco Company), TK and Elsie opened the El Morocco Club, which did fairly well. It was then that I had my first, and I think my only, father-to-son talk. I felt I was getting nowhere in the film business in England.

'How would you like to go to Hollywood?' he asked. I thought he was kidding. 'I'll give you letters to all my friends. You'll see Uncle Charlie [Chaplin] and Bryan Foy at Warner Brothers – one of them will get you in.' It was all settled. TK scraped together enough to pay my passage to New York, plus £80 ($400 at that time) in cash for the bus fare to Hollywood, and to get started. So I packed and left for the States.

TK was delighted with the idea of my going, but Elsie was heartbroken. She wrote regularly every week, and for the first six months until I got my IATSE union card, she would put from one to five pounds in her letters, whatever she could afford and sometimes even when she couldn't afford anything.

Business eventually fell away and they closed the El Morocco and went into the Stadium Club in Croydon with former boxer Marvin Hart, whose daughter Anne is married to that great little comedian Ronnie Corbett.

No sooner had TK and Elsie settled in, however, when a cable arrived from New York; 'Mother passed away peacefully on Friday [16 September 1938]. Dad OK. Everything taken care of. Don't worry. Tell the family. Love Lew.' TK took this very badly. He had not seen his mother for ten years and wanted to go over, but there was nothing he could do. Elsie told me years later that he sat in mourning and cried for over a week. He gradually overcame his grief and had settled into working at the club when he received another cable: 'Papa passed peacefully away on Friday [6 January 1939]. Tell everybody, everything taken care of, hope you and family well. Love Lew.' TK was distressed and once again he sat in mourning.

In the meantime, I had obtained my union card and was working at Warner Brothers Studios in Burbank. I wrote that they should start thinking of coming over, as Hollywood was full of old-time fighters, including a number of his old opponents, Maxie Rosenbloom, Jack Perry, and his first American opponent Phil Bloom, all making a living in films. I wrote and told TK that I had spoken to Bryan Foy, who had said TK would have no trouble making a fair living. Then there were his other friends, Victor McLagen, Jack Warner, Billy Sullivan and, of course, Chaplin. 'You know them all,' I wrote. 'And I could get a two-bedroom flat and we could manage quite comfortably.'

Elsie was all for the idea; they were disillusioned with England, where they still felt the effects of the recent trial, not to mention the Mosley affair. And war was just around the corner. TK wrote and said, 'Mummy and I like the idea of coming over, but I must get a little bankroll together. We can't come over like immigrants.' He went on to say they would make plans to come over in about six months' time. But the bell rang for The Big Fight. War was declared. The Lewis family were unable to 'pack up and leave', so travelling plans were shelved for the time being.

By now, TK and Elsie had grown to have the same outlook on life. It could be said that they were fatalists, but only after TK had realized that his fists could no longer change his fate. They had suffered many hard knocks, but they took things as they came. They would say, 'What is to be – will be,' and would be prepared to accept the good with the bad on equal terms. After all, there was always tomorrow – please God it will come right.

31 The Living Legend

'We were all lined up at an RAF camp when Winston
Churchill came to inspect us. I was standing to attention
in front of my squad when the great man stepped in front
of me. He said, 'We could do with more fighters like you,
Lewis.' I was so thrilled I said 'No, sir, we could do with
more fighters like you!'

TK

With the outbreak of war, TK immediately looked round for
something to do for his country. He volunteered for the Ambulance
Service, but wasn't satisfied. He wanted to be involved. He had been
an officer in the last war. He could have used that to get a similar
position, but he chose the hard path, and managed to talk his way
into the RAF by taking four years off his age.

His courage and determination saw him through the tough training
courses from which he emerged as a sergeant instructor. Wherever
TK was stationed, he would find that the commanding officer, or
one of the top brass, was an old friend. But all through his stint in the
RAF, TK never asked for special favours. He had a rapport with the
men under him and consequently never reported or put anyone on a
charge. Some of his immediate superiors would complain by saying
he must start putting men on a charge. TK's reply would always be,
'I never have any trouble with the men. They always do as I ask.' It
was not in his nature to hurt people – outside of the ring.

Recently, while checking through photographs and dates for
TK's biography, I came across a letter dated 26 October 1971,
the anniversary of TK's funeral. I had not been in the mood to
reply at the time and had put it to one side. It was from Squadron
Leader R.W.D. Hier, formerly TK's PT sergeant instructor when
he joined the RAF, enclosing a copy of TK's New York State boxing
licence for 1920/1, inquiring if I would like the original.

Now, of course, I was most intrigued and wanted to find out
how he had obtained it. So, nineteen years on, with the help
of the Birmingham directory inquiry, I called Mr Hier and,

after recovering from our amazement, we had a long and most enlightening conversation. He then sent me a seven-page letter and, with difficulty, I have chosen the following extracts, which I think say it all:

'I still can't believe it! After fifty years I hear from the son of Ted Kid Lewis. It's absolutely fantastic and not a little thrilling. Ted and Jimmy Wilde were my father's idols and can you imagine my feelings when I came face to face with the great man himself. Ted was one of thirty recruits assigned to me. They were all in civvies, tall, short, fat, thin, "mummy's boys" and, outstanding amongst them, was Ted.

'Each squad had to appoint a senior man and who better to have than your Dad? I couldn't put Ted on scrubbing floors, polishing the coal bins, cleaning windows, etc. In no time at all, Ted had all the men enjoying their work.

'One day Ted came to me. "Hey Kid," (he called everybody Kid) "is there a cinema here?" He had a couple of reels of films of his fights. We went to the local cinema, and Ted went up to the projection room. He came down smiling and we went and sat in the theatre. A few minutes later, a hand-written sign was superimposed on the screen with the words: "Ted Kid Lewis, ex-boxing champion at three weights, is in the audience and we will be showing some film of his fights."

'Well, I have never been so intrigued or excited in my life. The crowd loved it and Ted obligingly signed autographs for everybody.

'In those days Ted was, like us all, usually short of cash. He used to borrow my Austin Ruby saloon which I had bought for £4 10s and he would put in a gallon of petrol at one shilling and threepence, to pop up to town to see some friends. He would come back with money and food, saying that his friends, Curley Carr and Chummy Gaventa, would never let him down.

'Ted lived out of camp with your mother Elsie, and I soon realized why Ted always looked the best-dressed, his uniform pressed, shoes shining and well-groomed. Elsie would send Ted with something for me to "nosh" and I never turned down a dinner invitation from Elsie. What a cook she was! And what a lucky man Ted was, to have Elsie as manager, trainer, valet, housekeeper and wife. They were a wonderful couple.

'I put Ted in charge of the boxing squad – what a break for me. I even sparred with him! I was twenty-four and Ted was forty-seven, yet I never laid a glove on him. You would have thought I was 23 years older than him. It was one of the finest moments of my life – if only my father could have seen it.

Red Cross boxing tournament, Wembley 1940. Corporal Lewis talks to
Anthony Eden while the High Commissioners for Rhodesia and
South Africa look on

Night of the Champions: (left to right) Jimmy Wilde, Jack Kid Berg,
Harry Mason, TK, Bombardier Billy Wells and Jack Bloomfield

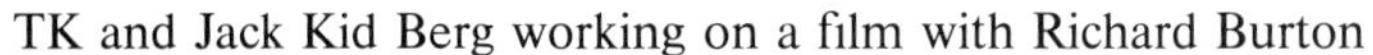

TK with life-long chum Curley Carr at Morton's wartime wedding, 1947

TK and Jack Kid Berg working on a film with Richard Burton

TK, Bud Flanagan and Henry Cooper at a charity boxing show

At the 75th anniversary of the NSC, 1966. Front row, left to right: Tommy Farr, TK, Georges Carpentier, Bombardier Billy Wells. Middle row: Charles Ledoux. Back row: Derek Lloyd, Johnny Cuthbert, Ken Buchanan, Howard Winstone, Henry Cooper, Carl Gizzi, Eddie Avoth, Eddie Thomas

Boxing Writers' Club chairman, Peter Wilson, presents TK with a special trophy, 1964

TK graciously acknowledges the applause of the Boxing Writers' Club at their annual dinner, 1969

Joe Louis, former heavyweight champion, discussing the past with TK
prior to boxing in his exhibition tour at Earl's Court, London

TK discusses strategy with Terry Downes for his bout with Paul Pender

Georges Carpentier presenting TK with a gold belt at the Empress Hall, 1950. Jack Fox holds the belt while Johnny Best Jr stands by

After the show there was no need for a referee to intervene in this clinch between TK and Georges Carpentier

The following day, Morton told Carpentier 'I've been waiting to do this for twenty-eight years!'

Fifty-five years after winning his first NSC belt, Stanley Baker presents TK with the NSC presentation belt for his services to boxing, 1969

TK and Morton at the 1968 Boxing Writers' annual dinner

TK enjoying life at the Nightingale Home, 1967

TK at the Anglo-American Sporting Club, 1967. 'Thank you for all the kind things you said about me.' Seated: Bill Martin and Terry Downes

'My squad were up to scratch in time for the "passing out" examinations and anyone failing would stay behind for another six weeks. I didn't want that to happen to Ted Kid Lewis, so, just in case, I sent him away sick on passing-out day (after a word with the MO). So your Dad got his PT Badge and was posted to another station. But I am sure he would have passed, because Ted was capable of anything. My squads were never the same. He was so kind and considerate, and everyone was "Kid" with him. His departure left a personality vacuum that was irreplaceable.'

I sent Taff, as he wished to be called, some of TK's RAF photographs and the one Taff had signed to TK. He replied, thanking me for sending him the photos in such good condition after fifty years: 'And to think my egoism must have been sky-high, to think of signing one of my photos to the greatest boxer of his time, if not ever. The memory of knowing your father and what a character and sportsman he was, will forever be with me.'

TK was moved to various RAF bases where Elsie found digs and set up home. No matter where, or what shape or size the accommodation, Elsie always made it look like home, and whatever the cooking facilities were, she would always be able to make a meal and entertain their friends. Elsie was very proud. They had lived the good life and now it was becoming more difficult to maintain the same standards. But Elsie was something special. She had dignity and whatever company TK and Elsie found themselves in, Elsie was always the centre of attraction. They made friends wherever they went. TK and Elsie looked and were a happy couple and that happiness was their main asset.

The war was now in full swing. I had been burned on my fingers as a child and had been left with a disability – I couldn't straighten two fingers on my left hand. Because of this, I was classified as 4F in the American call-up. But I volunteered for the British services and did not show my left hand. The British Council in Los Angeles accepted the offer unofficially, and made it clear that if I were to catch a boat from Halifax, Nova Scotia, and present myself to the authorities in London, I would be accepted into the Forces.

The Lewis family reunion at the Cumberland Hotel on 9 February 1942 was the answer to all our prayers. We were a family once again. TK, in uniform, was proud to take me to see his top brass friends in the RAF. But I was turned down and, because of my fingers, classified 3B. TK was disappointed but seemed satisfied once I started work as a cameraman for the Central Office of Information on instructional films for the services and for the Ministry of Information. TK was proud of his son. I had made the effort.

When TK had weekend leave, he and Elsie would stay at their friend Chummy Gaventa's bachelor apartment at the Athenaeum Court, Piccadilly, where Chummy made sure that Elsie and TK had everything they wanted. I later stayed there for a couple of months while looking for a permanent address.

The following years moved quickly for TK. He was demobbed from the Royal Air Force in 1944 and went into full-time management. He moved to Blackburn where Elsie set up home while TK acted as matchmaker for Northern promoter Tommy Catlow.

The next big event for TK and Elsie, however, was when they travelled to London to attend a wedding. I was getting married. The old cliché, 'You haven't lost a son, you've gained a daughter', really came true this time. TK and Elsie now had a daughter. Sally was proud of TK and Elsie and over the years proved her worth by the love and affection she gave to my parents.

And 1944 brought new joy and excitement to TK and Elsie. They were presented with Marsha, their first grandchild, whose arrival brought new life for them. The Lewis family was growing.

The Blackburn job lasted eight months and once again TK and Elsie returned to London. TK continued to manage a few boxers, and whenever possible, filled in with film work while I was always on the lookout for stunts or situations which would enable me to get publicity for TK.

In the meantime, Elsie's family and friends kept writing inviting them over for a holiday, but TK didn't think he was doing well enough to go without some sort of bankroll. He convinced Elsie, however, (with our help), to go, and that he would be alright. She reluctantly agreed and we saw her off at Southampton, her last words to me being, 'Promise me you'll look after Daddy, make sure his laundry is done and the flat kept clean.'

She dreaded leaving him alone, knowing how he relied on her. But she had a fantastic time. Her family and friends had not seen her for nearly twenty years, and she was on the go for the whole two months. In stark contrast, TK wandered about like a lost sheep, a signal to us of what would happen in the future. He couldn't count the days fast enough, waiting for her return and it took all my persuasive powers to convince him not to travel to Cherbourg, so that he could be with Elsie one day earlier.

We all travelled to meet the boat at Southampton, and every head turned as Elsie walked down the gangplank; she looked like a million dollar film star! TK began to shake with excitement and burst into tears of joy, 'Look, look, there's Mummy!' Yes, TK was back amongst the living again.

I was now producing fight films for Michael H. Goodman. The films were of most of the big fights being promoted by Jack Solomons, the number one promoter of that time. I had the idea of using Freddie Mills, whom Jack Solomons had built into a big name, and approached Freddie's manager, Ted Broadribb, telling him that I wanted to use Freddie in a number of sports films.

Ted replied, 'It's a good idea but we are planning to make a big benefit night for Freddie. Your idea will have to wait.'

Although I was a personal friend of Freddie's, I was incensed by this. Freddie had just finished making a fortune and here they were thinking of giving him a benefit night. If anyone was entitled to such a night, surely TK was.

I called to see Bill McGowran of the *Evening News* and asked if he thought that the British public would support a benefit night for TK. Bill was a great admirer of TK's and said, 'Yes,' and added that he would start the ball rolling immediately. I said I would gather a formidable committee to ensure the success of the benefit.

I went to see Marc Segal, Jack Fox and Ike Morris, leading members of that great charity organization, The Sportsman's Aid Society. Would they help? Would they?! They would be delighted. All those approached to join the committee accepted and the committee consisted of: Peter Wilson, Bill McGowran, Isidore Green, Jerry Doltis, Geoffrey Simpson, Bob Fabian, Dr Phil Magonet, Ike Morris, Jack Fox, Marc Segal, Bud Flanagan, Morris Woolf, Moss de Yong, Curley Carr, Joe Coral, Bob Scheffer, and others.

At that time I had an interest in the Empress Hall boxing shows, with promoters Braitman and Ezra. They had some dates they were finding difficult to fill, so I suggested that my committee should take one date off their hands. A Ted Kid Lewis night would be good publicity for them; they liked the idea and agreed. In fact, every big name in show business wanted to help, and things moved along smoothly despite several set-backs, such as the British Boxing Board of Control refusing the committee's application to televise the show without giving a reason; Ronnie Ezra waiting just before we went to the printers to tell us that he had decided the ringside seats be kept at £2.2.0 (their usual price) instead of the £5.5.0 ringside and special

£10 VIP seats we had intended to charge; and, finally, his demand for £1,000 for the loss of the date!

It was too late to change venues, and finally Ezra made us bring the date forward from 26 to 19 September 1950. In spite of all these setbacks, however, it was a night to remember.

The committee brought Georges Carpentier to London to present TK with an illuminated address and a miniature gold belt. The fans gave TK a five-minute standing ovation and, as always, TK was unable to control his emotions.

The Master of Ceremonies, Johnny Best Jr., son of the great Liverpool promoter, announced: 'My Lords, La . . . dies and Gentle . . . men, in this corner – Ted Kid Lewis – and in this corner. . . ' and at that moment a portly old gentleman squeezed between the ropes, 'Johnny Sharp!' The two lifelong friends embraced. It had been forty years since Johnny and TK had been in the same ring – forty-one years since TK had lost his first professional fight. The crowd loved it.

And this announcement was followed by many other old-timers until Johnny Best shouted: 'Last, but not least, Georges Carpentier!' Georges climbed through the ropes and he and TK embraced. The crowd went wild and it was some time before Johnny Best could control their enthusiasm. Georges made a speech and gave TK the belt. TK managed, between choking and crying, to say 'thank you'.

No, they had not forgotten Ted Kid Lewis, and the following week he was presented with a cheque for £3,000, after deducting the £1,000 demanded by Ezra. The money, of course, didn't change TK or Elsie. They were the same happy couple, with or without money. They bought a small flat in St John's Wood and lived on the balance, waiting to see what tomorrow would bring. The new flat gave them roots and I think they were more content with life than at any other time.

Whenever or wherever there was a boxing show, TK would show up. He was more than welcome and took me whenever possible. He would, almost without exception, be introduced as 'The one and only'. It never failed to bring the colour back into his face. His eyes glistened with pride that they still remembered him.

However, during the Jack Solomons reign as number one promoter, TK would have to wait in Solomons's gym with the hangers-on and the 'never-was-ers' for a ticket after the weigh-in, when Sam Burns, son of Syd Burns, the old-time boxer, would emerge from the office door and hand out tickets. On the occasion of the Sugar Ray Robinson/Randolph Turpin world middleweight title fight, Sam gave TK a ticket which was the end seat up in the top corner of Wembley. This was one fight in which Solomons could easily have introduced TK. The public would have appreciated it and the introduction would have boosted TK's morale.

I managed to exchange my ringside ticket with another ex-fighter who had an adjoining seat so that TK and I could sit together. TK was pleased I had made the exchange, that is, until we finally reached the seats, which were nearer Wembley Station than the ring. 'What's this?' he asked, and I quickly made up the story that it was the only way we could sit together.

He just shook his head and sat down and accepted the situation, but I found it hard to forget the times when Jack Solomons used to call TK at home and ask him to come to the Devonshire Club (where Solomons had started) to make a personal appearance, to referee, or to ask permission to use one of his fight films on his television programmes.

It was at this time that I was told that Solomons was annoyed I had arranged to have TK's show with Braitman and Ezra and not with him. However, he had known I was with them at the time and, besides, he had been approached by Bill McGowran at the outset and had turned it down. Only when he realized he was missing out on so much publicity had he changed his mind, but then it was too late. Jack had also been a big noise on the British Boxing Board of Control at the time they had refused to allow TK's show to be televised.

I was with TK at Solomons's gym after the weigh-in for the Bruce Woodcock/Jack Gardner fight. Sam Burns gave out the free seats, as usual, to managers, officials and former boxers. Gradually, the people left, leaving TK and a few boxers who had not received a ticket. TK asked, 'Have you got a ticket for me, Sam?' Sam shook his head, holding his arms out, with palms upturned. 'Sorry Ted, Jack said no.' He looked most embarrassed, turned and went back into the office.

I quickly grabbed TK before the refusal could penetrate and rushed him downstairs, and exchanged my ticket with a ticket-scalper for two seats together. TK couldn't believe what had happened. 'It must have been a mistake, Jack wouldn't do that to me.' He had tears in his eyes. I agreed and told him it must have been a mistake and that I would go and see Jack the following week.

TK let the subject drop and we enjoyed the evening. He received the usual pats on the back, and shook hands with all his friends and signed numerous programmes offered to him for his autograph.

However, the following week I went up to Solomons's office. Johnny Sharpe, who then worked for Jack, was there behind the box office window. I asked him to see if Jack could see me for a few moments. A few seconds later, Jack called out, 'Come in, Morton.' We shook hands and he asked, 'What can I do for you?'

I didn't feel like being diplomatic after the way he had treated TK. 'Have you got something against my father, don't you like him?' I blurted out.

Jack looked surprised. 'Why, I've known him all my life. He was at my wedding. Why?'

'Then why didn't you give him a ticket to your last show? Sam told him that you said there wasn't one for him!'

Waving his hands, Jack said, 'Don't be silly. It must be a mistake, I never said that to Sam.'

I had expected an answer like that; what else could he have said? But I had come to say my piece and wasn't going to be denied: 'Mistake or not – he was turned down like some bum! From now on, give him a ringside ticket for all your fights, before the weigh-in, and send me the bill. He thinks you're a great guy Jack, I don't want to disillusion him.'

He smiled. 'Don't be silly, Morton. I'll always leave him a ticket.'

'Well, do it with a good heart. Don't make him hang around to the end. Tell Sam what to do.' We shook hands, I had had my say, it was off my chest and TK continued to get his ticket – free.

It was only years later that I began to wonder why Sam Burns had left Solomons to join Jarvis Astaire. Perhaps it was because Sam became embarrassed about taking the blame for Jack Solomons's machinations.

When Harry Levene became the number one promoter, with Jarvis Astaire, Mike Barrett and Micky Duff, whether it was at Wembley or the Albert Hall, TK was paid the respect he deserved. They all made sure that TK had a ticket to their shows and I made it my business, with the help of the sporting press, that TK would be seen and remembered, not only for the deeds he had accomplished, but that he should know he had not been forgotten. I am satisfied that it was the one job in life I did well. TK always recognized how different his life and career might have been had he been managed by men like Jarvis Astaire and George Walker, brother of Billy. Of Jarvis he commented, 'He looks after his boxers, plays the game the way it should be played – he's fair.' And of George Walker he once remarked, 'I wish he'd been my brother: the kind a fighter needs, who relieves you of your worries, not your money.'

Jarvis Astaire, George Walker and Ted Kid Lewis – what a team they might have made.

TK concentrated on film work and this gave him a certain amount of independence, but he was beginning to age and developed a mild form of Parkinson's Disease, so that from time to time when he wasn't concentrating he would become forgetful. I was making documentary films in 1953 and my partner suggested we put TK on the board of directors, as our public relations officer. His appointment would make good press copy, and his name on our notepaper would create an interest with potential clients.

I asked TK what he thought of the idea of being our public relations officer. His eyes lit up with pride and he gave me his usual bear hug and kiss on the cheek (he didn't stand on my feet this time, I was too quick for him). He couldn't wait to call Elsie: 'Hello, darling, I'm working for Morton,' he exclaimed eagerly. Elsie must have asked him what his job was. I could hear the one-sided conversation from the adjoining office. I think I shed a few tears and glowed with pleasure as I heard him say, 'I'm – eh – a relations officer.' The relationship between us had reversed. I had become the father and would look after TK like a son.

However, the job lasted about eight months; he was not one for sitting around an office. It was the lack of activity and mixing with people that he missed, so he decided to take up film work again. We both had a good laugh when he gave me his notice, but I could understand – he needed to be on the go all the time. TK's attitude to money hadn't changed. I recall giving him his weekly allowance to take home to Elsie for housekeeping, only to see him pass a 'tapper', stop, go back and give him a pound. 'Why did you do that?' I asked him. But he just shrugged his shoulders. I wasn't satisfied. 'He didn't even ask you.' He broke into an embarrassed, disarming smile. 'Yeah, I know, but he looked like he needed it.' There was no answer to that. I just shook my head; TK was that kind of man.

Nineteen fifty-four was another great milestone in TK's life. Sally and I presented him with a grandson, Michael. There was no way of measuring the joy shared by TK and Elsie. 'God is being very good to us,' Elsie said, and added that it was because Daddy was a good man. That summed up their attitude to life; 'Be good to one another and others will be good to you.'

TK got a part as the barman in the Mae West show, *Diamond Lil*. The press were very generous when the show went on tour, and Mae West and TK were splashed all over the local papers in every town they played. The management were very pleased that their judgement in using TK had paid off, so the show came to London and had a fair run at the Prince of Wales Theatre.

When the show closed, TK opened a man's shop. With TK there to greet the customers, the press as usual gave him their support. They really must have loved the man, as they never seemed to let him down. Unfortunately, TK's partner chose middle-range goods, when they should have gone for top-line goods, as most customers would have bought anything, just to have the chance to talk and get TK's autographed picture!

Eventually the profits were insufficient and the shop was closed. TK still wanted to work, however, and was delighted when a friend, David Morris, a director of the Lewis Tobacco Company, offered to find him a job. Elsie, too, was pleased. 'It will help keep Daddy active.' He worked there for three months until one weekend TK and Elsie came to visit and I saw that his fingers were bandaged. He said it was nothing, but Elsie broke down. His hands, she revealed, were cut and blistered from wrapping parcels and pulling string in the packing department! TK's great friend, Dave Morris, after receiving the publicity for giving TK a job, had let him work in the dispatch department – some friend.

TK did not care what work he did; he would hold his head up, regardless of the job. Whatever he did had no bearing on the past – he had been somebody, and could not now be criticized for doing a menial job. However, I insisted that he quit then and there, but TK wouldn't hear of it. He would give a week's notice. He didn't want to let his employers down.

From there TK went to work for John Collins, the Battersea Fun Fair millionaire. John had great affection for TK; he was just what John needed, a celebrity to be seen, to walk around and keep an eye on the security men. This job suited TK; he knew everybody there, but John's acting brother-in-law didn't like it and made it his business to see TK was axed. Maybe TK saw too much – who knows?

He then got a job selling new and second-hand cars. They printed cards with his picture on the back, and he worked on a commission and expenses. He introduced a number of customers, but he couldn't sell second-hand cars. 'I couldn't kid them that the cars were great, when I wasn't sure.' He was too honest. If he tried to lie, he would go red in the face.

32 Final Days

'The best old boxer of this, or any other, year.'
Boxing Writers' Club, 1964

By the late 1950s, TK was beginning to slow up. It took him twice as long to get about and hammer toes didn't help, so I used to get my prop man to stretch his shoes to make him more comfortable. However, whatever he did, wherever he went, he always looked immaculately dressed, from top to toe. Elsie saw to that. It was important that he be kept active, so I would call all my friends in the business to ensure that he had a fair amount of film calls. He was more than satisfied with film extra work in the crowd scenes. Sometimes, I offered to pay his fees as long as they called him, to point out how important it was to me to keep him busy, but it wasn't necessary. My friends rallied around and he was kept occupied.

In 1961, however, Elsie became quite ill. I moved them into our flat, so that Sally and I could look after them. Elsie knew she didn't have long to go and she would constantly say, 'Promise me you will look after Daddy.' This was a constant worry to her dying day. I'm not sure if TK knew, but the worry began to take its toll on her. Eventually, Elsie was sent to a nursing home, then finally to a hospital. Then, in 1962, TK received his biggest blow ever, when, after returning from the hospital, I had the ordeal of telling him that Elsie had passed away.

He looked at me in a daze. 'She's gone,' he said, and I'm not sure whether he said it as a question, or simply a statement. Then he broke down and cried like a child. He had lost his rudder, his guiding light, and nobody thought he would survive six months after her death. Elsie had been TK's engine, his motivator. When TK had been a boxer, he had been dressed, fed and looked after by others. All that had stopped when he had retired, and Elsie had taken over as manager, trainer, valet, general cook and bottle-washer. TK had always looked immaculate. Elsie would press his suits every night. He would awake to find one hanging ready, with a clean shirt, socks, tie, underwear and handkerchief all waiting for him. Elsie had waited on TK hand and foot and enjoyed every minute of it. Her Teddy was not going to look like a bum. 'People don't respect bums, but they'll respect Daddy.' And that they did.

My family rallied round and Sally tried to take over where Elsie had left off. But TK was too independent and we eventually agreed that he should move back into his apartment. I would see him nearly every day. Money was no problem, but he needed our company.

I remember one day dropping him off for an appointment outside the Athenaeum Hotel in Green Park. He was just getting out of my car, when a bus hit us in the back. TK managed to hang on, half out and half in the car. I quickly ran round and grabbed him, but he pushed me off with, 'I'm all right.' He was too proud to complain, but he was shaking. I told him to sit down. 'I'm all right,' he said again, and my reply caused us both to laugh for many years afterwards. It was, 'Sit down, or I'll knock you down.' It must have been the way I said it, because he sat down.

The bus driver came running over, full of apologies. His foot had slipped on the accelerator, he said. Then he spotted TK. The poor fellow went green. 'My God, it's Kid Lewis. What have I done?' Then I had the added problem of consoling the driver!

We called an ambulance and TK reluctantly went to the hospital. X-rays showed nothing broken, but I don't think he ever fully recovered from the impact and shock. I sent him away for a holiday to recover, after which he carried on making the rounds. Thereafter, my constant worry was to keep TK occupied, to ensure that he always had company, but it was difficult to give him orders.

TK was now past seventy – elderly for a normal person, let alone for an ex-boxer with a record of nearly three hundred fights. He had a breakdown in 1963, and his doctor put him straight into a nursing home. The press, as usual, were generous with their sympathy and TK received hundreds of letters from well-wishers, most of whom he did not know. He spent six weeks in the nursing home, and his will to survive remained as strong as ever.

After his recovery, I sent him to New York for a holiday. He stayed with his brother Lew and wife Lee in New York. Lew took TK to various boxing shows, where the fight fans were delighted and gave him the sort of reception they save for former champions. He made the usual rounds, meeting up with old friends, and lunching regularly at Jack Dempsey's, often sitting under a large framed photograph of himself. He also received another 'First' to be added to his many, when he became the first British boxer to be elected into the Boxing Hall of Fame.

The month's visit to New York was a hectic time for TK; he received a good press and was invited everywhere. It was like old times for him to be with Lew, sister Flo, Elsie's sister Rose and brother Harry and their families. Thirty-five years had passed since his departure from the States and he was still remembered. The visit did him the world of good.

He returned in great spirits and, after a few weeks living alone at his flat, I felt he should move to the Seven Hotel in Brighton, where he would have plenty of company. He only agreed to go, providing I promised to keep his flat. 'It was our home,' he said. I kept that promise until after he passed away.

TK was a great ambassador for Great Britain. When travelling abroad, he never failed to make it clear that he was British-born. But when bestowing honours, his country passed him over. Other boxers have been honoured, as have jockeys, trainers, athletes, rugger and football players, golfers, and sports officials – but not TK. However, in 1964, the people who counted did just that.

TK used to look forward to the annual dinner of the Boxing Writers' Club where everybody who's anybody in the boxing world gathered. The membership of the club consisted, then as now, of journalists who are top in their trade, their experience in boxing spanning the period from when TK was in his prime to the present-day era. At the annual dinners, after the speeches and the presentation to the best young boxer of the year, who usually turned out to be a British champion, they would introduce the present-day champions followed by the presentation of the old-time champions. Without exception, the last champion to be introduced would be TK and, year in and year out, he would receive a standing ovation from the toughest boxing critics in the country. They wrote what they thought and said what they liked, and they liked TK and said so. It goes without saying that they helped extend his life-span.

Thus, it was appropriate that the Boxing Writers' Club should be the first official body to honour him. In 1964 they presented him with a special trophy. It was inscribed: 'To the best old boxer of this, or any other, year, Ted "Kid" Lewis, from the Boxing Writers' Club 1964'. It was presented to him by the then chairman, Peter Wilson. TK considered this the greatest compliment he had ever received. We both cried with pride on our way home. I will always display it in the forefront of my father's trophies.

TK spent two happy years at the Seven Hotel as their star resident. When the weather was good, he could be seen strolling along the Brighton promenade, where he would be stopped every few yards by old friends, or by someone wanting his autograph. Sally's and my Sundays were shared, alternately with my son Michael in boarding school and the other with TK in Brighton. We would take TK out along the front and watch with amazement as the people crowded around. It was incredible that so many people, forty years after his retirement, still remembered him with such affection. TK would call me every day; he was lonely even though he was never alone at the hotel. He kept calling in the doctor, who told me, 'There's nothing wrong; he's just lonely.'

It was in 1966 that I was able to get him into the Nightingale Home for Aged Jews, where he spent his last and most comfortable four years. It gave him a new lease of life. The staff treated TK as if he was still champion. Either Sally, Marsha or I would visit him every day; it was only a mile and a half from our house. He would hug and kiss us when we arrived, asking 'How's everybody?' We would tell him, then he would say, 'You don't want to hang around with all these fogeys! See you tomorrow.' He was satisfied with just seeing us. That was all he needed and we made sure he got what he wanted. He would then return to watch a card game. He didn't play any more; he had finally learnt his lesson!

He was never without visitors. Friends used to call me at the office, asking permission to take TK to a boxing show, or a Ladies Night. The nurses would dress him up in his dinner jacket and wait up for him to return; they were marvellous. He was fast becoming the elder statesman of boxing; after all, he was Britain's greatest living boxer.

Jarvis Astaire and Micky Duff asked TK to be the guest of honour at their Anglo-American Sporting Club boxing night. There was a record crowd present of over eight hundred guests in evening dress to pay their respects to TK, and the TV cameras were there to record the event. I had the pleasure of accompanying TK, and the honour of sitting beside him at the top table. After dinner and the speeches, Terry Downes, on behalf of the club, presented TK with a silver salver. The inscription on it was read out by the Master of Ceremonies: 'To the Crashing, Smashing, Dashing Ted Kid Lewis, for Winning the Welterweight Championship of TED World. The Greatest of Them All, for His Contribution to Boxing. London 20 March 1967.' TK, holding the salver, tears in his eyes, stood up and faced the microphone. 'Thank you very much for the kind things you said about me,' and sat down to tumultuous applause, with everyone clamouring for autographs.

Before the evening's actual boxing commenced, Micky Duff had arranged to project some of TK's old fights. Those present saw the last rounds of three fights, two with Johnny Basham and one with Tom Gummer. Bill Martin, the then Chairman of the Boxing Writers' Club and boxing correspondent for the Press Association, added to the excitement by giving a running commentary to the old silent films. The fans loved it. They were calling out, 'Go on, Ted!' and 'Two hands, Ted!' and roared with delight as two of the best left-hook knockouts proved just how good TK was. One had the feeling that it was actually all happening at that moment. TK was in his glory. Everybody wanted to shake his hand as if the victories had just taken place. Those old boxing films and the TV recording of the evening are now part of my boxing collection.

The again in October 1967, Jarvis and Micky brought Jack Dempsey over to be the club's guest of honour and at the same time for Jack to present TK with a birthday cake. TK and Jack met and embraced in Jarvis's office. It was a touching scene as the two giants of the ring talked over old times with tears in their eyes. It was 'house full' again, and the TV recording shows how the club member's were delighted to be present on such an occasion. These recordings will always remind me of how lucky I was to have had the privilege of being with TK at these events.

A few months later, TK was again guest of honour at the Manchester Anglo-Sporting Club, run by TK's old pal, Moss Goodman. I was again privileged to be present when Moss presented TK with a silver cigarette box. The box had the usual inscription – The Crashing, Smashing, Dashing, etc., dated 30 October 1967.

I used to take TK to the National Sporting Club's boxing evenings, when well-known celebrities were honoured. Their names were listed on the scroll of honour board in the club room, together with a cabinet filled with trophies loaned by various honoured guests. Included there was TK's World Welterweight Championship Cup and the Boxing Sports Writers' Trophy. I approached Dai Thomas and asked why only two boxers were honoured, Georges Carpentier and Bombardier Billy Wells, the rest being jockeys, footballers, cricketers, golfers and tennis players. After all, it was a Boxing Club and the name of Ted Kid Lewis should be there. Hadn't he won his first title at the old NSC?

Dai agreed but said his hands were tied, and suggested I talk to the new club secretary, Danny Blanchflower, the former Northern Ireland footballer. I put the idea to Danny and suggested that 6 October 1969 – a Monday, the usual NSC Boxing Night – would be the perfect date. It would be the fifty-sixth anniversary of the night TK beat Alec Lambert at the NSC for the featherweight championship of Great Britain. The bout had taken place on 6 October 1913.

Danny thought it would be a good idea and, as there was over six months until the date, he would have ample time to prepare and make it a truly bumper evening. It was agreed that I would buy the silver belt that Young Joseph's family had put up for sale – which Joseph had received when he had won the British welterweight title in 1908. I would have it refurbished and engraved as being presented to TK by the NSC to commemorate the date and for his services to boxing. I would split the cost of the belt and engraving with the NSC and they would also donate £250 to the Nightingale Home where TK was then living.

Danny called me in mid-September to say that, due to some mix-up of dates, he would have to put back the date to 10 November, but that I should not worry, as the advertising had not yet been sent out. However, I had to have the engraving re-done, removing the date.

In fact, very little pre-publicity was sent out for 10 November. Nevertheless, it was a full house, I made sure of that. I invited forty-two old friends of TK's just to make sure. On the Thursday before the big night, I received another call from Danny. He had forgotten to book a celebrity to present the belt! Fortunately, that afternoon, I bumped into Stanley Baker, the film actor, and he agreed to do the honours.

It was a great night in spite of the setbacks. Stanley Baker made a speech from the ring and called TK up. TK climbed through the ropes, not as nimbly as in the past, but the reception was tremendous. He bowed to the fans and Stanley read out the inscription, 'Presented by the National Sporting Club to Ted Kid Lewis, former Welterweight Champion of the World. For His Contribution to Boxing', and presented TK with the belt, together with a large framed photographic montage of TK from photographs I had supplied to Danny. TK felt honoured and enjoyed the congratulations from all the guests. He sat between his grandson Michael and me, and was the third proudest man in the hall, because Michael and I tied for first and second.

I could never tell TK that I paid for the belt, or that the NSC had never sent the £250 donation to the Nightingale Home. I did consider complaining to Sir Charles Forte who owned both the NSC and the Café Royal, where the event took place. However, I decided to accept the situation, as Sir Charles most likely did not know anything about it. But I resolved that that would be the last time anyone took advantage of my father. When the Club was being redecorated, I went to collect TK's trophies and noticed that the scroll of Honour Board had thirty-five celebrity names dating from 1956 to 1977, only four of which were boxers: Carpentier, Wells, Lewis and Henry Cooper. It was sad to think how the great National Sporting Club had declined.

TK continued to make the rounds, going to many boxing shows and thoroughly enjoying himself. Then one day in September 1970 I received a call from Jack Solomons inquiring how TK was. I was delighted he showed interest. He said he needed a favour. Could TK be the guest of honour at the World Sporting Club on 13 October 1970? It sounded like old times or, as they say, '*déjà-vu*'. It seems he was stuck for a big name, but I would have even accepted another invitation from Danny Blanchflower, because I reasoned such an occasion would be good therapy for TK.

Thus, his dinner jacket was cleaned and pressed and everything made ready for TK to have another big night. However, on the morning of the big day I received a call from Asher Corren, the Executive Director of the Home, saying that TK had caught a chill and that he would not recommend TK went out that evening. I went straight to the Home. He didn't look too well, but smiled when he saw me. I told him that the show was cancelled and that a top-of-the-bill fighter had damaged his hand. TK, propped up in bed, replied, 'So what, he's still got one good hand, hasn't he?' I had great difficulty in keeping a straight face. But he was satisfied; he wasn't going to miss the show.

I then called Solomons, who said he was sorry to hear TK wasn't well, but would I come instead and receive the presentation on TK's behalf? I was in TK's seat, feeling inadequate and completely out of place. I tried to convince myself it was all right, that I was doing it for TK. Then Lord Manny Shinwell rose and informed the gathering that TK was indisposed and that his son would stand in for him. I got up, accepted the silver plated salver on behalf of TK, nodded my thanks – and then broke down. Nearly everyone in the hall came over to console me and to wish TK well.

But TK's health deteriorated. His fighting heart could stand no more. Even his stamina and courage could not help and on 20 October 1970, he passed peacefully away. It was the end of a living legend.

TK had chosen the life he loved and wanted. His fists had sky-rocketed him to fame and into a society for which he was ill-prepared. But he had more than held his own. He had achieved his goal. Through his charity, he had brought happiness and pleasure to the sporting world. He would not have asked for more.

And the sporting world came in their hundreds to show their respect at TK's funeral. It was Sunday, 25 October 1970, on my birthday, that TK was laid to rest. TK had lost his final fight but he would always be remembered.

Epilogue

It is nearly twenty years since TK died but hardly a week goes by when his name is not drawn to my attention, when I am not suddenly reminded of him by unsolicited testimonials that leap out at me from books, films and TV. TK is alive out there in the world of boxing.

Recently I watched Harry Carpenter interview the present undisputed heavyweight champion of the world 'Iron' Mike Tyson on BBC TV. Tyson, despite his ferocious image, is a boxing history connoisseur. His late manager, Jim Jacobs, was the owner of the world's largest library of fight films and consequently young Mike grew up watching and learning from the great fighters. When Harry asked him whether there were any old-time British fighters that he was particularly keen on Mike replied: 'I was hoping you would ask. There was Owen Moran – and the great Ted Kid Lewis.'

Mike smiled, 'He's probably the greatest fighter ever to come out of here, if you really think about it. Because you rate a fighter by his longevity and for years Ted Kid Lewis beat the greatest American fighters, for years . . . why, he won the title twice and it's unbelievable, the guys he had to fight! Benny Leonard, Jack Britton, Mike Gibbons, Willie Richie – the *Who's Who* of boxing, the greatest of the great, and yet he still prevailed as number one.'

Tyson was no more than two years old when TK passed away and yet, for him, TK is alive and an inspiration. And although Tyson is undoubtedly one of the greatest himself, he is just one of many modern champions who have cited TK as a standard, a beacon of excellence, a reference point by which to judge themselves.

There are still, however, people alive today who knew TK as a contemporary, incredible as that may seem. Chummy Gaventa is one, who, because of his love and respect for my mother and father, will always have a special place in my heart. I recently visited Chummy, now a well-known London bookmaker, at his West End office. I first remember Chummy back in 1922, pedalling his bicycle like mad to keep up with our car as we left the Stag's Head – TK's pub – for a day's outing. I was sitting in the dicky seat with TK's sister Dolly and she was trying to introduce her new

boy-friend Chummy to TK and Elsie who were seated in the front!
I have been friends with him ever since.

I visited Chummy with some photographs to see if he could name
some of the people, which he did. At the same time I asked him
about a court case involving himself and TK back in 1926–7, and
he immediately recalled: 'We were coming out of the Premierland
and somebody must have "mixed it", because Ted came over to me
looking very annoyed and said, "What did you say?" and before I
could reply he slapped me across the face and walked away!'

Why, I asked Chummy, did he go to court?

'I'm not sure,' he replied. 'I didn't want to go, but Issy Farrar
insisted. I was working for Issy at the time, so I went. But I couldn't
stop laughing all through the trial! The judge didn't think it was
funny, so he dismissed the case. I've been telling everybody since,
that "I fought a draw with Kid Lewis!".'

Such people with their memories, still fresh as though they were
yesterday, are precious to me. Another such, this time a great boxer
in his own right, is Jack Kid Berg. In fact, my interest in boxing has
taken on a new lease of life through my friendship with 'Yiddle' as he
is affectionately known, and his wife Moya. I get immense pleasure
out of going to fights with 'The Whitechapel Whirlwind', as he was
known. It gives me the opportunity to be in the company of a real
champion again and I can give him the same care and attention as I
did to TK, enjoying the same kind of familial feeling.

I now take great delight in reminding everyone that Berg is
Britain's greatest living fighter, but Yiddle will always chip in
with, 'Only because Ted's no longer with us'. I love it when he
kisses me goodnight and says, 'If I had had a son, I would have
liked him to be like you.'

When Whitbreads named the top ten sporting personalities and
held a public poll of one hundred people to choose the best in each
sport, Jack and I went along – I was invited because TK had been
named as one of the ten best greats in boxing – and we sat next to
Henry Cooper. When it was announced that Henry had been chosen
as Britain's number one and TK number two, Henry turned to me
and said, 'Morton, I'm glad Ted isn't here.'

I'm sure he meant it – he is that kind of fellow and a fighter
who has upheld the dignity of boxers ever since his retirement.
Henry is one of the old school, a gentleman in and out of
the ring, and today, when I show my tapes of TK, I see
not just his undoubted ability, but also how a boxer should
behave.

He would climb into the ring with his hands gripped over his head giving a warrior's handshake as he turned to each corner of the hall, smiling from cauliflower ear to cauliflower ear. Then he would walk over to his opponent, smile, shake hands and show his bandages, allowing his opponent to inspect them. Walking back to his own corner he would lean through the ropes to shake hands with friends and colleagues, and even when seated on his stool would respond to people passing by, leaning through to shake hands again.

He looked and acted at all times like the perfect gentleman, the true British sportsman – no eyeball to eyeball confrontations, no snarling and no 'fierce' looks. That was, until the bell rang. Then Ted Kid 'Jekyll' would become Ted Kid 'Hyde'!

After knocking out his opponent he would quickly walk over to his opponent's corner, shake hands with him or pat him on the back, say a few words and wave to the crowd. There was no jumping for joy, no somersaulting, no banging the chest. He had done what he had been paid for and what he had come to do.

I now look forward each year to the Boxing Writers' Club Annual dinner as the guest of Bill Martin who, through TK, has become a personal friend. One gets the opportunity to talk to old and famous friends, the people who count in boxing, all of them gathered in one place.

It is only after dinner, when they introduce present and past champions, that I have to battle to control my tears – and usually lose. If only he were there to take the bows and receive the plaudits from the boxing writers, the genuine admirers who would rise to their feet to acknowledge his greatness.

But I still see in my mind's eye that gentle, lovable, shy man, as he prepares to rise as the Chairman announces, 'Last but not least, Britain's greatest, the former Welterweight Champion of the World, Ted Kid Lewis!'

Oh yes, he's there, as I wipe away the tears. He will never let me down.

Ring Record 1909–1929

Year	Mth	Day	Opponent	Decision		Venue
1909	Sep	13	Johnny Sharp	L pts	6	Judaeans A C
		19	Joe Lipman	W pts	6	J A C
	Oct	9	Alf Cohen	W pts	6	J A C
		30	George Thomas	W KO	1	J A C
	Nov	27	Pte Joe Marks	W pts	6	J A C
	Dec	6	Dick Hart	Drew	6	J A C
		18	Jack Kid Levene	W KO	3	J A C
1910	Jan	8	Bill March	W pts	6	J A C
		16	Alf Jacobs	W pts	6	J A C
		31	Jim Brown	L pts	6	J A C
	Feb	13	George Powell	W rsf	1	J A C
		27	Piper Holmes	W pts	6	J A C
		28	George Marks	W pts	6	J A C
	May	15	Jack Kid Levene	W pts	6	J A C
		22	Young Morris	W pts	6	J A C
		29	Young Sullivan	W KO	3	J A C
	Jun	5	Joe Madden	W KO	2	J A C
	Jul	17	Jack Greenstock	Drew	6	J A C
		24	Alf Jacobs	W pts	6	J A C
		31	Joe Madden	Drew	6	J A C
	Aug	6	Ted O'Neil	W KO	5	J A C
		13	Young Smith	W rsf	3	J A C
		16	Sid Venner	W pts	6	J A C
	Oct	8	Curley Bume	W pts	6	J A C
	Nov	12	Boyo Lambert	W pts	6	J A C
1911	Jan	1	Dick Murray	W pts	6	J A C
		8	Bill Marsh	W pts	6	J A C
		15	Jack Marks	W pts	6	J A C
		22	Alf Jacobs	W pts	6	J A C

	25	Joe Madden	W pts	6	J A C
	29	Joe Jacobs	W pts	6	J A C
Feb	2	Young Kline	W KO	3	J A C
	5	Alf Small	W rsf	2	J A C
	9	Billy Smith	W KO	4	J A C
	12	Young Sullivan	L pts	6	J A C
	19	Joe Madden	Drew	6	J A C
	26	Jack Kid Levene	W pts	6	J A C
Mar	5	Jim Butler	W KO	1	J A C
	12	Charlie Smith	W KO	4	J A C
	19	Jack Ginnion	W rsf	3	J A C
	26	Joe Ross	W pts	6	J A C
Apr	2	Young Hyams	W pts	10	J A C
	9	Nat Brooks	W pts	10	J A C 8st 4lb Comp
	16	Jack Marks	W pts	10	J A C
	23	Jack Fisher	L pts	6	J A C
	30	Nat Brooks	L pts	15	J A C
May	7	Joe Madden	W pts	12	J A C
	14	Alf Small	W pts	10	J A C
	18	Tom Chinnery	W pts	6	Chelsea
	21	Young Greenstock	Drew	6	J A C
	28	Jack English	W KO	3	J A C
Jun	1	Sid Vinner	W pts	6	J A C
	4	Young Kline	W KO	3	J A C
	11	Alf Small	W KO	12	J A C
	18	Dick Murray	W pts	6	J A C
Jul	25	George Marks	W pts	6	J A C
	29	Pte. Joe Marks	W rsf	7	J A C
Aug	9	Curley Hume	W pts	6	J A C
	16	Tom Perkins	W pts	10	J A C
	23	Jack Harbour	W dis	3	J A C
Sep	2	Fred Halsband	Drew	6	J A C
	4	Walter Marshall	W rsf	3	Ring Blackfriars
	17	Billy Smith	W rsf	4	J A C
	20	Ted O'Neill	W rsf	5	J A C
	30	Tom Perkins	W pts	6	J A C
Oct	5	Lew Cohen	W KO	3	J A C
	8	Harry Ray	W pts	6	Ring Blackfriars
	10	Tom Perkins	W pts	6	J A C
	18	Tom Perkins	Drew	6	J A C
	21	Alf Small	W pts	6	J A C
	23	Jack Bunner	W pts	10	J A C
	29	Tom Perkins	W pts	10	J A C
Nov	2	Dick Murray	W pts	10	J A C
	9	Jim Hales	W pts	6	Hoxton

	12	Alf Small	W KO	2	Ring Blackfriars
	19	Kid Olds	W pts	6	J A C
	26	Billy Griggs	W KO	1	Ring Blackfriars
Dec	3	Frank Warner	W pts	6	Poplar
	7	Jimmy Butler	W rsf	2	Ring Blackfriars
	10	Billy Taylor	W pts	8	Poplar
	17	Jim Shires	W pts	10	Ring Blackfriars
	24	Frank Fay	W pts	6	J A C
	31	Eddie Foy	W pts	6	J A C
1912 Jan	6	Jewey Murray	W KO	1	Premierland
	13	Billy Taylor	W pts	8	Premierland
	16	Harry Wilson	W pts	10	Premierland
	20	Darky Harris	W KO	3	Premierland
Feb	10	Tom Mack	W pts	6	Premierland
	17	Duke Lynch	W pts	10	Premierland
	24	Alf Mitchell	W pts	10	Premierland
Mar	2	George Buswell	W pts	10	Premierland
	16	Alan Porter	W pts	10	Premierland
	18	Jim Shires	W KO	2	Premierland
Apr	1	Duke Lynch	L KO	1	N S C
	3	Leon Truffler	W pts	10	Paris
	6	Gus Venn	W KO	7	Premierland
	27	Gus Venn	W pts	10	Premierland
May	5	Jim Hales	W pts	6	Premierland
	25	Leon Truffler	W pts	10	Premierland
Jun	8	Jack Chinnery	W pts	6	Premierland
	22	George Ruddick	W pts	10	Premierland
	29	Darkey Haley	W pts	6	Premierland
Jul	6	Seaman Hayes	W pts	10	Premierland
	13	Harry Wilson	W pts	10	Premierland
	27	Jack O'Neill	W KO	3	Premierland
Aug	10	Young Brooks	L pts	10	Premierland
	31	Fred Halsband	L pts	10	Premierland
Sep	7	Tom Clifford	W pts	6	Premierland
	14	Sam Russell	W pts	10	Premierland
	21	Fred Blake	W pts	6	Premierland
	28	Tom Allen	W pts	10	Premierland
Oct	5	Con Houghton	L dis	6	Premierland
	12	Jim Lloyd	W pts	10	Premierland
	19	Jack Chinnery	W KO	3	Premierland
	24	Jim Campbell	W pts	6	Premierland
Nov	9	Fred Halsband	W pts	10	N S C
	16	Alf Small	W KO	5	Premierland
	30	George Ruddick	W pts	12	Premierland

Dec	2 Darky Harris	W KO	3	Premierland
	9 Jack Harrison	W KO	3	Premierland
	16 Jim Shires	W pts	10	Ring Blackfriars
	22 Harry Berry	W pts	15	Premierland
1913 Jan	2 Jim Lloyd	W pts	10	Liverpool
	4 George Buswell	W KO	14	Ring Blackfriars
	16 Nat Williams	Drew	15	Liverpool
	27 Johnny Condon	W pts	20	Ring Blackfriars
Mar	3 Johnny Condon	W pts	20	Ring Blackfriars
Apr	7 Young Brooks	W pts	15	N S C
Jun	2 *Joe Starmer	W pts	15	N S C
Jul	19 Harry Sterling	W rtd	7	Ring Blackfriars
	26 Duke Lynch	W pts	20	Ring Blackfriars
Aug	23 Harry Sterling	W pts	20	Ring Blackfriars
Sep	15 Ferdinand Quendraux	W KO	10	Ring Blackfriars
Oct	6 **Alec Lambert	W KO	17	N S C

*Eliminator for Featherweight Title
**British Featherweight Title

1914 Jan	5 George Buswell	W KO	2	Ring Blackfriars
Fed	2 *Paul Til	W dis	12	Premierland
Mar	14 Harry Berry	W KO	3	Premierland
	18 Ted Saunders	W KO	6	Coventry
May	30 Herb McCoy	W pts	20	Sydney
Jun	12 Hughie Mehegan	W pts	20	Sydney
	26 Young Shugrue	W pts	20	Sydney
Jul	11 Herb McCoy	L pts	20	Melbourne
Aug	1 Bobby Moore	W pts	20	Melbourne
Nov	9 Phil Bloom	Nd	10	New York
Dec	25 Young Jack O'Brien	Nd	6	Philadelphia

*European Featherweight Title

1915 Jan	1 Willie Moore	Nd	6	Philadelphia
Mar	10 Frankie Mack	W pts	20	Havana
	26 Jack Britton (1st)	Nd	10	New York
Apr	6 Harry Lenney	Nd	10	New York
	16 Johnny Lore	Nd	10	Montreal
	30 Johnny Lustig	Nd	10	Montreal
Jun	9 Kid Graves	Nd	10	New York
	23 Johnny Marto	Nd	10	New York
	25 Mike Mazie	Nd	10	New York
Jul	21 Charlie White	Nd	10	New York

Aug	3	Mike Glover	W pts	12	Boston
	11	Kid Curley	Nd	10	Buffalo
	17	Fighting Zunner	Nd	10	Buffalo
	31	*Jack Britton (2nd)	W pts	12	Boston
Sep	28	Jack Britton (3rd)	W pts	12	Boston Defend Title
Oct	18	Willie Moore	Nd	6	Philadelphia
	26	Joe Mandot	W pts	12	Boston Defend Title
Nov	2	Milburn Sailor	W pts	12	Boston Defend Title
	23	Jimmy Duffy	W KO	1	Boston Defend Title
	30	Mike Glover	L pts	12	Boston
Dec	28	Willie Richie	Nd	10	New York Defend Title

*World Welterweight Title

1916 Jan	1	KO Brennan	Nd	10	Buffalo
	13	Mike Glover	W pts	12	Boston
	17	Kid Graves	Nd	10	Milwaukee Defend Title
	20	Jack Britton (4th)	Nd	10	Buffalo Defend Title
Feb	5	Marty Farrell	Nd	6	Philadelphia
	9	Soldier Bartfield	Nd	10	Buffalo
	15	Jack Britton (5th)	Nd	10	New York Defend Title
	21	Jimmy Duffy	Nd	10	Buffalo
	24	Harry Trendall	W KO	7	St Louis
Mar	1	Harry Stone	W pts	20	New Orleans Defend Ti
Apr	19	Jack Able	W pts	8	Chattanooga
	24	*Jack Britton (6th)	L pts	20	New Orleans Defend Ti
May	18	Mike Gibbons	Nd	10	New York
	24	Eddie Moha	W KO	12	Dayton Ohio
Oct	17	Jack Britton (7th)	L pts	12	Boston Title
	24	Young Denny	Nd	12	St Louis
Nov	14	Jack Britton (8th)	Drew	12	Boston Title
	23	Johnny Griffiths	Nd	10	Cleveland
Dec	21	Johnny Griffiths	Nd	10	Cleveland

*Lost World Welterweight Title

1917 Jan	29	Willie Beechner	Nd	10	New York
	31	Sam Robideaux	W pts	15	Providence
Feb	6	Kid Graves	W KO	9	New York
	26	Johnny Griffiths	Nd	12	Akron, Ohio
Mar	19	Willie Moore	W KO	1	New York
	26	Jack Britton (9th)	Nd	12	Cincinnati Title
Apr	4	Jimmy Coffey	W KO	1	New York
	12	Billy Weeks	W KO	12	Dayton, Ohio
	28	Johnny Griffiths	Nd	12	Columbus

May	4 Jimmy O'Hagen	W KO	2	New York
	19 Jack Britton (10th)	Nd	10	Toronto Title
	22 Joe Egan	W pts	12	Boston
	24 Mike O'Dowd	Nd	10	New York
Jun	6 Jack Britton (11th)	Nd	10	St Louis Title
	14 Jack Britton (12th)	Nd	10	New York Title
	25 *Jack Britton (13th)	W pts	20	Dayton, Ohio Title
Jul	4 Johnny Griffiths	Nd	15	Akron, Defend Title
Aug	7 Jimmy O'Hagen	Nd	10	Saratoga
	17 Mike O'Dowd	Nd	10	New York
	28 Mike O'Dowd	L pts	12	Boston
	31 Albert Badoud	W KO	1	New York Defend Title
Sep	3 Soldier Bartfield	Nd	10	Buffalo
	11 Soldier Bartfield	Nd	10	Rochester
	14 Jimmy O'Hagen	Nd	10	Brooklyn
	15 Italian Joe Gans	Nd	10	Brooklyn
	24 Frankie Carbone	Nd	10	New York
Oct	24 Battling Ortega	Drew	4	Oakland Defend Title
Nov	13 Johnny McCarthy	W pts	4	San Francisco Defend Title
Dec	17 Bryan Downey	Nd	12	Columbus Defend Title

*Regained Welterweight Title

1918 Jan	14 Soldier Bartfield	Nd	12	Columbus
	23 Solidier Bartfield	Nd	10	Toronto
Feb	4 Johnny Tillman	W KO	6	Philadelphia
	18 Jimmy Duffy	W KO	1	Toledo
	25 Soldier Bartfield	Nd	6	Philadelphia
	26 Willie Langford	Nd	10	Buffalo
Mar	6 Jack Britton (14th)	Nd	10	Atlanta
Apr	16 Joe Eagan	Nd	10	Milwaukee
May	2 Jack Britton (15th)	Drew	10	Scranton
	17 Johnny Tillman	W pts	20	Denver Defend Title
	24 Jack Britton (16th)	Nd	6	New York
Jun	20 Jack Britton (17th)	Nd	6	New York
	25 Tommy Robson	W pts	12	Boston
Jul	4 Johnny Griffiths	Nd	20	Akron Defend Title
Aug	3 Tommy Robson	W pts	12	Boston
	17 Walter Mohr	Nd	8	Jersey City
Sep	23 Benny Leonard	Nd	8	Newark Defend Title

1919 Jan	1 Bryan Downey	Nd	12	Columbus
	15 George Rivet	Nd	10	Montreal
Mar	10 Johnny Griffiths	Nd	8	Memphis Defend Title
	17 *Jack Britton (18th)	L KO	9	Canton Defend Title

Jul	14	Steve Latzo	Nd	6	Philadelphia
	28	Jack Britton (19th)	Nd	8	Jersey City Title
Aug	4	Steve Latzo	Nd	6	Philadelphia
Sep	1	Mike O'Dowd	Nd	10	Syracuse
Oct	11	K O Laughlin	W KO	1	Portland
	16	Jimmy McCabe	W KO	1	Atlanta
	29	Jack Able	W pts	10	Atlanta
Dec	26	Matt Wells	W TKO	12	Albert Hall, London

*Lost World Welterweight Title

1920 Jan	13	Frank Moody	W KO	1	Manchester
Feb	14	Maurice Prunier	W KO	6	Paris
	28	Jerry Shea	W KO	1	Mountain Ash
Mar	4	Gus Platts	W TKO	18	Sheffield
	11	*Johnny Bee	W KO	4	Holborn Stadium
Apr	5	Kid Doyle	W KO	11	Liverpool
	30	Kid Doyle	W KO	5	Holborn Stadium
Jun	9	**Johnny Basham	W TKO	9	Olympia Defend Title
Sep	23	Mike O'Dowd	Nd	12	Jersey City
Oct	12	Marcel Thomas	Nd	8	Jersey City
Nov	19	***Johnny Basham	W KO	19	Albert Hall Defend Title

*Won British Welterweight Title
**Won European and Empire Welterweight Titles
***Relinquished European Welterweight Title

1921 Feb	7	Jack Britton (20th)	L pts	15	New York Title Challenge
Mar	16	Jack Perry	Nd	10	Detroit
Apr	8	Nate Siegel	L pts	10	Boston
	13	Augie Ratner	L pts	15	New York
Jun	27	*Jack Bloomfield	W pts	20	Holland Park
Sep	21	Ernie Barrieau	W KO	10	Toronto
Oct	14	**Johnny Basham	W TKO	12	Albert Hall Defend Title
Nov	17	***Boy McCormick	W KO	14	Albert Hall

*Won British Middleweight Title
**Won European Middleweight Title & Defend British Welter Title
***Won British Light-Heavyweight Title (unofficial)

1922	Feb	16	Tom Gummer	W KO	1	Dome Brighton
	May	11	*Georges Carpentier	L KO	1	Olympia
	Jun	19	**Frankie Burns	W KO	11	Holland Park
	Sep	4	Marcel Thomas	W rtd	4	Premierland
	Nov	20	***Roland Todd	W pts	20	Holland Park

*World Light-Heavyweight Title Challenge
**Won Empire Middleweight Title
***Won British, European & Empire Middleweight Titles

1923	Feb	15	*Roland Todd	L pts	20	Albert Hall Defend Titles
	Jul	30	Augie Ratner	L pts	20	Albert Hall
	Oct	4	Frankie Burns	W pts	20	Premierland
	Nov	8	Fred Archer	W pts	20	Premierland
	Dec	26	Fred Davies	W pts	20	Premierland

*Lost British, European & Empire Middleweight Titles

1924	Jan	22	Sid Pape	W rtd	2	Bradford
	Feb	12	Bruno Frattini	W KO	17	Milan, Italy
	Mar	18	Francis Charles	W pts	15	Paris
	Apr	5	Chic Nelson	Drew	15	Hamburg
	Apr	12	Eric Milenz	W KO	8	Berlin
	Jun	1	Piet Hobin	Drew	20	Paris
	Jul	3	*Johnny Brown	W pts	20	Albert Hall
	Nov	26	**Tommy Milligan	L pts	20	Edinburgh Defend Titles

*Defend British, European & Empire Welterweight Titles
**Lost British, European & Empire Welterweight Titles

1925	Jan	22	Francis Charles	W pts	20	Albert Hall
	Mar	19	Tommy Milligan	L dis	5	Albert Hall
	Jul	10	Bob Sage	W pts	10	Hollywood
	Oct	8	Marcel Thuru	L dis	1	Albert Hall
	Nov	8	Simon Rossman	L dis	8	Premierland
		27	Len Johnson	L rtd	9	Manchester

1926	Mar	7	Billy Prichard	W KO	10	Premierland
	Mar	21	Billy Mattick	W dis	5	Premierland

1927	Aug	4	Joe Green	W rtd	4	Ilford
		14	Jim Carr	W KO	3	Premierland
		28	Nol Steenhorst	W rtd	9	Premierland

Sep	11	Ted Coveney	W TKO	6	Premierland
Oct	6	Young Ansemes	W KO	1	Premierland
	16	Joe Rolfe	W KO	11	Premierland
Dec	3	Alex Storbeck	W KO	1	South Africa
		(Light-Heavyweight Champion South Africa)			
1928 Jan	7	Johnny Squires	Drew	15	South Africa
		(Heavyweight Champion South Africa)			
Jul	23	Maxie Rosenbloom	L dis	6	Long Island City
Dec	17	Charley Belanger	L dis	1	Toronto
1929 Dec	13	Johnny Basham	W KO	3	Hoxton, London

(W pts=won on points; W KO=Knockout; W rsf=Won, referee stopped fight; W rtd=Won, opponent retired; W TKO = won, Technical Knockout; Nd= No decision; L pts = lost on points; L dis= Lost, disqualified)

Index

Able, Jack, 97, 136
Adams, Harry, 183
Addenskolski, Count, 196, 197
Akron, 113
Anderson, George, 169
Anderson, 'Fireman', 203
Ansemes, 202
Archer, Fred, 173
Astaire, Fred, 72
Astaire, Jarvis, 244, 245, 250
Athletic Club, (135th St), 68
Atlanta, 126, 136
Atlas Athletic Club, 74
Attel, Abe, 22, 32

Badoud, Albert, 101, 114, 143
Baer, Max, 145
Baker, 'Snowy', 45, 47, 50, 53, 57
Barnes, 'Binnie', 90
Barrett, Mike, 244
Barrieu, Ernest, 151
Barry, Bros, 138
Barrymore, John, 187
Bartfield, Soldier, 69, 71, 73, 96,
    114, 120
Basham, Johnny, 140, 143, 144,
    147, 148, 151–3, 165, 221–3,
    251
Bauman, Lou, 112
Beckett, Joe, 43, 137, 142, 153,
    230, 231
Bee, Johnny, 143

Beechner, Willie, 106, 108
Beery, Wallace, 187
Belanger, Charlie, 215, 216, 217
Benjamin, Joe, 158
Bennett, Richard, 186
Berg, Jack, 201, 256
Berlin, 196–8, 200, 201
Berliner, Victor, 172, 190
Bernstein, Freeman, 63, 64, 65, 67
Berry, Harry, 28
Bettinson, 'Peggy', 26, 29, 45, 51,
    67, 71, 82, 163, 165
Birkenhead, 143
Blake, Jack, 231
Blanchflower, Danny, 252–3
Bland, Gus, 87
Bloom, Phil, 60, 69, 187, 235
Bloomfield, Jack, 145, 151
Boan's Gym, 133
Boston, 64, 73, 74, 76, 113, 122,
    150
Boxing Club de Paris, 140
Bournemouth, 229, 230
Braddock, James, 212, 231
Brennan, 'Kayo', 93
Briggs, Tom, 16
Brighton, 43, 143, 152, 154,
    157, 244, 250
Britt, Jimmy, 7
Britton, Jack, 60, 62, 68–71, 73,
    75, 76–8, 89, 90, 94, 96,
    97, 104, 105, 108–13, 120,

121, 127–9, 134–6, 146,
147, 150–52, 181,
255
Broadribb, Ted, 50, 53, 241
Broadway Sporting Club, 96
Brooks, Nat, 19
Brooks, (Young), 17, 27, 30–32,
34
Bronson, Ray, 68
Brown, Johnny, 177, 178
Brown, Sam, 183, 184
Browns, Far Rockaway, 71
Budapest, 196
Buffalo, 75, 93, 96, 106, 114
Bunner, Jack, 19, 24
Burge, Dick, 30, 33, 35
Burke, Dick, 97
Burns, Fred, 163, 164, 166, 172
Burns, Sam, 242–4
Burns, Sid, 7, 12, 16, 19, 27, 33,
42, 138
Buswell, George, 29, 41

Callaghan, Jack, 43, 154
Callaghan, Tommy, 220–22, 224
Canton, Ohio, 127
Cape Town, 168, 205
Caplin, Benny, 174
Carbone, Frank, 114
Carpenter, Harry, 255
Carpentier, Georges, 24, 25, 39,
41, 42, 142, 145–7, 153–62,
165, 171, 175–6, 190, 242,
251, 253
Carr, 'Curley', 163, 171, 172,
190, 201, 205, 220, 238
Carr, Jim, 202
Carter, Kid, 204
Cavell, Edith, 79
Chaplin, Charlie, 8, 117, 186, 187,
235
Chaplin, Sydney, 117–19, 186
Charles, Francis, 176, 182
Chevalier, Maurice, 175
Chicago, 66

Churchill, Winston, 237
Cirque de Paris, 24
Clabby, Jimmy, 51, 57, 68
Cochran, Charles, 143
Coffey, Jim, 108
Cohen, (Cockney), 16
Cohen, (Young), 11, 20, 22, 43
Collins, Josie, 158
Condon, Johnny, 29
Connolly, Johnny, 83, 84
Conrad, Con, 158
Coogee, 48, 50
Cooper, Henry, 253, 256
Corbett, Ronnie, 235
Corbett, W.F., 50, 52
Corrie, Eugene, 33, 34
Coveney, Ted, 202
Croffoth, James, 57
Cross, Leach, 44, 60, 62
Curley, Jack, 66
Curley, Kid, 75
Curzon, Bill, 19

Davies, Danny, 144
Davies, Fred, 173
Day, Edith, 158
Dayton, (Ohio), 79, 100, 109, 110
De Ponthieu, 45
Delaney, Jack, 45
Dempsey, Jack, 134, 142, 147,
156, 158, 160–62, 185, 248,
250
Denny, Young, 105
Denver, 120
Descamps, Francois, 159, 160
Detroit, 150
Dolling, Dai, 33, 35
Donovan, Mike, 60
Downey, Brian, 126
Douglas, J.H., 142, 151
Doyle, Kid, 20, 143
Driscoll, Jim, 25, 26, 30–2,
37–40, 42, 44, 49, 52
Dresner, Nat, 181
Duff, Micky, 244, 250, 251

Duffy, Jimmy, 79, 96, 120
Dundee, Johnny, 121, 185
Durban, 168

Eagan, Joe, 120
Erzle, George, 123
Evernden, Arthur, 42

Fairbanks, Douglas, 186, 187
Farrar, Issy, 201, 256
Farrell, Marty, 96
Fender, Percy, 167
Finch, Teddy, 180
Fitzsimmons, Bob, 51, 145
Fleischer, Nat, 98
Flowers, 'Tiger', 212
Flynn, Leo, 66, 67
Foley, Larry, 47, 51
Ford, Johnny, 72
Fox, Joe, 12
Frattini, Bruno, 174
Fremantle, 48
Frisch, Paul, 171
Future City Athletic Club, 105,
    109

Gans, Joe, 114
Gardner, Jack, 243
Gaventa, 'Chummy', 238, 240,
    255, 256
Gibbons, Mike, 60, 93, 97–9, 126
Gibson, Bill, 101, 102
Glover, Mike, 68, 69, 73, 74, 79,
    91, 94
Goldsmith, Jack, 84–8
Goldswain, Jack, 42
Goodman, Albert, 184, 185
Goodman, Alec, 17, 25, 30, 33,
    43, 44, 48, 50, 57–9, 64, 67,
    70, 72–6, 83, 87, 89, 94–5, 99,
    105, 111, 112, 115, 128, 134,
    135, 137, 139, 141, 150, 151,
    152, 157, 171, 177, 178
Goodman, Moss, 184, 251
Goodwin, Jack, 152, 171

Gould, Willie, 101, 102
Graves, Kid, 71, 94, 108
Greb, Harry, 121
Green, Harry, 158
Green, Joe, 202
Greenstock, Jack, 12
Griffo, Young, 51
Griffiths, Johnny, 105, 108, 113,
    122, 127
Grupps Gym, 57, 84, 89, 94, 105,
    107, 185
Gummer, Tommy, 143, 154–5,
    165, 251
Gunther, George, 24

Haley, 'Patsy', 76
Halsband, Fred, 12, 16, 17, 26, 49
Hamburg, 176
Hart, Marvin, 235
Harvey, Charlie, 57–9, 61, 62, 68,
    71, 89, 101, 102, 122, 124,
    125, 126, 127, 133–8, 141,
    146, 147, 149, 151, 152,
    157–9, 181, 185, 200, 207–10,
    212, 215–17, 219
Havana, 64, 65, 68, 70
Hawkins, Dai, 59
Hayes, Seaman, 25, 26
Hier, R., 237
Hobin, Piet, 176
Hogan, 'One Round', 119
Hollywood, 117, 185, 187, 235
Hollywood Legion, 187, 188
Honeyman, Mike, 12
Hulls, J.T., 139

Jack, Fred, 42
Jack the Ripper, 6
Jackson, Peter, 51
Jacobs, Harry, 19–23, 27, 40, 182
Jacobs, Jim, 255
Jeanette, Joe, 101
Jersey City, 124
Joel, Woolf, 158
Johannesburg, 168, 203

Johnson, Len, 188, 189
Johnson, Jack, 33, 64–6, 69,
        145
Johnston, Jimmy, 58–62, 67, 68,
        71, 72, 75, 78–80, 82, 89, 96,
        97, 100–102, 104, 106, 108,
        110, 112–15, 117, 119, 121–4,
        146, 147, 149–52, 185, 207,
        210–12, 215, 216, 218, 219
Joseph, Young, 7, 12, 15, 30, 43,
        251
Judean Club, 9, 10, 12, 13, 17, 38,
        62, 107

Lambert, Alec, 31, 32, 35–8,
        177, 251
Lane, Lupino, 158
Langford, Sam, 101, 102
Langford, Willie, 120
Latzo, Steve, 134, 135, 212
Lauder, Harry, 39, 51
Laughlin, K.O., 136
Ledoux, George, 40, 43
Lee, Tommy, 50
Lenny, Harry, 69
Leonard, Benny, 52, 101, 109,
        123–5, 185, 255
Lethorr, Ira, 229
Levene, Harry, 57, 171, 172,
        244
Levinsky, 'Battling', 121, 145, 147
Levy, Albert, 173, 189
Lewis, Elsie, 85–103, 106, 107,
        108, 110, 113–15, 117, 119,
        124, 126, 127, 133, 135, 137,
        138, 140, 141, 146, 147, 150,
        151–6, 159, 164, 166–8, 170,
        174, 175, 177–86, 189–91,
        195–210, 213, 214–16, 218,
        220–3, 226, 230, 234–7, 240,
        241, 245, 246, 247, 256
    Marsha, 240, 250
    Michael, 245, 252
    Morton, 113, 119, 124, 137,
        138, 143, 149, 151, 159,

        167, 168, 173–5, 177–80,
        182, 184–6, 188, 190, 201–4,
        215, 220, 222, 224, 229,
        255
    Sally, 240, 245, 247, 250
Lewis, Harry, 7, 8, 30, 31, 68
Littlestone, Manny, 172, 190,
        205
Liverpool, 29, 71, 72, 181
Lloyd, Jim, 30
Lomski, Leo, 210–12
London, 4, 50, 60, 90, 95, 137,
        147, 151, 152, 168, 173, 177,
        180, 195, 200–2, 205, 208,
        219, 220, 223, 225, 229,
        232, 239, 240, 246
Lonsdale, Belt, 23, 28, 35, 37, 41,
        43, 46, 47, 49, 66, 70, 133,
        143, 151, 153, 164, 166
Lopez, Vincent, 101
Lore, Johnny, 70
Los Angeles, 119, 185, 187, 239
Loughran, Tommy, 212
Louis, Joe, 115
Lupino, Stanley, 158
Lustig, Johnny, 70
Lynch, Duke, 23, 25–7, 32
Lytell, Bert, 183, 186, 187

Mace, Jem, 51
Mach, Billy, 181
Mack, Frankie, 64, 66
Madden, Joe, 175–9
Madison Square Garden, 79, 97,
        98, 121, 150, 208, 210, 212
Maidenhead, 154
Manassa, Mauler, 142
Manchester, 189, 223
Mandot, Joe, 60, 79
Mann, F.T., 167
Mansfield, Alf, 17
Mansfield, Harry, 19, 33
Marks, Joe, 78, 185, 186
Martin, Bill, 251, 257
Marto, Johnny, 71

Index

271

Marx, Bros, 158
Masterton, 'Bat', 61, 129
Mattick, Billy, 190, 191
Mazie, Mike, 71
McCarthy, Johnny, 117
McCloud, Tex, 90
McCorkindale, Don, 168
McCormick, 'Boy', 153
McCoy, Al, 135, 146
McCoy, Herb, 49–53
McFarland, 'Packy', 69, 97, 126
McLaglen, Victor, 185, 187,
    235
McTigue, Mike, 212
McVey, Sam, 101
Mehegan, Hughie, 45, 46, 49–52
Melbourne, 53
Memphis, 127
Mendeloff, Gershon, 3, 5, 12, 14,
    19, 58, 107
Mendeloff, Leah, 3, 4, 91
Mendeloff, Solomon, 3–6, 13,
    14, 16, 18, 19, 20, 21, 96,
    103, 106, 110, 133, 140
Milan, 174, 175
Milenz, Eric, 176
Miller, Freddie, 174
Milligan, Tommy, 181–3, 195
Mills, Bertram, 47
Mills, Cyril, 47
Mills, Freddie, 241
Mogford, Ernest, 23, 33, 140, 141
Moha, Eddie, 100
Mohr, Walter, 124
Montreal, 70, 127
Moody, Frank, 140
Moore, Bobby, 50, 53
Moore, Pal, 52, 61
Moore, Ted, 153
Moore, Willie, 61, 79, 108
Moran, Owen, 31, 32, 45, 52, 59,
    255
Morgan, Dan, 69, 75–8,
    109, 110, 121, 146, 150, 151,
    160

Morgan, Eddie, 33
Morris, Dave, 246
Morris, Harry, 40
Morris, Joe, 153, 164, 172, 188,
    201, 205
Mortimer, Harry, 93
Mosley, Oswald, 220, 224–8
Muhammed, Ali, 211
Mussolini, Benito, 224

National Athletic Club, (Phil), 61
National Sporting Club, 10, 23,
    24, 26, 27, 29, 31, 32, 39, 43,
    45, 71, 112, 143, 149, 151,
    165, 166, 251, 252
Nebraska, 71
Neil, 'Young', 79
Nelson, B, 32
Nelson, C, 176
Newark, (NJ), 124
New Orleans, 96
New York, 57, 58, 60, 67, 69, 70,
    79, 84, 89, 92, 93, 95, 100,
    102, 105, 106, 107, 109, 110,
    114, 126, 137, 145, 147, 149,
    150, 152, 185, 203, 207, 208,
    216, 219
Niblo, Fred, 88
Niagara Falls, 106

Oakland, 117
O'Brian, Jack, 61, 71
O'Dowd, Mike, 106, 113, 114,
    120, 135, 146
O'Hagen, Jimmy, 113, 114
Ohio, 70
Ortega, 'Battling', 115, 116, 117

Palace Sporting Club, 108
Palmer, Billy, 171
Palmer, Joe, 157, 160, 161
Palmer, 'Pedlar', 171
Pape, Sid, 173
Papke, Billy, 62
Paragon Music Hall, 7

Paris, 24, 140, 162, 174, 175, 176,
    178, 182
Perry, Jack, 150, 187, 235
Philadelphia, 61, 79, 96, 100
Phillips, Jackie, 16
Pickford, Mary, 186
Pittsburgh, 62
Platts, Gus, 142
Poesy, Jean, 42
Premierland, 16, 19, 20, 22, 25,
        26, 28, 29, 40, 43, 45, 164,
        172, 190, 201, 202, 256
Preston, Harry, 154, 155, 156, 158
Pritchard, Billy, 190, 191
Providence, Rhode Island, 108
Prunier, Maurice, 141, 142

Quendraux, Ferdinand, 32, 33, 34

Ratner, Augie, 101, 121, 150,
        168, 172, 209
Read, A., 32
Reeve, Ada, 50
Reeve, Harry, 12, 19
Rice, 'Bandsman', 33, 142, 231
Richards, Phil, 173, 175
Richie, Willie, 45, 53, 80, 90, 93,
        97, 255
Ring, (Blackfriars), 29, 31, 32, 41,
        159
Rivet, Georges, 127
Robideaux, Sam, 108
Robson, Tommy, 122, 123
Rochester, New York, 114
Rogers, Will, 90
Rolf, Joe, 202
Rose, Charlie, 3, 133
Rosenbloom, Maxie, 208, 209,
        210, 212, 235
Rossman, Simon, 188, 189

Sage, Bob, 187
Sailor, Milburn, 49, 52, 72, 79
San Diego, 117, 118
San Francisco, 51, 57, 58, 59, 117,
        134

San Rafael, 115
Saratoga, 113
St Louis, 105, 109
St Nicholas Rink, 71, 114
Scales, Jack, 7, 16
Seaman, Manny, 115, 116, 117,
        211
Segal, Dave, 86, 87, 88
Segal, Hans, 199
Seigal, Nate, 150
Sharp, Johnny, 11
Shea, Jerry, 142
Shear, Sam, 20, 21, 22, 23, 26, 29,
        30, 32, 33, 40
Sheffield, 142, 223
Shinwell, Manny, 253
Shugrue, Joe, 45, 50, 52, 53
Simmonds, Nat, 233
Slogg, Sid, 139
Smith, Dick, 142, 173
Smith, 'Gunboat', 121, 134
Smith, Jewey, 15, 172
Solomons, Jack, 241, 242, 243,
        244, 253
Somerset, Pat, 158
Southampton, 137, 138, 185,
        205, 230, 240, 241
Southend, 201
Sports Palatz, 176
Squires, Johnny 167, 168, 204, 205
Stanley, 'Digger', 29, 39, 42
Starmer, Joe, 31
Steenhorst, Noel, 202
Stokes, Harry, 33, 159, 163
Stone, Harry, 96
Storbeck, Alex, 203, 204
Sullivan, Billy, 187, 236
Sullivan, Dan, 33
Sullivan, Mike, 68
Summers, Johnny, 7, 27, 40, 138
Sydney, 48, 49, 50, 51

Tendler, Lew, 121
Terry, Ellen, 48
Thomas, Dai, 251

Thomas, Marcel, 147, 164
Thuru, Marcel, 188
Til, Paul, 42, 43, 44, 45,
  164
Tillman, Johnny, 120, 121
Todd, Roland, 165, 166
Toronto, 151, 216
Trendell, Harry, 96
Truffler, Leon, 24, 25
Tucker, Sophie, 163
Tunney, Gene, 101
Turpin, Randolph, 242
Tyson, Mike, 255

Venn, Gus, 42

Walker, George, 158, 244
Walker, Micky, 151, 212
Warner, Jack, 236
Warner, 'Young', 50
Warner Bros, 183, 185, 235
Washington, 126
Weeks, Billy, 108
Wells, 'Bombardier', 42, 142, 231,
  251
Wells, Matt, 68, 73, 94, 136, 137,
  139, 153

Welsh, Freddie, 39, 42, 45, 53, 61,
  62, 68, 70, 72, 76, 80, 109,
  110, 123
Welterweight title, 81, 112
West, Mae, 246
Westchester, (NY), 59
White, Charlie, 71, 72, 73, 79
White, Jimmy, 231
Wilde, Jimmy, 238
Willard, Jess, 65, 66, 134
Williams, Billy, 164
Williams, Ike, 74
Williams, Nat, 29
Williams, Tom, 23, 25, 33
Wills, Harry, 101, 102
Wilson, Arnold, 147, 153, 156,
  168, 177, 197
Wilson, Gus, 171, 174, 175, 187
Wilson, Johnny, 146
Wilson, Woodrow, 105, 106
Wolgast, Ad, 32, 59, 60, 62, 80
Wonderland, 7, 15, 16, 19
Woodcock, Bruce, 243
Woolf, Jack, 19
Woolley, Frank, 167, 168

Zunner, 'Fighting', 75